T0328972

Central Banks as Fiscal Players

It is well known that the balance sheets of most major central banks significantly expanded in the aftermath of the financial crisis of 2007–2011, but the consequences of this expansion are not well understood. This book develops a unified framework to explain how and why central bank balance sheets have expanded and what this shift means for fiscal and monetary policy. Buiter addresses a number of key issues in monetary economics and public finance, including how helicopter money works, when modern monetary theory makes sense, why the Eurosystem has a potentially fatal design flaw, why the fiscal theory of the price level is a fallacy and how to escape from the zero lower bound.

WILLEM BUITER is Visiting Professor of International and Public Affairs at Columbia University. He was an academic economist for twenty-eight years. He was a founding external member of the Monetary Policy Committee of the Bank of England from 1997 to 2000 and has been an adviser to the IMF, the World Bank, the Inter-American Development Bank, the European Commission, central banks and finance ministries across the world.

FEDERICO CAFFÈ LECTURES

This series of annual lectures was initiated to honour the memory of Federico Caffè. They are jointly sponsored by the Department of Public Economics at the University of Rome, where Caffè held a chair from 1959 to 1987, and the Bank of Italy, where he served for many years as an advisor. The publication of the lectures will provide a vehicle for leading scholars in the economics profession, and for the interested general reader, to reflect on the pressing economic and social issues of the times.

Other Books in This Series

Nicola Acocella, *Rediscovering Economic Policy as a Discipline* (2018)

Samuel Bowles, *The New Economics of Inequality and Redistribution* (2012)

János Kornai and Karen Eggleston, *Welfare, Choice and Solidarity in Transition: Reforming the Health Sector in Eastern Europe* (2010)

Paolo Sylos Labini, *Underdevelopment: A Strategy for Reform* (2010)

Serge-Christophe Kolm, *Reciprocity: An Economics of Social Relations* (2009)

Augusto Graziani, *The Monetary Theory of Production* (2009)

Luigi L. Pasinetti, *Keynes and the Cambridge Keynesians* (2009)

Jean-Jacques Laffont, *Regulation and Development* (2005)

Robert M. Solow, *Monopolistic Competition and Macroeconomic Theory* (1998)

Edmond Malinvaud, *Diagnosing Unemployment* (1994)

Central Banks as Fiscal Players

The Drivers of Fiscal and Monetary Policy Space

WILLEM BUITER
Columbia University

CAMBRIDGE
UNIVERSITY PRESS

CAMBRIDGE
UNIVERSITY PRESS

University Printing House, Cambridge CB2 8BS, United Kingdom

One Liberty Plaza, 20th Floor, New York, NY 10006, USA

477 Williamstown Road, Port Melbourne, VIC 3207, Australia

314–321, 3rd Floor, Plot 3, Splendor Forum, Jasola District Centre,
New Delhi – 110025, India

79 Anson Road, #06–04/06, Singapore 079906

Cambridge University Press is part of the University of Cambridge.

It furthers the University's mission by disseminating knowledge in the pursuit of
education, learning, and research at the highest international levels of excellence.

www.cambridge.org
Information on this title: www.cambridge.org/9781108842822
DOI: 10.1017/9781108904292

First published 2021

A catalogue record for this publication is available from the British Library.

ISBN 978-1-108-84282-2 Hardback
ISBN 978-1-108-82276-3 Paperback

This book is dedicated to Anne

Contents

Figures

Tables

Introduction

The original inspiration for this volume was the Frederico Caffè Lectures I gave in Rome on December 13–14, 2011. Quite a lot of water has flown down the Tiber since then and my thinking about the monetary and fiscal policy issues I addressed in the lectures has evolved and, I hope, become more coherent.[1]

The simple idea that motivates most of this book is that central banks make a significant, indeed at times essential, contribution to the fiscal space of the sovereign. This is because the ability to issue monetary liabilities, especially currency, is a source of profits to the central bank. This is the case for two reasons. First, currency carries a zero nominal interest rate and central bank reserves often have policy-determined interest rates below the safe rate of return on non-monetary financial instruments of comparable duration and risk. Unless the economy is at the effective lower bound (ELB), issuing money and investing it in low-risk securities is therefore a profitable business. The second reason is that central bank money is irredeemable. It is an undoubted asset to the holder but not in any meaningful sense a liability to the issuer. This makes monetary issuance profitable even if the economy is at the ELB. We operationalize this by including the present discounted value of the terminal stock of central bank money as an asset in the solvency constraint of the private sector but not as a liability in the solvency constraint of the central bank.

The reason the profits from monetary issuance are a source of revenue to the sovereign is that the central government fiscal authority (Treasury) is the beneficial owner of the central bank. We therefore

---

[1] I would like to thank three anonymous referees of an earlier version of this manuscript for extensive, detailed and constructive comments and suggestions. Anne Sibert and Ebrahim Rahbari contributed important insights.

should, in order to understand the fiscal space of the sovereign, consolidate the accounts of the Treasury and the central bank, and do our analyses and forecasts in terms of the accounts of this consolidated entity – henceforth referred to as the State. The profits of the central bank thus help relax the intertemporal budget constraint (IBC) of the State or, equivalently, boost net worth on the comprehensive balance sheet of the State. This is a key feature our analysis shares with Modern Monetary Theory.[2]

A direct implication of the unique position of the central bank as the liquid window of the Treasury is that the central bank is uniquely qualified to fulfill the key financial stability roles of lender of last resort (LLR), to deal with funding liquidity crises, and market maker of last resort (MMLR), to deal with market liquidity crises.

Chapter 1 starts with a brief overview of the facts about the advanced economy central bank balance sheet explosion since the Great Financial Crisis (GFC). The increase in profit remittances by the Fed to the US Treasury during the post-GFC years of extraordinarily low policy rates stands out. The Chapter then delves into the analytics of seigniorage arithmetic and how seigniorage revenues can boost fiscal space. Away from the ELB, when the demand for real base money is constrained by a conventional base money demand function, the real value of the seigniorage (as a share of GDP) that can be extracted at a target rate of inflation of, say, 2 percent is rather small – typically well under 0.5 percent of GDP for most advanced economies. At the ELB, however, seigniorage can be truly massive because the demand for real base money is infinitely interest-sensitive.

Chapter 1 also considers the noninflationary loss absorption capacity of central banks and provides estimates for the Fed, the ECB, the Bank of Japan (BoJ) and the Bank of England (BoE). Even away from the ELB, the present discounted value of current and future seigniorage when inflation is at its target value of, say, 2 percent, can

---

2   See Bell (2000), Tcherneva (2002), Forstater and Mosler (2005), Mosler (2010), Wray (2015), Roche (2019) and Fullwiler et al. (2019).

be a quite impressive number. This means that these central banks can survive large losses without this forcing them into solvency-preserving monetary issuance on a scale that threatens the inflation target.

Another implication of this approach is that the conventional (financial) net worth of a central bank can be significantly negative without this posing a threat to the solvency of the central bank. The key missing asset from the conventional balance sheet is the present discounted value of future seigniorage. This transforms the solvency of the central bank if the central bank (or the national Treasury that is the beneficial owner of the central bank) has discretionary control over current and future issuance of the monetary base. This is the case for the Fed, the Bank of Japan, the Bank of England and the People's Bank of China (PBoC) but not for the nineteen national central banks (NCBs) that, together with the European Central Bank (ECB), make up the Eurosystem. Monetary issuance for each national central bank of the Eurozone is a collective decision made by the Governing Council of the ECB. There is no national discretion. From the perspective of an individual NCB (and its sovereign) all its euro-denominated liabilities are effectively denominated in a foreign currency over which it has no discretionary control. Sovereign default and insolvency of the associated NCB therefore can occur in the Eurozone under circumstances where this could be avoided by a central bank and sovereign that are not part of a monetary union that eliminates national discretionary control over seigniorage.

Chapter 2 derives the comprehensive balance sheet (or intertemporal budget constraint of the central bank and the Treasury (or general government) and of the consolidated State and contrasts these with the conventional balance sheets. We then consider, theoretically and quantitatively, the arithmetic of fiscal sustainability by focusing on the net nonmonetary debt of the consolidated general government and central bank and the seigniorage-augmented primary surplus of the State. The fact that Japan's general government gross debt was 237.6 percent of GDP at the end of 2017, while the net nonmonetary debt of the consolidated State was only 67.4 percent of GDP, under-lines the importance of our approach. Japan does not yet have a serious public debt stock problem. It has a bit of a public sector flow deficit problem: its general government cyclically adjusted primary budget deficit was 3.8 percent of GDP in 2017. But because it is at the ELB and has been for years, it can extract massive seigniorage – more than 10 percent of GDP each year in the five years leading up to 2017. That suggests that, if Japan ever were to escape the ELB, it could have both a stock and a flow monetary overhang problem.

Chapter 3 considers the analytics of helicopter money drops – monetized fiscal stimuli. These will always boost nominal aggregate demand because central banking is profitable (interest rates on assets exceed those on liabilities and/or central bank money is irredeem-able). This Chapter also summarizes some of the key results of the first three chapters in the following seven propositions.

1. A central bank can be solvent with negative conventional equity or net worth.
2. Central bank current and future resources are "tax payers' money," regardless of whether the central bank is fully dependent, operationally independent or operationally and goal independent. All that is required for this is to be true is that the Treasury is the beneficial owner of the central bank.
3. Consider the purchase of additional Treasury debt by the central bank funded by the permanent/irreversible issuance of additional base money equal in present discounted value (PDV) to the purchase of Treasury debt. The cancellation (wiping out/forgiving) of that additional Treasury debt purchased by the central bank is equivalent to the central bank holding that additional Treasury debt forever (rolling it over as it matures). Holding consols (perpetuities) on a permanent basis is another equivalent strategy.
4. A permanent increase in the monetary base used by the central bank to purchase additional private domestic or foreign assets is equivalent to an equal-size permanent increase in the monetary base used by the central bank to purchase Treasury debt.[3]

---

[3] We assume the rate of return on private domestic and foreign assets is the same as that on Treasury debt.

5. Quantitative Easing (QE) that is permanent/irreversible in present discounted value terms creates fiscal space for a deferred helicopter money drop.

6. Assume the interest rate on base money is zero. A helicopter money drop today boosts demand even in a permanent liquidity trap, when the nominal interest rate is at the zero lower bound (ZLB) forever. It relaxes the intertemporal budget constraint of the state by an amount equal to the permanent increase in the stock of base money

7. Lack of nominal effective demand is a policy choice or the result of a failure of cooperation and coordination between the central bank and the Treasury, not an unavoidable fate, even for an economy apparently stuck at the ELB. A sufficiently large helicopter money drop will always boost nominal aggregate demand. If necessary, public spending on real goods and services can be boosted by the required amount. Whether the higher nominal aggregate demand manifests itself as higher real aggregate demand or higher inflation depends on the amount of excess capacity in economy.

Chapter 4 reviews how not to use the intertemporal budget constraints of the central bank and the State. It analyses, using a simple two-sector model, why the fiscal theory of the price level (FTPL) is fatally logically flawed. The elementary error is the confusion of the intertemporal budget constraint of the State with a mis-specified equilibrium nominal bond pricing equation. The IBC of the state, holding with equality and with sovereign bonds priced at their contractual values (free of default risk), despite essentially arbitrary (non-Ricardian) fiscal-financial-monetary programs, is used as an equilibrium condition that is supposed to set the general price level at the level required to make the real value of the outstanding stock of nominal government bonds consistent with sovereign solvency. It does so by equating the real value of the outstanding stock of nominal sovereign debt to the present discounted value of current and future augmented primary surpluses of the State.

A fundamental problem with this approach is that this IBC of the State, holding with equality and with bonds priced at their contractual values, has already been used as an equilibrium condition in the form of the IBC of the private sector, holding with equality and with sovereign debt priced at its contractual value. In equilibrium, if the IBC of the private sector holds with equality and with sovereign debt priced at its contractual value, this implies that the IBC of the State also must hold with equality and with sovereign debt priced at its contractual value. This private-sector IBC, holding with equality, is necessary to fully characterize optimal private consumption behavior. It cannot be used again disguised as the IBC of the State.

Not surprisingly, the FTPL generates a number of anomalies and inconsistencies.

Anomaly 1: The price level can be negative.

Anomaly 2: If the public debt is index-linked and/or denominated in foreign currency, there is no FTPL.

Anomaly 3: The FTPL can price phlogiston – it can determine the general price level in a model in which money exists only as a numeraire. It is not uncommon in the recent literature to determine the price of money (phlogiston) without there being a stock of money (phlogiston) outstanding, through the simple expedient of assuming there is a nonzero stock of money-denominated (phlogiston-denominated) bonds outstanding. We object to the introduction of this ultimate nondeliverable forward contract for money (phlogiston) when there is no corresponding deliverable market. It is not good economics to be able to determine a price without an associated quantity.

Anomaly 4: If the logic of the FTPL holds, we could have the Mrs. Jones theory of the price level (MJTPL). The IBC of any private agent, holding with equality and with private debt priced at its contractual value, can be used to determine the general price level the same way the FTPL does, if the private agent pursues a non-Ricardian consumption and asset allocation program.

Anomaly 5: When we distinguish properly between the contractual value of government debt (free of default risk) and its market value (which can reflect default risk), that is, when we use the IBC of the State as an equilibrium sovereign debt pricing equation in the proper manner, the FTPL vanishes. The FTPL relies on the fact that, when there is nominal government debt outstanding, the general price level can sometimes appear to perform the role of a "sovereign debt discount factor" or sovereign debt revaluation factor – give or take six anomalies and two inconsistencies. The sovereign debt discount factor converts the contractual value of sovereign bonds (absent default risk) into the market value of these bonds (which can reflect default risk). When we introduce the sovereign debt discount factor explicitly (which turns the IBC of the State, holding with equality, into a legitimate sovereign bond pricing equation), the FTPL vanishes.

Anomaly 6: When viewed as an equilibrium selection criterion in a model with multiple equilibria, the FTPL in general produces explosive or implosive solutions for the general price level and the rate of inflation when the nominal money stock is exogenous and constant.

Inconsistency 1: If the FTPL is not viewed as an equilibrium selection rule but is imposed as another equilibrium condition when the nominal money stock is exogenous and the fundamental equilibrium has been selected (a constant growth rate of the nominal money stock supports a constant rate of inflation), then the model is overdetermined.

Inconsistency 2: When the price level is predetermined (as in models with Keynesian nominal wage and price rigidities), adding the IBC of the State (holding with equality and with sovereign bonds priced at their contractual values) as an equilibrium condition, in addition to the IBC of the household sector (holding with equality and with bonds priced at their contractual values), the result is an overdetermined system, even when the nominal interest rate is exogenous.

Chapter 5 uses the model of the previous Chapter to discuss three ways to eliminate the zero lower bound on nominal interest rates: (1) abolish currency, (2) tax currency and (3) introduce a variable exchange rate between currency and bank reserves (deposits) with the central bank. We come down in favor of getting rid of cash as the most robust of these three options. This would have the further advantage of eliminating a preferred store of value and means of payment for illegal activities. There are both economic and political costs associated with the abolition of cash, however. Some of these can be addressed or at least mitigated by eliminating only the larger denomination currency notes. This would lower the ELB without eliminating it.

We confirm that helicopter money drops stimulate nominal aggregate demand even when the economy is permanently at the zero lower bound. This is because of the irredeemability of central bank money that causes the intertemporal budget constraint of the State to be relaxed when there is a monetary injection, as long as the growth rate of the nominal money stock in the long run is equal to or greater than the interest rate on the monetary base (zero in the case of currency).

Chapter 6 uses an extension of the comprehensive balance sheet framework of Chapter 2 to demonstrate why the Eurosystem is not an operationally decentralized central bank (like the Fed), but a system of currency boards with twenty independent profit and loss centers that is at risk of collapse because individual national central banks (NCBs) can go bankrupt.

A "regular" NCB of the kind outlined in the earlier chapters (including the Fed, the BoJ, the BoE and the PBoC) can, in principle, issue base money at will. Unless it has significant foreign-currency-denominated or index-linked liabilities, it cannot be forced into default. The ECB and the nineteen NCBs that make up the Eurosystem represent twenty independent profit and loss centers. No individual NCB can decide on the amount of monetary issuance it can engage in. That is a collective decision of the Governing Council of the ECB. An NCB in the Eurosystem is therefore categorically different from the central banks analyzed in the rest of this book. The same applies to the nineteen sovereigns in the Eurozone, none of which can control the monetary issuance of "their" NCB.

The implication is that, from the perspective of an individual NCB (and indeed from the perspective of their sovereigns) it is as if all its euro-denominated debt is foreign-currency denominated. Own-risk activities undertaken by NCBs (that is, activities for which the individual NCB is responsible and for which there is no profit and loss sharing with the rest of the Eurosystem) have vastly increased in scope and scale. Individual NCBs therefore can become insolvent even if the consolidated Eurosystem (treating all risk as shared risk) is solvent.

We argue that this is more than a theoretical curiosum. The exposure of the Banca d'Italia to high-risk Italian sovereign debt, both directly (through the Public Sector Purchase Programme) and indirectly, thought its exposure to Italian banks that hold a large amount of Italian sovereign debt, is such that its solvency could be at risk should there be a material Italian sovereign debt restructuring. The Chapter then discusses how to cure this affliction. Reducing or, preferably, eliminating own-risk activities by NCBs is one obvious solution. Another is reducing the riskiness of the assets that some NCBs and the commercial banks in their jurisdictions are exposed to. This could be done through financial engineering, through sovereign risk sharing or through regulatory measures limiting the exposure of banks to any counterparty, including their own sovereign.

A key message of this book is that it is time to move from the conventional balance sheet of the State (and of its constituent entities) to the comprehensive balance sheet or intertemporal budget constraint. The fiscal options open to the State can only be understood if we have a clear understanding of the IBC of the State. The IBC of the State is central to understanding the fiscal space available to the authorities and to designing sustainable countercyclical and structural fiscal policies. This key role of the IBC of the State also makes it all the more important that its improper use in the FTPL be exposed.

Whatever the degree of operational independence of a central bank, it remains the liquid monetary window of the Treasury, which is also its beneficial owner. There is an unavoidable tension between the beneficial ownership of the central bank by the national Treasury and the operational independence of the central bank. Operational independence requires accountability. At the very least, operational independence of a central bank requires that there be clarity and transparency about all its fiscal and quasi-fiscal transactions. Temporary confidentiality may make sense during financial upheavals; full disclosure has to be the rule once financial order has been restored.

I The Central Bank Balance Sheet: Why It Matters

I.I THE POST–GREAT FINANCIAL CRISIS CENTRAL BANK
BALANCE SHEET EXPLOSION

The size of central bank balance sheets in many advanced economies has increased massively since the start of the Great Financial Crisis (GFC) in the second half of 2007.[1] Even before central bank policy rates hit the effective lower bound (ELB), there were significant balance sheet increases due to the lender-of-last-resort (LLR) and market-maker-of-last-resort (MMLR) operations of the Fed, the Bank of England and the ECB. Figures 1.1 through 1.6 tell the story.

Once the policy rate (generally a short, risk-free nominal interest rate) hit the ELB, and the authorities were unable or unwilling to eliminate or materially lower the ELB, there were only three options open to the monetary policy makers. The first was to change the size and composition of the balance sheet. The second was "open mouth operations," including forward guidance about policy rates and the size and composition of the balance sheet. The third was to target some other financial asset price, like a long-term interest rate or the exchange rate.[2] Of the major monetary authorities, only the Japanese chose the third option when the Bank of Japan (BoJ) introduced "Quantitative and Qualitative Monetary Easing with Yield Curve Control" in September 2016. It pegged the overnight rate (the

---

[1]   GFC is often expanded as *Global* Financial Crisis. This is inaccurate; the financial crisis was confined to the North Atlantic region; hence our preference for *Great* Financial Crisis.

[2]   In a Modigliani–Miller world in which the relative supplies of different nonmonetary assets do not affect yields, credible forward guidance about the (short) policy rate would also pin down longer-maturity rates (over the horizon of the forward guidance). Term premia can, of course, be present even in a Modigliani–Miller world.

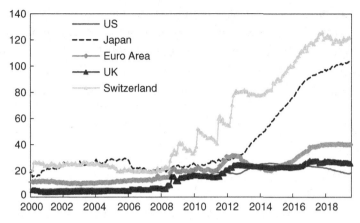

FIGURE I.I Central bank assets

uncollateralized overnight call rate) at –10bps and targeted the ten-year Japanese Government Bond (JGB) yield at close to zero (strictly a target range between 0 percent and 10bps), which meant that the size of the Bank of Japan's purchases of longer-dated sovereign debt became endogenous.[3]

The Fed's balance sheet as a share of GDP was 5.98 percent at the end of June 2007. It peaked as a share of GDP at the end of 2014 at 25.81 percent. At the end of June 2018, it was 21.09 percent. The decline since the end of 2014 reflects the growth of nominal GDP, the tapering that started in December 2013, followed by the end of QE on October 29, 2014, and the start of quantitative tightening (QT) or balance sheet shrinking) in October 2017, which ended in August 2019.

The Bank of England had a balance sheet equal to 6.38 percent of GDP in February 2008. This grew to 24.14 percent of GDP in February 2013, fluctuated a little and reached 24.4 percent of GDP at the

[3]   The ten-year JBG target was changed on July 31, 2018, to a target range between 0 percent and 20bps. The BoJ could, in principle, set both price and quantity in the JGB market by choosing a "rationing equilibrium" that is not on the market supply curve of JGBs – specifically an equilibrium where at the pegged JGB yield the quantity bought by the BoJ is less than the quantity offered by the market. We don't think this is how the yield curve control is implemented.

beginning of 2017. It appears to have remained roughly constant in nominal terms since then, with the ratio to GDP declining gently as nominal GDP continued to increase. The balance sheet of the consolidated Eurosystem was 12.85 percent of Eurozone GDP at the end of June 2007. It stopped expanding in nominal terms with the end of the first QE programme in December 2018. The Eurosystem actually shrank its balance sheet by around €1 tn between June 2012 and November 2014. Its balance sheet peaked as a share of GDP at 40.04 percent at the end of 2017, a level from which it declined very gently since then despite continued balance sheet expansion until December 2018, because of growth in nominal GDP. QE was set to resume at a rate of €20 bn a month in November 2019.

The Bank of Japan's balance sheet was 18.82 percent of GDP in June 2007. At the end of June 2018 this had risen to 96.60 percent and it can be expected to rise further if the Bank of Japan succeeds in hitting its current quantitative and qualitative easing plans (¥80 tn at an annual rate) or manages to continue its (lower) actual volume of asset purchases (¥ 40 to ¥50 tn at an annual rate).

The balance sheet of the Swiss National Bank was 18.99 percent of GDP in June 2007. Largely driven by foreign currency inflows, it now stands at 120.72 percent of GDP (June 30, 2018).

Among the advanced economies, New Zealand, Denmark, Norway, Australia and Canada stand out by having no material increases in the size of their central banks' balance sheets as a share of GDP since the GFC.

Some details about the composition of the assets and liabilities of the Fed can be found in Figures 1.2a and 1.2b.

In the United States, on the asset side of the balance sheet, the initial explosion involved "other assets," reflecting emergency asset purchases and collateralized lending operations during the initial panic phase of the GFC. Such LLR and MMLR operations were no longer as significant when financial chaos had been subdued in 2010. Since then, mortgage-backed securities (MBS) and Treasury debt have

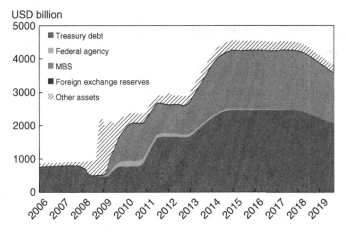

FIGURE 1.2A US Federal Reserve assets

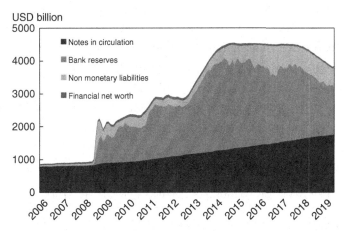

FIGURE 1.2B US Federal Reserve liabilities

accounted for effectively all of the balance sheet expansion on the asset side, and the shrinkage, since October 2017.

On the liability side of the Fed's balance sheet, the explosion in excess reserves since 2008 is a familiar story. What is perhaps more surprising is that the stock of currency (notes in circulation) more than doubled from $811 bn to $1,661 bn between June 2007 and June 2018. US population in 2018 is about 326.8 million, so there is just over $5,000 of currency outstanding for every man, woman and child in the United States. Rogoff (2016, 2018) estimates that around 44 percent of the stock of US currency (by value) is held abroad, but that still leaves more than $2,800 in cash for each US resident. This suggests that cash holdings in the United States are distributed highly unevenly, with the anonymity of cash making it a favorite store of value and medium of exchange for illegal activities.

The recent growth in the size of nonmonetary liabilities reflects continued attempts by the Fed to move its practices for managing the size and composition of its balance sheet into the twenty-first century, for instance by using reverse repos (called repos outside the USA) which include nonbank counterparties, something that is clearly sensible in a country where banks account for only just over 30 percent of financial intermediation (see Financial Stability Board (2018)).[4]

The US Treasury, like any central government Treasury or ministry of finance, is the beneficial owner of the central bank, regardless of the often rather esoteric formal ownership arrangements history may have bestowed on the central bank. That means the US Treasury receives something akin to the "profits" of the Federal Reserve System – and has a material role in determining how such profits are

---

[4]   The New York Fed conducts overnight reverse repo operations each day as a means to help keep the federal funds rate above the floor of the target range set by the Federal Open Market Committee (FOMC). An overnight reverse repurchase agreement (ON RRP) is overnight secured borrowing by the Fed from eligible counterparties. When the Fed conducts an ON RRP, it borrows overnight in a secured manner by selling a security to an eligible counterparty and simultaneously agreeing to buy the security back the next day at a price set today. There is a reduction in reserve balances on the liability side of the Federal Reserve's balance sheet and a corresponding increase in reverse repo obligations while the trade is outstanding. The FOMC sets the ON RRP offering rate, which is the maximum interest rate the Federal Reserve is willing to pay in an ON RRP operation; the actual interest rate that a counterparty receives is determined through an auction process. It is a complement to the interest rate on excess reserves as an instrument for setting a floor on the overnight market rate. In a Fed overnight repo (called a reverse repo outside the USA) it buys a security from an eligible counterparty and simultaneously agrees to sell the security back the next day at a price set today. It amounts to a secured overnight lending rate for the Fed. In principle, the overnight repurchase operations could be used to keep the overnight market rate below the ceiling of the Fed's federal funds target rate. See Board of Governors of the Federal Reserve System, Policy Tools, Overnight Reverse Repurchase Agreement Facility; www.federalreserve.gov/monetarypolicy/overnight-reverse-repurchase-agreements.htm.

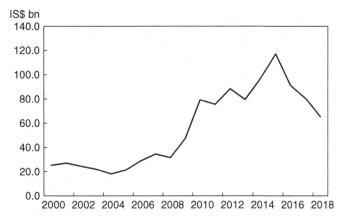

FIGURE I.3 Fed payments to US Treasury

defined and measured. As shown in Figure 1.3, in the years prior to the GFC, profit remittances from the Fed to the Treasury ranged between $20 bn and $40 bn. They peaked in 2015 (paid in 2016) at $97.7 bn. The decline since 2015 is mostly due to the Fed paying interest on excess reserves (and on required reserves) at a quite generous level, currently (September 19, 2019), 1.80 percent.

Not satisfied with a mere $97.7 bn, Congress in late 2015 raided the reserves of the Regional Reserve Banks to the tune of $19.3 bn to help fund the Fixing America's Surface Transportation (FAST) Act. The 2017 FRB payment to the US Treasury was $80.6 bn and the 2018 payment $65.3bn.

The evolution of central bank assets and liabilities since the GFC for the United Kingdom, the Eurozone and Japan are shown in, respectively, Figures 1.4a,b, 1.5a,b, and 1.6a,b.

I.2 A LITTLE SEIGNIORAGE ARITHMETIC

To put some analytical structure on these expanding central bank balance sheets, and especially on the fiscal and quasi-fiscal implications, the concept of seigniorage is indispensable. Seigniorage is the stream of profits earned by the central bank through its ability to issue base money at negligible marginal cost. It is a key driver of the

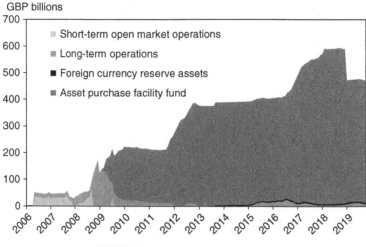

FIGURE 1.4A UK BoE assets

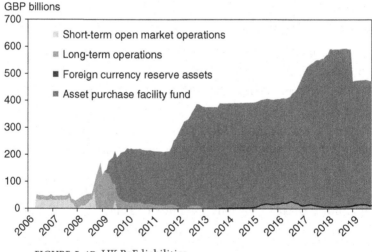

FIGURE 1.4B UK BoE liabilities

contribution of the central bank to the sovereign's funding needs. What follows relies on Buiter (2003, 2007a and 2014a).

In a modern fiat money economy, base money, M, is the sum of the stock of currency, J, and commercial bank reserves held with the central bank, Z, itself the sum of required reserves, Z^r, and excess

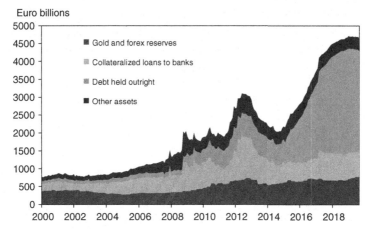

FIGURE I.5A Eurosystem assets

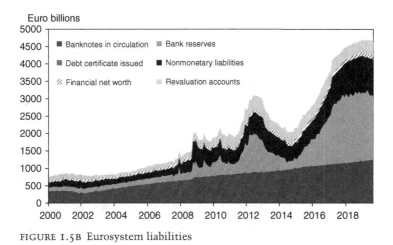

FIGURE I.5B Eurosystem liabilities

reserves, Z^e. All three components pay interest rates that are typically below the risk-free market rate of interest, $i_{t,t-1}$, the interest rate on one-period safe government debt paid in period t. Currency typically pays a zero interest rate, $i^l_{t,t-1} = 0$. The interest rate on required reserves, $i^r_{t,t-1}$, and on excess reserves, $i^e_{t,t-1}$ are set by the central bank. In addition, currency is *irredeemable* – the holder of a given amount of currency has no other claim on the issuer (the central bank) than for that same amount of currency. For all practical purposes, the

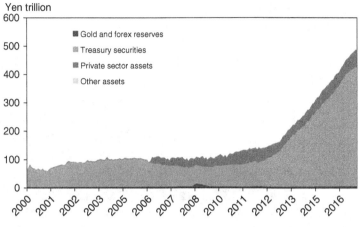

FIGURE I.6A Japan BoJ assets

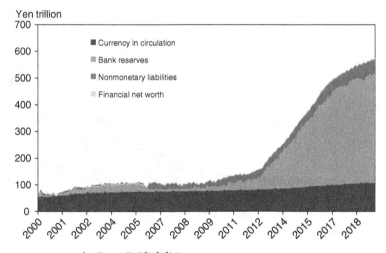

FIGURE I.6B Japan BoJ liabilities

stock of bank reserves can also be viewed as irredeemable – at most the holder can insist on redemption in the form of currency, and even that is not self-evident.

So

$$M = J + Z$$

$$Z = Z^r + Z^e$$

1.2.a   Two Measures of Seigniorage and the Present Value Seigniorage Identity

Two useful measures of "flow seigniorage," the current revenue obtained by the central bank from its issuance of base money, are:[5]

$$\Omega_t^1 \equiv M_{t+1} - (1 + i_{t,t-1}^M)M_t$$
$$= \Delta M_{t+1} \quad \text{if } i_{t,t-1}^M = 0 \tag{1.1}$$

and

$$\Omega_t^2 \equiv (i_{t,t-1} - i_{t,t-1}^M)M_t$$
$$= i_{t,t-1}M_t \quad \text{if } i_{t,t-1}^M = 0 \tag{1.2}$$

where $i_{t,t-1}^M$ is the average interest rate on the monetary base:

$$i_{t,t-1}^M = i_{t,t-1}^J \left(\frac{J_t}{M_t}\right) + i_{t,t-1}^r \left(\frac{Z_t^r}{M_t}\right) + i_{t,t-1}^e \left(\frac{Z_t^e}{M_t}\right)$$

The first measure, Ω^1, represents the command over real resources achieved in period t by the issuance of base money in that period. When the nominal interest rate on base money is zero (as it is for its currency component), Ω^1 is just the change in the monetary base. The second measure represents the interest saved in a period by having borrowed through the issuance of base money liabilities rather than through the issuance of nonmonetary debt or, equivalently, the profit earned in a given period by holding monetary liabilities and an equal amount of nonmonetary assets.

A few more bits of notation are required: I_{t_1,t_0} is the nominal stochastic discount factor between periods t_1 and t_0.[6] It is related as follows to the risk-free, one-period nominal interest rate: $\frac{1}{1+i_{t+1,t}} = E_t I_{t+1,t}$; R_{t_1,t_0} is the real stochastic discount factor between periods t_0 and t_1; it is related to the risk-free, one-period real interest rate as follows: $\frac{1}{1+r_{t+1,t}} = E_t R_{t+1,t}$; $\Pi_{t_1,t_0} = \frac{P_{t_1}}{P_{t_0}}$ is the inflation factor between periods t_0 and t_1. The three factors are related by:

---

5   $\Delta X_t \equiv X_t - X_{t-1}$. The time subscripts of asset stocks refer to the beginning of the period in which they are held.

6   The mathematics of stochastic discount factors can be found in the Appendix to Chapter 1.

$R_{t_1,t_0} = I_{t_1,t_0} \Pi_{t_1,t_0}$. The real growth–corrected stochastic discount factor between periods t_0 and t_1, $\overline{R}_{t_1,t_0}$ is defined analogously. Let Y_t be real GDP in period t. The real growth factor between periods t_0 and t_1 is defined by $\Gamma_{t_1,t_0} = \frac{Y_{t_1}}{Y_{t_0}}$. The real growth–corrected stochastic discount factor is defined by $\overline{R}_{t_1,t_0} = R_{t_1,t_0}\Gamma_{t_1,t_0}$.

We also define the following notation: For any sequence of nominal payments X_j, $j = 1, 2, \ldots.$, the present discounted value (PDV) at the beginning of period t of all current and future values of X_j, P_j is defined as $V_t(\{X, I\}) \equiv E_t \sum_{j=t}^{\infty} I_{j,t} X_j$. For any sequence of real payments $X_j/P_j, j = 1, 2, \ldots.$, the PDV at the beginning of period t of all current and future values of X_j/P_j is defined as $V_t\left(\left\{\frac{X}{P}, R\right\}\right) \equiv E_t \sum_{j=t}^{\infty} R_{j,t} \frac{X_j}{P_j}$.

For any sequence of payments as a share of GDP, $X_j/(P_j Y_j), j = 1, 2, \ldots.$, the PDV at the beginning of period t of all current and future values of x_j using growth-adjusted real discount rates is defined as $V_t\left(\left\{\frac{X}{PY}, \overline{R}\right\}\right) \equiv E_t \sum_{j=t}^{\infty} \overline{R}_{j,t} \frac{X_j}{P_j Y_j}$

It can be shown by brute force that the two seigniorage measures are related as follows by the intertemporal seigniorage identity (see also Buiter (2007a)):

$$E_t \sum_{j=t}^{\infty} I_{j,t} \left(M_{j+1} - (1 + i_{j,j-1}^M) M_j \right) \equiv E_t \sum_{j=t}^{\infty} I_{j+1,t}(i_{j+1,j} - i_{j+1,j}^M) M_{j+1}$$
$$-(1 + i_{t,t-1}^M)M_t + \lim_{j \to \infty} E_t I_{j,t} M_{j+1} \qquad (1.3)^7$$

In words, the PDV of current and future changes in the monetary base (corrected for any interest paid on the monetary base) equals the PDV of current and future profits earned from investing the current and future money stocks, minus the initial value of the stock of base

---

[7] In continuous time, without uncertainty, the intertemporal seigniorage identity is:

$$\lim_{v \to \infty} \left(\int_t^v e^{-\int_t^s i(u)du} \left(\dot{M}(s) - i^M(s)M(s) \right) ds \right)$$
$$= \lim_{v \to \infty} \left[\int_t^v e^{-\int_t^s i(u)du} \left(\left(i(s) - i^M(s) \right)M(s) \right) ds + e^{-\int_t^v i(u)du} M(v) \right] - M(t)$$

money plus the PDV of the terminal stock of base money. We can write (1.3) more compactly as:

$$V_t(\{\Omega^1, I\}) = V_t(\{\Omega^2, I\}) + V_t(\lim_{j \to \infty} M_{j+1}, I)$$
$$-(1 + i^M_{t,t-1})M_t \tag{1.4}$$

If we want to study the behavior of an economy that is permanently stuck at the effective lower bound, as we do in Chapter 5, it is not sensible to assume that the PDV of the terminal base money stock, $\lim_{j \to \infty} E_t I_{j,t} M_{j+1} = V_t(\lim_{j \to \infty} M_{j+1}, I)$ equals zero in the long run. This may well be the case for Japan, as is clear from Figure 1.7, which shows the uncollateralized overnight call rate since 1998.

Except in such a permanent liquidity-trap equilibrium, the assumption that the stock of nominal base money does not forever grow at a rate equal to or greater than the short nominal interest rate is probably unobjectionable.

Our two flow seigniorage measures as a share of GDP, $\omega^1_t = \frac{\Omega^1_t}{P_t Y_t}$, and $\omega^2_t = \frac{\Omega^2_t}{P_t Y_t}$ are given by:

$$\omega^1_t = \frac{\Delta M_{t+1} - i^M_{t,t-1} M_t}{P_t Y_t} = (1 + \pi_{t+1,t})(1 + \gamma_{t+1,t})m_{t+1}$$
$$-(1 + i^M_{t,t+1})m_t$$
$$\omega^2_t = \frac{(i_{t,t+1} - i^M_{t,t+1})M_t}{P_t Y_t} = (i_{t,t+1} - i^M_{t,t+1})m_t \tag{1.5}$$

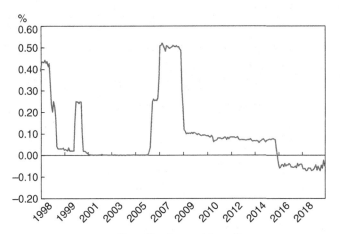

FIGURE I.7 Yen uncollateralized overnight call rate

where $m_t = \frac{M_t}{P_t Y_t}$ is the monetary base as a share of GDP (the reciprocal of the income velocity of circulation of base money), $1 + \pi_{t+1,t} = P_{t+1}/P_t$ and $1 + \gamma_{t+1,t} = Y_{t+1}/Y_t$.

1.2.b How Much Seigniorage Can Be Extracted?

What would the values of these two seigniorage measures be for the USA if the economy were at its inflation target, assumed to be 2.0 percent, and real GDP growth were, say, 2.0 percent – a reasonable number for the growth rate of potential output of the USA? We will assume that the interest rate on required and excess reserves is zero (i.e. we set $i^M = 0$ in equation (1.5)), which flatters the magnitude of the seigniorage calculations.

As of March 13, 2019, the total monetary base was $3,430 bn, split almost equally between currency in circulation ($1,717 bn) and total balances maintained ($1,713 bn).[8] The US nominal GDP in 2018 was $20,513 bn. The monetary base is therefore 16.72 percent of annual GDP. The "noninflationary" seigniorage that can be extracted according to the ω^1 measure (assuming that $m_{t+1} = m_t$) is therefore 0.68 percent of GDP. If we narrow down the seigniorage concept to just the change in the stock of currency in circulation, the noninflationary seigniorage as a share of GDP would be 0.34 percent of GDP. This number no doubt comes as a disappointment to some proponents of Modern Monetary Theory (MMT), who at times appear to confuse the large amount of monetary deficit financing that is feasible and safe at the ELB, when the economy is in a liquidity trap, with the noninflationary monetary deficit financing that is possible away from the ELB (see, e.g., Bell (2000), Tcherneva (2002), Forstater and Mosler (2005), Wray and Forstater (2005), Mosler (2010), Wray (2015, 2018) and Roche (2019)). Fullwiler et al. (2019) do not make this mistake.

Note that at the ELB, when the economy is in a liquidity trap, the stock of money balances as a share of GDP can be increased through nominal base money issuance; that is, m_{t+1} can be made

---

[8]   See Federal Reserve Board; www.federalreserve.gov/releases/h3/current/.

larger than m_t in equation (1.5) by possibly highly significant amounts, because the demand for real money balances at the ELB is infinitely interest-elastic. This accounts for the extraordinarily large seigniorage numbers in some of the years following the GFC, shown in Table 2.11 in Chapter 2.

The ω^2 measure of seigniorage (interest saved) would be the same as the ω^1 measure if the nominal interest rate were 4 percent. Current estimates of the short-term neutral nominal interest rate in the USA tend to be 3 percent or less, however. With $i = 0.03$, and again assuming $i^M = 0$, the interest saved would be 0.5 percent of GDP if we include the entire monetary base in the calculation. It would be 0.25 percent of GDP if we included just currency in circulation.

Instead of asking how much seigniorage can be extracted with inflation at its target value, we might be interested in the maximum amount of seigniorage as a share of GDP that can be extracted at any *constant* rate of inflation. This rules out hyperinflation equilibria. To answer this question, we need to know how the demand for real money balances varies with the rate of inflation. That means we have to have an estimate of a base money demand function. We restrict the analysis in what follows to the demand for currency in circulation, in part because the current US interest rate on required and excess reserves is very close to the market interest rate (it was 2.40 percent on March 16, 2019, and 1.80 percent on September 23, 2019), so very little seigniorage is currently earned on this component of the monetary base.

A standard Cagan-style demand function for currency takes the form:[9]

$$\frac{J}{P} = kY^\alpha e^{-\beta(i-i^J)}$$
$$k, \alpha, \beta > 0 \tag{1.6}$$

---

[9] The Cagan (1956) base money demand function does not have the property, used elsewhere in this book, that the demand for real base money becomes infinitely interest-sensitive when the nominal interest rate is zero. From equation (1.6), when $i = i^J = 0$, $\frac{J}{P} = kY^\alpha$.

With the interest rate on currency, i^I, equal to zero, it follows that, at a constant nominal interest rate, the growth rate of the stock of currency, μ, the rate of inflation, π, and the growth rate of real GDP, γ, are related as follows:

$$1 + \mu = (1 + \pi)(1 + \gamma)^\alpha \tag{1.7}$$

The steady-state values of the two seigniorage measures as shares of GDP – if a steady state exists – are given by:

$$\begin{aligned} \omega^1 &= \left((1+\pi)(1+\gamma) - (1+i^M)\right)m \\ \omega^2 &= (i - i^M)m \end{aligned} \tag{1.8}$$

In the case of revenue from currency alone, this becomes, using (1.6) and $i^M = i^I = 0$:

$$\begin{aligned} \omega^1 &= \left((1+\pi)(1+\gamma) - 1\right)kY^{\alpha-1}e^{-\beta i} \\ \omega^2 &= ikY^{\alpha-1}e^{-\beta i} \end{aligned} \tag{1.9}$$

Of course, we can only have a steady state if either α, the output elasticity of currency demand, equals 1 or if the growth rate of real GDP is zero.

The Global Economics team at Citi have produced estimates of long-run currency demand functions for the euro, the US dollar, the pound sterling and the Japanese yen, based on equation (1.6), allowing for nonstationarity, common trends and structural breaks in the relevant series (see, e.g., Buiter (2013)).

The estimation yields a robust estimate for the output elasticity of currency demand, α, for the euro, the US dollar and sterling of around 0.8 (and around 1.0 for the yen), implying that every 1 percent increase in real output calls forth a 0.8 percent (1.0 percent for the yen) increase in real money balances demanded. The interest rate semi-elasticity of currency demand is somewhat less precisely estimated. The average coefficient value estimated for β is around 3 for the euro area (but considerably higher for the United States at 7.2), implying that a 1 percentage point increase in a short-term nominal market interest rate (our opportunity cost measure) implies a 3 percent decrease in the demand for real euro currency balances.

To continue the steady-state analysis, we set $\alpha = 1$, which will mean an overestimate of long-run seigniorage for the euro, the US dollar and sterling at any constant rate of inflation. We assume that the one-period, risk-free nominal interest rate and the one-period, risk-free real interest rate are related through the Fisher equation:

$$1 + i = (1 + r)(1 + \pi) \tag{1.10}$$

This gives us:

$$\omega^1 = \left((1 + \gamma)(1 + \pi) - 1\right)ke^{-\beta((1+r)(1+\pi)-1)}$$
$$\omega^2 = \left((1 + r)(1 + \pi) - 1\right)ke^{-\beta((1+r)(1+\pi)-1)} \tag{1.11}$$

Taking the real interest rate and the growth rate of real GDP as given, the inflation rate that maximizes ω^1 is given by:

$$\hat{\pi}_{\omega^1} = \frac{1}{(1+r)\beta} - \frac{\gamma}{1+\gamma} \tag{1.12}$$

and the inflation rate that maximizes ω^2 is given by:

$$\hat{\pi}_{\omega^2} = \frac{1}{(1+r)\beta} - \frac{r}{1+r} \tag{1.13}$$

The maximum steady-state values of our two flow seigniorage measures are:

$$\hat{\omega}^1 = \frac{(1+\gamma)}{(1+r)\beta}ke^{-\left(1+\beta\left(\frac{r-\gamma}{1+\gamma}\right)\right)} \tag{1.14}$$

and

$$\hat{\omega}^2 = \left(\frac{1}{\beta}\right)ke^{-1} \tag{1.15}$$

The two seigniorage maximizing inflation rates and the maximized value of seigniorage as a share of GDP are the same if the real interest rate equals the growth rate of real GDP – if the economy is at the Golden Rule.

For the USA, our point estimate of β is 7.2 (a rather high number). Assume for illustrative purposes that the real growth rate and the real interest rate are both 2 percent. We estimate k by taking the ratio

Table 1.1 *Steady-state inflation rate that maximizes seigniorage as a share of GDP*

Country/ currency	Year	β	k=Ratio of currency to annual GDP	$r = \gamma$ (%)	$\hat{\pi}^1$ (%)	$\hat{\omega}^1$ (%)
Eurozone	2013	2.9	0.096	1.0	33.2	1.22
US	2014	7.2	0.073	2.0	11.7	0.37
Japan	2015	2.0	0.185	0.5	49.3	3.40
UK	2016	1.7	0.039	1.5	56.5	0.84

Source: own calculations

of currency in circulation to GDP in the most recent year when the interest rate on excess reserves was (near) zero. For Japan this is 2016, for the United States 2014, for the Eurozone 2013 and for the United Kingdom 2016.

Given these assumptions (including the counterfactual one for the United States, the United Kingdom and the Eurozone that the output elasticity of currency demand equals 1), the constant rate of inflation that maximizes the share of seigniorage in GDP in the USA is a low 11.66 percent. The maximum share of seigniorage in GDP in the USA is a low 0.37 percent. Both these low numbers reflect the high value of β. If we assume instead that the interest semi-elasticity of US dollar currency demand is 2.0, the constant inflation rate that maximizes steady-state seigniorage as a share of GDP for the USA is 47.1 percent and the maximum constant share of seigniorage in GDP is 1.34 percent. Japan's maximum sustainable seigniorage is 3.4 percent of GDP at an inflation rate of 49.3 percent.

Although 1.34 percent of GDP on a recurrent basis is nothing to be sniffed at, it is a useful qualifier to the PDV calculations in the next subsection. When you are considering an infinite horizon, dramatic things can happen if the gap between the discount rate and the growth rate of what is discounted is small.

I.2.C The Present Value of Seigniorage Revenues

We are interested in the empirical magnitude of the present discounted value of current and future seigniorage at the beginning of period t, denoted $V_t(\{\Omega^1, I\})$, that is:

$$V_t(\{\Omega^1, I\}) = E_t \sum_{j=t}^{\infty} I_{j,t-1} \left(M_{j+1} - (1 + i^M_{j,j-1}) M_j \right) \tag{1.16}$$

The reason for our interest is that $V_t(\{\Omega^1, I\})$, the PDV of current and future seigniorage, is a key asset in the comprehensive balance sheet (or intertemporal budget constraint) of the central bank and the State – an asset that is absent from the conventional balance sheet but that is essential in assessing the solvency of the central bank and the State. These ideas are developed further in Chapter 2. Clearly, central bank solvency should never be a problem unless the central bank has significant foreign-currency-denominated or index-linked liabilities.[10] If this is not the case, the central bank should always be able to service its debt obligations by adding to the monetary base ("printing money"). The only (political) constraint on this is the inflation that will be generated, sooner or later, if the nominal stock of base money grows at a sufficiently high rate for a sufficiently long period of time. An interesting benchmark is the PDV of current and future seigniorage if the inflation rate is at its target level. If that PDV is a sufficiently large number, we can be reasonably confident that the central bank will be able to discharge all its financial obligations without having to engage in excessively inflationary monetary base expansion.

An empirical implementation of equation (1.16) is a heroic task, which we tackle by making the heroic simplification of stationarity. Specifically, we assume that the proportional growth rate of the monetary base is a constant μ and that the short nominal interest rate is a constant i. We also restrict the consideration of the monetary base to the currency component, omitting required and excess reserves

---

[10] Strictly speaking, only "deliverable" index-linked securities – bonds promising to pay a given amount of physical real output each period – create unavoidable default risk.

issuance as a source of seigniorage. This means that we set $M = J$ and $i_j^J = 0$ in equation (1.16). We therefore err on the side of underestimating the size of the NPV of future seigniorage.

The PDV of current and future currency issuance can now be written as

$$V(\{\Omega^1, I\}) = \left(\frac{1+i}{1+i-(1+\pi)(1+\gamma)^{\alpha}}\right)\left((1+\pi)(1+\gamma)^{\alpha} - 1\right)J_0 \quad (1.17)$$

where J_0 is the initial value of the stock of currency.

To arrive at estimates of the present discounted value of seigniorage when inflation is at its target rate, we need to combine our estimated coefficients with assumptions about future real growth rates for the euro area and discount rates for the stream of seigniorage revenue. A reasonable estimate for the long-run real growth rate of the euro area would be around 1 percent pa. The long-run nominal discount rate presents something of a problem in this age of extraordinarily low nominal and real interest rates. It is very easy to get infinite values for the PDV of future seigniorage revenues (and for the PDV of future central bank operating costs, discussed in Chapter 2) even with interest rates in excess (for the Eurozone, Japan and the United Kingdom *well* in excess) of their current values.

We now use this PDV of current and future seigniorage framework to make estimates of the noninflationary loss absorption capacity (NILAC) of a number of central banks. This analysis draws on writings by Buiter (2010, 2013) and Buiter and Rahbari (2012a, b). "Noninflationary" here again means an inflation rate of 2 percent for the GDP deflator – a reasonable approximation to the inflation targets of the monetary authorities we are considering. Table 1.2 presents the estimates for the value of the PDV of Eurosystem seigniorage based on our benchmark assumptions about the output elasticity of currency demand, α, the semi-elasticity of currency demand with respect to the short nominal interest rate, β, the rate of inflation, π, as well as a number of alternative assumptions for real GDP growth rates, γ, and nominal interest rates, i. As Table 1.2 indicates, the resulting value

Table 1.2 *Present discounted value of future seigniorage in the euro area (α=0.8; β=2.9; π=0.02)*

EUR (bn)	Interest/Discount Rate (i)				
Real Growth Rate (γ)	2.5%	3.0%	3.5%	4.0%	4.5%
0.5%	30,428	4,692	2,520	1,712	1,290
1.0%	infinite	17,579	4,698	2,690	1,873
1.5%	infinite	infinite	13,256	4,689	2,827
2.0%	infinite	infinite	infinite	11,064	4,669

Note: α represents the long-run income elasticity of the money demand function, and β the corresponding interest rate semi-elasticity.
Source: Citi Investment Research and Analysis

would be just under €2.7 tn at a 1 percent average real growth rate and with a nominal discount rate of 4 percent. Raising the average growth rate of real GDP to 1.5 percent raises the estimate of the present discounted value of seigniorage by 74 percent. Note that the relevant growth rate here is the average growth rate in the future, with the horizon being infinite. Even with a real GDP growth rate as low as 0.5 percent, a nominal discount rate of 2.5 percent would generate a PDV of seigniorage of just over €30 tn. A 2 percent nominal discount rate would result in an infinite PDV of seigniorage, even with real GDP growth at 0.5 percent – the long-run growth rate of the nominal stock of currency exceeds the nominal discount rate in this case.

The corresponding estimates and calculations for US dollar, sterling and yen currency demand and seigniorage are given in Tables 1.3, 1.4 and 1.5, respectively.

By any standards, these estimates of the PDV of noninflationary seigniorage are large numbers. For the euro area, as noted, at 2 percent inflation, 1 percent real GDP growth and a 4 percent nominal interest rate, it comes to €2.7 tn (see Table 1.2). For the USA, with 2 percent inflation, real GDP growth at 2 percent and a 4 percent nominal discount rate, the PDV of future noninflationary seigniorage is $13.7 tn (see Table 1.3). For the United Kingdom, with 2 percent inflation,

Table 1.3 *Present discounted value of future seigniorage in the United States (α=0.8; β=7.2; π=0.02)*

US$ (bn)	Interest/Discount Rate (i)				
Real Growth Rate (γ)	2.5%	3.0%	3.5%	4.0%	4.5%
0.5%	40,093	6,051	3,180	2,115	1,560
1.0%	infinite	22,670	5,930	3,322	2,265
1.5%	infinite	infinite	16,731	5,793	3,418
2.0%	infinite	infinite	infinite	13,668	5,645
2.5%	infinite	infinite	infinite	infinite	11,760

Note: α represents the long run income elasticity of the money demand function, and β the corresponding interest rate semi-elasticity.
Source: Citi Investment Research and Analysis

Table 1.4 *Present discounted value of future seigniorage in the United Kingdom (α=0.8; β=1.7; π=0.02)*

UK£ (bn)	Interest/Discount Rate (i)				
Real Growth Rate (γ)	2.5%	3.0%	3.5%	4.0%	4.5%
0.5%	1,956	303	164	112	85
1.0%	infinite	1,137	306	176	123
1.5%	infinite	infinite	862	307	186
2.0%	T	infinite	infinite	724	307
2.5%	infinite	infinite	infinite	infinite	640

Note: α represents the long run income elasticity of the money demand function, and β the corresponding interest rate semi-elasticity.
Source: Citi Investment Research and Analysis

1.5 percent real growth and a 4 percent discount rate, the PDV is £307bn. With 2 percent real growth this becomes £724 bn (see Table 1.4). For Japan, with a 0.5 percent trend real GDP growth and a 4 percent discount rate, the PDV is ¥172 tn (see Table 1.5). If we used discount rates closer to what has been the norm since the start of QE

Table 1.5 *Present discounted value of future seigniorage in Japan*
(α=1.0; β=2.0; π=2.0)

Yen (tn)		Interest/Discount Rate (i)			
Real Growth Rate (γ)	2.5%	3.0%	3.5%	4.0%	4.5%
0.5%	infinite	529	261	172	128
1.0%	infinite	infinite	647	315	208
1.5%	infinite	infinite	infinite	768	370
2.0%	infinite	infinite	infinite	infinite	893

Note: α represents the long run income elasticity of the money demand
function, and β the corresponding interest rate semi-elasticity
Source: Citi Investment Research and Analysis

(say, 2 percent) the PDV of future seigniorage would be robustly
infinite.

The numbers in Tables 1.2 to 1.5 underestimate the noninflationary loss-absorbing capacity or NILAC of the central bank for a
number of reasons. First, it excludes required and excess reserves from
the exercise, or assumes they are paid the market opportunity cost and
therefore don't represent a source of profit to the central bank. Even if
this were correct currently, it is at the discretion of the central bank,
which sets both the reserve requirement and the rates of remuneration
on required reserves and excess reserves. The required reserve ratio for
the euro area was lowered (on December 8, 2011) to 1 percent of
eligible deposits from 2 percent. The United Kingdom has no required
reserves other than those required to be held under the *de minimis*
Cash Ratio Deposit Scheme. As regards excess reserves, the availabil-
ity of private and other sovereign substitutes limits the ability of the
central bank to extract rents from these liabilities. The new liquidity
requirements of Basel 3 (the Liquidity Coverage Ratio (LCR) and the
Net Stable Funding Ratio (NSFR)) have, however, made holding excess
reserves with the central bank more attractive to banks, and the
central bank could extract greater rents from "excess reserves"
because of that.

Second, it ignores the conventional loss-absorption capacity of central banks. In the case of the Eurosystem, this amounted, as of December 31, 2017, to €102.7 bn of Capital and reserves, plus €357.9 bn worth of revaluation accounts – mostly revaluation gains on gold and foreign exchange reserves. For the Bank of England on February 28, 2018, capital plus reserves was £4.5 bn. There is not enough detail in the published accounts to uncover the existence and valuation of the Bank of England's revaluation gains.[11]

Finally, from the intertemporal seigniorage identity (equations (1.3) or (1.4)) (see also Chapter 2 and Buiter (2007a)), the intangible asset that has to be added to the conventional balance sheet of the central bank (which already contains the outstanding stock of base money as a liability, of course) to obtain its noninflationary loss absorption capacity is not just the PDV of future currency issuance but the sum of the PDV of future currency issuance and the initial stock of currency, about €1,171 bn for the euro area stock of banknotes at the end of December 2017.[12] This means that the noninflationary loss-absorption capacity of the Eurosystem with $y = 1\%$, $\pi = 2\%$ and $i = 4\%$ is €4.3 tn. For the Bank of England, with $y = 1.5\%$, $\pi = 2\%$ and $i = 4\%$, the total contribution to the NILAC from seigniorage is £386 bn, of which about £74 bn comes from the outstanding stock of currency (as of March 31, 2017) and about £4.8 bn from capital and reserves.[13]

We must of course, subtract the PDV of the operating costs – the cost of running the monetary authority – to get a correct measure of the PDV of the fiscal space potentially created by the central bank. For these purposes, we should estimate the cost of running the central

[11]   Bank of England Annual Report and Accounts, 1 March 2017–28 February 2018. The Bank of England publishes data for the consolidated balance sheet (banking and issue departments) only with a five-quarter lag. Most other leading central banks provide this information at monthly or even weekly frequencies with minimal lags.

[12]   I assume for the purpose of these calculations that the NPV of the terminal stock of base money is zero.

[13]   Bank of England, Annual Report 2014, page 54, www.bankofengland.co.uk/publica tions/Documents/annualreport/2014/boereport.pdf. I could not make heads or tails of the treatment of the £41 bn off-balance sheet Funding for Lending Scheme item, including whether this was an asset, a liability or both, so it has been ignored in the calculation.

bank acting as a narrow monetary authority, stripping out the cost of its supervisory and regulatory functions. There is no fully satisfactory way to do this, however, because the ECB (since 2014), many of the Eurosystem national central banks, the Fed, the Bank of England (since 2015) and the Bank of Japan all combine the role of monetary authority with material supervisory responsibilities. Estimates of the cost of running the monetary authority based on the cost of running these central banks will be biased upwards (other things being equal).

The total annual operating cost of the Eurosystem were €9,7 bn in 2017. If we assume constant real operating costs, 2 percent inflation and a 4 percent nominal discount rate, we obtain a PDV of current and future operating costs of €504.4 bn. If instead we assume that the real operating costs rise at the same rate as real GDP, 1 percent, say, the PDV of operating costs is €1,029.4 bn. Note that this does include costs associated with the supervisory and regulatory activities of the ECB and the nineteen NCBs. The Eurosystem's "net" NILAC, that is NILAC minus the PDV of operating costs, is around €3 tn.

The total operating costs of the Banking Department and the Issue Department of the Bank of England in 2017 was £518 mn. This excludes the operating costs of the Prudential Regulatory Authority (PRA), which accounts for most of the supervisory and regulatory activities now undertaken by the Bank of England. If we assume constant real operating costs, 2 percent inflation and a 4 percent nominal discount rate, this results in a PDV of current and future operating costs of £26.9 bn. If instead we assume that the real costs rise at the same rate as real GDP, 1.5 percent, say, the PDV of operating costs is £114.6 bn. In the latter case, the net NILAC of the Bank of England is therefore around £271 bn.

These numbers are large enough to get excited about. These resources are, of course, tax payers' resources and should be accounted for properly. In Chapter 2, we consider in greater detail the implications of the consolidation of the accounts of the Treasury and central bank that is a logical implication of the Treasury's beneficial ownership of the central bank.

Appendix to Chapter 1: Stochastic Discount Factors

I_{t_1,t_0} is the nominal stochastic discount factor between periods t_1 and t_0, defined recursively by

$$I_{t_1,t_0} = \prod_{k=t_0+1}^{t_1} I_{k,k-1} \qquad \text{for } t_1 > t_0$$

$$= 1 \qquad \text{for } t_1 = t_0$$

The interpretation of I_{t_1,t_0} is the price in terms of period t_0 money of one unit of money in period $t_1 \geq t_0$. There will in general be many possible states in period t_1, and period t_1 money has a period t_0 (forward) price for each state. Let E_t be the mathematical expectation operator conditional on information available at the beginning of period t. Provided earlier-dated information sets do not contain more information than later-dated information sets, these stochastic discount factors satisfy the recursion property

$$E_{t_0}(I_{t_1,t_0} E_{t_1} I_{t_2,t_1}) = E_{t_0} I_{t_2,t_0} \quad \text{for } t_2 \geq t_1 \geq t_0$$

Finally, the risk-free nominal interest rate in period t, $i_{t+1,t}$, that is, the money price in period t of one unit of money in every state of the world in period $t+1$ is defined by

$$\frac{1}{1 + i_{t+1,t}} = E_t I_{t+1,t} \tag{1.1}$$

The real stochastic discount factor between periods t_0 and t_1, R_{t_1,t_0} is defined analogously. The inflation factor between periods t_0 and t_1 is defined by

$$\Pi_{t_1,t_0} = \frac{P_{t_1}}{P_{t_0}} = \sum_{j=t_0+1}^{t_1} (1 + \pi_{j,j-1}) \qquad \text{for } t_1 > t_0$$

$$= 1 \qquad \text{for } t_1 = t_0$$

where $\pi_{j,j-1} = \frac{P_j - P_{j-1}}{P_{j-1}}$ is the rate of inflation between periods $j-1$ and j. The real stochastic discount factor is defined by:

$$R_{t_1,t_0} = I_{t_1,t_0} \Pi_{t_1,t_0}$$

It has the same recursive property as the nominal discount factor:

$$R_{t_1,t_0} = \prod_{k=t_0+1}^{t_1} R_{k,k-1} \qquad \text{for } t_1 > t_0$$

$$= 1 \qquad \text{for } t_1 = t_0$$

$$E_{t_0}(R_{t_1,t_0} E_{t_1} R_{t_2,t_1}) = E_{t_0} R_{t_2,t_0} \quad \text{for } t_2 \geq t_1 \geq t_0$$

Finally, the risk-free real interest rate in period t, $r_{t+1,t}$, that is, the price in terms of output in period t of one unit of output in every state of the world in period $t+1$, is defined by

$$\frac{1}{1 + r_{t+1,t}} = E_t R_{t+1,t} \tag{1.2}$$

The real growth-corrected stochastic discount factor between periods t_0 and t_1, $\overline{R}_{t_1,t_0}$ is defined analogously. Let Y_t be real GDP in period t. The growth factor between periods t_0 and t_1 is defined by

$$\Gamma_{t_1,t_0} = \frac{Y_{t_1}}{Y_{t_0}} = \sum_{j=t_0+1}^{t_1} (1 + \gamma_{j,j-1}) \qquad \text{for } t_1 > t_0$$

$$= 1 \qquad \text{for } t_1 = t_0$$

where $\gamma_{j,j-1} = \frac{Y_j - Y_{j-1}}{Y_{j-1}}$ is the growth rate of real GDP between periods $j-1$ and j.

The real growth-corrected stochastic discount factor is defined by:

$$\overline{R}_{t_1,t_0} = R_{t_1,t_0} \Gamma_{t_1,t_0}$$

It has the same recursive property as the other discount factors:

$$\overline{R}_{t_1,t_0} = \prod_{k=t_0+1}^{t_1} \overline{R}_{k,k-1} \qquad \text{for } t_1 > t_0$$

$$= 1 \qquad \text{for } t_1 = t_0$$

$$E_{t_0}(\overline{R}_{t_1,t_0} E_{t_1} \overline{R}_{t_2,t_1}) = E_{t_0} \overline{R}_{t_2,t_0} \quad \text{for } t_2 \geq t_1 \geq t_0$$

2 A Stylized Set of Accounts for the Treasury, the Central Bank and the State

In this chapter, we first construct, in Section 2.1, the flow of funds accounts and conventional balance sheets of the Treasury and the central bank. We then obtain the intertemporal budget constraints (IBCs) or comprehensive balance sheets of the Treasury and the central bank. Finally, we consider the conventional balance sheet of the consolidated Treasury and central bank (the State) and the IBC of the State or, equivalently, the comprehensive balance sheet of the State. We show that the difference between the common starting point for one of the key parameters for fiscal sustainability analysis, the gross or net debt of the general government, and the final destination, the net nonmonetary debt of the State, can be vast. We then, in Section 2.2, go on to a simple debt sustainability exercise for a number of advanced economies.

As noted earlier, sovereign insolvency is always a choice rather than a necessity if the public debt is denominated in domestic currency and the authorities have discretionary control over current and future base money issuance (seigniorage). If, and to the extent that inflation is driven by current and future seigniorage, inflation tolerance ultimately determines fiscal sustainability for nations that possess monetary sovereignty. Limits to public debt sustainability are therefore reflections of limits on inflation tolerance for nations that have discretionary control over current and future seigniorage. For countries that have given up national monetary sovereignty, like the member states of the Economic and Monetary Union (EMU), sovereign debt sustainability is constrained by the centrally decided limits on each national sovereign's ability to create central bank money.

2.1   THE ANALYTICS OF THE ACCOUNTING FRAMEWORK

The central bank has as liabilities the monetary base $M \geq 0$ and non-monetary liabilities (term deposits, central bank bills and bonds, central bank repos (called reverse repos in the USA), securities lending etc.), N. The average nominal interest rate on the monetary base is as before denoted i^M. For simplicity, all nonmonetary debt instruments issued by both the central bank and the Treasury are assumed to be one-period maturity, domestic-currency-denominated safe nominal bonds, with a nominal interest rate i^N for the nonmonetary liabilities of the central bank and i for government bonds held by the public or by the central bank.

As assets, the central bank holds the stock of gold and international foreign exchange reserves, R^f (measured in foreign currency), earning a risk-free one-period nominal interest rate in foreign currency i^f, and the stock of domestic assets, which consists of central bank holdings of nominal, interest-bearing Treasury bills, B^{cb}, earning a risk-free nominal interest rate i, and central bank claims on the private sector, L, with domestic-currency nominal interest rate i^L. This includes financial instruments bought outright, collateralized lending and reverse repos (called repos in the USA). The stock of Treasury debt (all assumed to be denominated in domestic currency) held by the public outside the central bank is denoted B^p. T^p is the nominal value of the tax payments by the domestic private sector to the Treasury; it is a choice variable of the Treasury and can be positive or negative; T^{cb} is the nominal value of payments made by the central bank to the Treasury; it is a choice variable of the Treasury and can be positive or negative.

H is the nominal value of the transfer payments made by the central bank to the private sector (a "helicopter drop of money" if the increase in T^{cb} is financed through an increase in the monetary base). We can have helicopter money in this set-up if we assume H to be a choice variable of the central bank. In most countries, the central bank is not a fiscal principal and can neither impose explicit taxes nor make explicit transfer payments. It can and does of course, as we shall see, engage in actions that are, from an economic perspective, equivalent to taxation or engaging in transfers or subsidy payments. We leave H in the central bank's budget constraint for three reasons. First, even though in the real world only the Treasury can make explicit transfer payments to the private sector, – that is, $H \equiv 0$ and the central bank cannot engage in helicopter money, – the Treasury and the central bank together can engage in a joint policy action equivalent to helicopter money. This would be a tax cut or increase in transfer payments by the Treasury (a reduction in T^p) with a matching increase in "taxes" paid by the central bank to the Treasury (an increase in T^{cb} that keeps $T^p + T^{cb}$ constant), which the central bank then finances with an increase in the monetary base.

The second reason for introducing helicopter money is because it highlights the fiscal and quasi-fiscal roles of the central bank. Even when we set $H \equiv 0$ and thus rule out any explicit fiscal tax-transfer actions by the central bank (but not the equivalent combined Treasury–central bank operations described in the previous paragraph), the central bank can (and in practice often does) engage in a variety of implicit quasi-fiscal actions by lending to private (and sometimes public) counterparties at rates different from the appropriate risk-adjusted opportunity cost/fair rate of return. The central bank frequently subsidizes and occasionally taxes its (private) counterparties, and it tends to do so in ways that are less than transparent.

Third, a lot of popular and political debate appears to be based on the assumption that central banks can engage in helicopter money drops. It is instructive to analyze what would happen if indeed they could do so.

Total taxes net of transfer payments received by the State – the consolidated Treasury and central bank – are $T^s = T^p - H$; e is the value of the spot nominal exchange rate (the domestic currency price of foreign exchange); $C^g \geq 0$ is the real value of Treasury spending on current goods and services and $C^{cb} \geq 0$ the real value of central bank spending on current goods and services. Total real current spending by the consolidated Treasury and central bank (the State) is $C^s \equiv C^g + C^{cb}$. The central bank is assumed not to hold real assets, but the general government/Treasury can. The stock of real assets held by the Treasury is denoted K, the money price of a unit of this real asset is P^K (this should be viewed as the market price of a unit of real public sector capital), each unit of physical capital earns a nominal rental ρ and depreciates at a constant proportional rate δ. For simplicity, we assume that only the central bank holds foreign assets (the official gold and foreign exchange reserves) and that neither the Treasury nor the central bank issue foreign currency-denominated liabilities.

Equation (2.1) is the single-period budget constraint (really budget identity) of the Treasury and equation (2.2) that of the central bank.

$$
B^p_{t+1} + B^{cb}_{t+1} - P^K_t K_{t+1} \equiv P_t C^g_t - T^p_t - T^{cb}_t + (1 + i_{t,t-1})(B^p_t + B^{cb}_t)
$$
$$
- \left(\rho_t + P^K_t (1 - \delta) \right) K_t \tag{2.1}
$$

$$
M_{t+1} + N_{t+1} - B^{cb}_{t+1} - L_{t+1} - e_t R^f_{t+1} \equiv
$$
$$
P_t C^{cb}_t + T^{cb}_t + H_t + (1 + i^M_{t,t-1})M_t + (1 + i^N_{t,t-1})N_t
$$
$$
- (1 + i_{t,t-1})B^{cb}_t - (1 + i^L_{t,t-1})L_t - (1 + i^f_{t,t-1})e_t R^f_t \tag{2.2}
$$

The solvency constraint of the Treasury is the familiar no-Ponzi finance condition: the expected present discounted value (PDV) of the terminal stock of net financial liabilities minus tangible assets must be nonpositive:

$$
\lim_{j \to \infty} E_t I_{j,t-1}(B^p_{j+1} + B^{cb}_{j+1} - P^K_j K_{j+1}) \le 0 \tag{2.3}
$$

The solvency constraint of the central bank is that the present discounted value of its terminal stock of net *nonmonetary* financial liabilities has to be nonpositive:

$$
\lim_{j \to \infty} E_t I_{j,t-1}(N_{j+1} - B^{cb}_{j+1} - L_{j+1} - e_j R^f_{j+1}) \le 0 \tag{2.4}
$$

The reason monetary liabilities are not included in the solvency constraint of the central bank is that currency is *irredeemable*: the holder cannot demand, at any time, its exchange by the issuer for anything else. An irredeemable financial instrument is an asset to its owner but not, in any meaningful sense, a liability to the issuer. We extend this irredeemability property to the other components of the monetary base, commercial bank-required and excess reserves held with the central bank.

These solvency constraints and the single-period budget constraints of the Treasury and central bank imply the following intertemporal budget constraints (IBCs) for the Treasury and the central bank:

$$P_{t-1}^K K_t - (B_t^p + B_t^{cb}) \geq E_t \sum_{j=t}^{\infty} I_{j,t-1}\left(P_t C_j^g - (T_j^p + T_j^{cb}) + S_j^g\right) \quad (2.5)^1$$

$$
\begin{aligned}
B_t^{cb} + L_t + e_{t-1}R_t^f - N_t \geq E_t \sum_{j=t}^{\infty} I_{j,t-1}\left(P_j C_j^{cb} + T_j^{cb} + H_j + S_j^{cb}\right. \\
\left. - \left(M_{j+1} - (1 + i_{j,j-1}^M)M_j\right)\right)
\end{aligned}
\quad (2.6)
$$

where

$$S_j^g = \left(1 + i_{j,j-1} - \left(\frac{\rho_j}{P_{j-1}^K} + (1 - \delta)\frac{P_j^K}{P_{j-1}^K}\right)\right)P_{j-1}^K K_j \quad (2.7)$$

and

$$
\begin{aligned}
S_j^{cb} = (i_{j,j-1} - i_{j,j-1}^L)L_j + \left(1 + i_{j,j-1} - (1 + i_{j,j-1}^f)\frac{e_j}{e_{j-1}}\right) \\
e_{j-1}R_j^f - (i_{j,j-1} - i_{j,j-1}^N)N_j
\end{aligned}
\quad (2.8)
$$

Here S^g and S^{cb} are, respectively, the (implicit) losses (profits if negative) incurred (earned) by the Treasury on its real assets (in equation (2.7)) and by the central bank (in equation (2.8)). The central bank incurs implicit quasi-fiscal losses (profits if negative) by getting a (risk-adjusted) return on its loans to the private sector and on its foreign exchange reserves below their opportunity cost and/or by paying an interest rate on its nonmonetary liabilities above their opportunity

---

[1]   Note that $E_t E_{t-1} I_{t,t-1} = E_{t-1} I_{t,t-1} = \frac{1}{1+i_{t,t-1}}$.

cost – the safe rate of interest on government bonds. Total implicit losses of the consolidated Treasury and central bank on its portfolio are denoted $S^s \equiv S^g + S^{cb}$.

Using the intertemporal seigniorage identity (1.3) we can rewrite equation (2.6) as:

$$B_t^{cb} + L_t + e_{t-1}R_t^f - M_t - N_t \geq$$
$$E_t \sum_{j=t}^{\infty} I_{j,t-1} \left(P_j C_j^{cb} + T_j^{cb} + H_j + S_j^{cb} - (i_{j,j-1} - i_{j,j-1}^M)M_j \right)$$
$$+ \lim_{j \to \infty} E_t I_{j,t-1} M_{j+1} \tag{2.9}$$

The single-period budget constraint of the consolidated general government/Treasury and central bank – the State – is

$$M_{t+1} + N_{t+1} + B_{t+1}^p - L_{t+1} - e_t R_{t+1}^f - P_t^K K_{t+1} \equiv$$
$$P_t C_t^s - T_t^s + (1 + i_{t,t-1}^M)M_t + (1 + i_{t,t-1})B_t^p + (1 + i_{t,t-1}^N)N_t \tag{2.10}$$
$$- (1 + i_{t,t-1}^L)L_t - (1 + i_{t,t-1}^f)e_t R_t^f - (\rho_t + P_t^K(1 - \delta))K_t$$

The IBC of the State is

$$P_{t-1}^K K_t + L_t + e_{t-1}R_t^f - N_t - B_t^p \geq$$
$$E_t \sum_{j=t}^{\infty} I_{j,t-1} \left(P_t C_j^s - T_j^s + S_j^s - \left(M_{j+1} - (1 + i_{j,j-1}^M)M_j \right) \right) \tag{2.11}$$

or equivalently

$$P_{t-1}^K K_t + L_t + e_{t-1}R_t^f - M_t - N_t - B_t^p \geq$$
$$E_t \sum_{j=t}^{\infty} I_{j,t-1} \left(P_j C_j^s - T_j^s + S_j^s - (i_{j,j-1} - i_{j,j-1}^M)M_j \right)$$
$$- \lim_{j \to \infty} E_t I_{j,t-1} M_{j+1} \tag{2.12}$$

Finally, using the less-cluttered net present discounted value operator notation of equation (1.4) we can rewrite the intertemporal budget constraints as follows:

For the Treasury:

$$P_{t-1}^K K_t + V_t(\{T^p, I\}) + V_t(\{T^{cb}, I\}) \geq B_t^p + B_t^{cb}$$
$$+ V_t(\{PC^g, I\}) + V_t(\{S^g, I\}) \tag{2.13}$$

For the central bank either

$$B_t^{cb} + L_t + e_{t-1}R_t^f + V_t(\{\Omega^1, I\}) \geq N_t + V_t(\{PC^{cb}, I\})$$
$$+ V_t(\{T^{cb}, I\}) + V_t(\{H, I\}) + V_t(\{S^{cb}, I\}) \tag{2.14}$$

or, equivalently,

$$B_t^{cb} + L_t + e_{t-1}R_t^f + V_t(\{\Omega^2, I\}) + V_t(\lim_{j \to \infty} M_{j+1}, I) \geq$$
$$M_t + N_t + V_t(\{PC^{cb}, I\}) + V_t(\{T^{cb}, I\}) + V_t(\{H, I\}) + V_t(\{S^{cb}, I\})$$
$$\tag{2.15}$$

For the consolidated Treasury and Central bank either

$$P_{t-1}^K K_t + L_t + e_{t-1}R_t^f + V_t(\{T^s, I\}) + V_t(\{\Omega^1, I\})$$
$$\geq N_t + B_t^p + V_t(\{PC^s, I\}) + V_t(\{S^s, I\}) \tag{2.16}$$

or, equivalently,

$$P_{t-1}^K K_t + L_t + e_{t-1}R_t^f + V_t(\{T^s, I\}) + V_t(\{\Omega^2, I\}) + V_t(\lim_{j \to \infty} M_{j+1}, I)$$
$$\geq M_t + N_t + B_t^p + V_t(\{PC^s, I\}) + V_t(\{S^s, I\}) \tag{2.17}$$

Tables 2.1 to 2.5 help to illustrate why governments too may require a lender of last resort (LOLR).[2] Table 2.1 presents a stylized general government (Treasury) conventional balance sheet and Table 2.2 the stylized central bank conventional balance sheet. On the asset side of Table 2.1, we find marketable (and often relatively liquid) assets, including in principle (but omitted here for simplicity) general government holdings of gold, foreign exchange and other foreign investments, equity in partially or wholly publicly owned firms, and less liquid real assets, including land, structures and real estate, but also natural resource rights, from subsoil minerals, oil and gas to band spectrum. All these financial and real assets are captured by $P_t^K K_t$. On the liability side, there is marketable and nonmarketable public debt, $B_t^p + B_t^{cb}$. Conventional general government/Treasury net worth,

---

[2]   We prefer, for esthetic reasons, not to have to enter the stock of base money as $(1 + i_{t,t-1}^M)M_t$ rather than as M_t and to engage in similar notational clutter for other balance sheet items. In the balance sheet presentations, time should be thought of as continuous rather than discrete.

Table 2.1 *Stylized general government (Treasury) conventional balance sheet*

Assets		Liabilities	
$P_t^K K_t$	Value (at actual sale or purchase prices) of land, real estate, structures, mineral assets and other real assets, equity in public enterprises and other financial assets	Marketable and nonmarketable general government debt	$B_t^p + B_t^{cb}$
		General government financial net worth	W_t^g

Table 2.2 *Stylized central bank conventional balance sheet*

Assets		Liabilities	
$e_t R_t^f$	Gold and foreign exchange holdings and other foreign investments	Base money	M_t
B_t^{cb}	Treasury debt	Nonmonetary central bank liabilities	N_t
L_t	Private sector debt and loans to the private sector	Central bank financial net worth	W_t^{cb}

W_t^g, is the difference between the value of the tangible assets plus the financial assets and the financial liabilities.

Table 2.2 has the financial assets of the central bank, $B_t^{cb} + L_t + e_t R_t^f$, the financial liabilities of the central bank (monetary and nonmonetary) and the conventional financial net worth of the central bank W^{cb}.

Table 2.3 presents the general government or Treasury comprehensive balance sheet, which also features the intangible assets and liabilities that are omitted from the published financial or conventional balance sheets (see also Buiter (2010)). The comprehensive balance sheet of the general government *is* its intertemporal budget constraint (equation (2.13)), with the familiar no-Ponzi finance terminal condition imposed: the expected present discounted value of the terminal conventional net worth of the general government must be nonnegative. Tables 2.4 and 2.5 present two equivalent versions of the central bank's comprehensive balance sheet, corresponding, respectively to equations (2.14) and (2.15), the two equivalent representations of the intertemporal budget constraint of the central bank.

The most important intangible asset in Table 2.3 is the present value of taxes, levies and social security contributions, $V_t(\{T^p, I\})$. We also single out for future reference one particular stream of general government revenues: the net payments by the central bank to the general government, mostly to the central government Treasury, $V_t(\{T^{cb}, I\})$.[3] The present value of transfers, entitlement spending and exhaustive general government primary current expenditure, $V_t(\{PC^g, I\})$, appears on the liability side. We could have entered $V_t(\{S^g, I\})$, the present value of the subsidies paid by the general government on its real assets as a liability on the right-hand side of Table 2.3. Instead we subtract it from the market value of the real assets (the price at which these assets can be bought from or sold to the private sector) to get the fair value of the assets were they to remain in the public sector for at least one more period: $P_t^K K_t - V_t(\{S^g, I\})$.

Using the intertemporal seigniorage identity from equation (1.3) or (1.4), Table 2.4 turns into Table 2.5.

The comprehensive balance sheet of the central bank also includes an intangible asset and several intangible liabilities not included in its conventional financial balance sheet. Consider, for instance, Table 2.5 and contrast it with Table 2.2. The additional asset of the central bank is the PDV of future interest saved by having borrowed through the issuance of base money rather than through the issuance of nonmonetary debt instruments, $V_t(\{\Omega^2, I\})$ plus the PDV of the terminal stock of base money $V_t(\lim_{j \to \infty} M_j, I)$. The

---

[3]   These payments need bear no obvious relationship to the true profits or the conventional operating profits of the central bank. They are, in the final analysis, determined by the Treasury.

additional liabilities of the central bank are (1) the PDV of the net payments made by the central bank to the Treasury, $V_t(\{T^{cb}, I\})$, which we encountered as an asset of the Treasury in Table 2.3; (2) the PDV of the transfer payments to the private sector made by the central bank, $V_t(\{H, I\})$, (zero in most real-world economies); and (3) the PDV of the implicit, quasi-fiscal subsidies made by the central bank on its financial assets and liabilities, $V_t(\{S^{cb}, I\})$.

Even when central banks cannot engage in "helicopter money" drops, that is, even if $V_t(\{H, I\}) \equiv 0$, it can provide implicit subsidies/transfers to private counterparties through subsidized lending rates, through the term $V_t(\{S^{cb}, I\})$ in Table 2.4 or 2.5. Take the two three-year longer-term refinancing operations (LTRO) of the ECB in December 2011 and February 2012. These loans were made at an interest rate linked to the official policy rate, the refi rate. At the time, it stood at 1.0 percent but was expected to come down to 0.5 percent by the end of the year and to remain at that level over the life of the LTRO. Over the three years of the LTRO, the bank's cost of borrowing could be as little as 60 basis points. In addition, collateral requirements for the loans were weakened dramatically. There can be little doubt that these LTROs involved a significant subsidy from the ECB to the borrowing banks, in our view at least 3.0 percent per year. With just over 1 trillion worth of LTROs undertaken, the annual subsidy would be €30 bn; over three years the PDV of the subsidy would be around €85.6 bn, using a 4 percent discount rate for the PDV calculations.

When the ECB's deposit rate was set at −0.4 percent in March 2016, the ECB also announced targeted longer-term refinancing operations (TLTRO). These had a four-year maturity, with the possibility of repayment after two years. Counterparties exceeding the lending benchmark were able to borrow at a rate that could be as low as the rate on the deposit facility at the time of allotment. For highly risky Eurozone banks to be able to borrow from the Eurosystem, using high-risk collateral like Italian sovereign debt,

Table 2.3 *Stylized general government comprehensive balance sheet*

Assets		Liabilities	
$P_t^K K_t - V_t(\{S^g, I\})$	Fair value of land, real estate, structures, mineral assets and other real commercial assets, equity in public enterprises and other financial assets under public ownership in period t	Marketable and nonmarketable general government debt	$B_t^p + B_t^{cb}$
$V_t(\{T^p, I\})$	Present value of taxes, levies and social security contributions	Present value of general government primary current expenditure	$V_t(\{PC^g, I\})$
$V_t(\{T^{cb}, I\})$	Present value of payments made by the central bank to the Treasury		
		Comprehensive general government net worth	$\hat{W}_t^g$

for a four-year period at –0.4 percent represents a significant transfer from the Eurosystem (i.e. the Eurozone tax payers and beneficiaries of public spending) to the Eurozone banks.

As noted earlier, the main asset of the sovereign is highly illiquid: the PDV of future taxes, levies and social security contributions, denoted $V_t(\{T^p, I\})$. It may be possible to securitize some future tax flows and thus to turn the PDV of such taxes into tradable instruments, but this has only been attempted on a limited scale, and mostly

Table 2.4 *Stylized central bank comprehensive balance sheet*

Assets		Liabilities	
$e_t R_t^f$	Gold and foreign exchange holdings and other investments	Nonmonetary central bank liabilities	N_t
B_t^{cb}	Treasury debt	Present value of current primary expenditure by central bank	$V_t(\{PC^{cb}, I\})$
	Private sector debt and loans to the private sector	Present value of payments made by the central bank to the Treasury	$V_t(\{T^{cb}, I\})$
$V_t(\{\Omega^1, I\})$	Present value of future base money issuance by the central bank	Present value of transfer payments by the central bank to the private sector	$V_t(\{H, I\})$
		Present value of implicit subsidies paid by the central bank	$V_t(\{S^{cb}, I\})$
		Central bank comprehensive net worth	$\hat{W}_t^{cb}$

at the local and state/provincial level. Among the revenue streams of the Treasury are the "remittances" by the central bank of part of its profits, $V_t(\{T^{cb}, I\})$. The national Treasury is the beneficial owner (and in some cases, as in the United Kingdom, the legal owner) of the central bank, and the nonretained part of central bank profits are paid out as a form of dividends to the national Treasury. The equity in the central bank, even in those cases where the central bank is formally a joint stock company, is usually not traded, however, so the Treasury, even where it holds most or all of the central bank's equity, cannot realize the PDV of future central bank profits by selling the equity. The actual stream of payments made by the central bank to the

Table 2.5 *Alternative but equivalent stylized central bank comprehensive balance sheet*

Assets		Liabilities	
$e_t R_t^f$	Gold and foreign exchange holdings and other investments	Base money	M_t
B_t^{cb}	Treasury debt	Nonmonetary central bank liabilities	N_t
L_t	Private sector debt and loans to the private sector	Present value of current primary expenditure by central bank	$V_t(\{PC^{cb}, I\})$
$V_t(\{\Omega^2, I\})$	Present value of interest saved by the central bank through its issuance of base money	Present value of payments made by the central bank to the Treasury	$V_t(\{T^{cb}, I\})$
$V_t(\lim_{j \to \infty} M_j, I)$	Present value of terminal base money stock	Present value of transfer payments by the central bank to the private sector	$V_t(\{H, I\})$
		Present value of implicit subsidies paid by the central bank	$V_t(\{S^{cb}, I\})$
		Central bank comprehensive net worth	$\hat{W}_t^{cb}$

Treasury in any given period need bear little relationship to economic profits earned in that period. The value of T^{cb} in one or more periods and even of $V_t(\{T^{cb}, I\})$ could be negative if the Treasury makes transfers to the central bank, say to recapitalize it following losses on the central bank's assets.

Another key future stream of funding resources for the sovereign comes from *foregone* public spending, that is, a reduction in $V_t(\{PC^s, I\})$. The PDV of primary (noninterest) current public spending is a key intangible liability. If it were possible to turn commitments to future cuts in public spending – a reduction in an illiquid liability – into a matching capacity to issue new liquid liabilities, one would have achieved a financial engineering miracle: the de facto securitization of future public spending cuts. This may be possible when optimism, confidence and trust in the government are high. But when pessimism rules, confidence has vanished and trust is weak, the government may be unable to translate promises of future public spending cuts or of future tax increases into a present ability to fund itself in the markets at affordable interest rates. Even during normal times the bulk of the intangible assets of the sovereign is illiquid and of long maturity, and during times of financial stress even a determined attempt to reduce the intangible liabilities of the government through promises of future tax increases or public spending cuts need not translate into any significant increase in its ability to borrow today.

In addition to holding significant amounts of illiquid intangible assets and liabilities, many governments have nontrivial financial deficits and/or a sizeable stock of sovereign debt, part of which matures and requires re-financing each period. Most governments therefore have regular, recurrent funding needs. Like banks, governments therefore suffer from maturity and liquidity mismatch among their assets and liabilities. So even if the government is solvent – provided it can get funded at yields that reflect the market's belief that the government *is* solvent – this government could be tripped into a fundamentally unwarranted payments default should the market instead adopt the "self-fulfilling fear equilibrium belief" that the government is (most likely) not solvent. A lender of last resort capable of issuing an unquestionably liquid instrument (for instance, base money) in any amount, may well be necessary to trump the "fear equilibrium" or "government debt run equilibrium" that always threatens the government, just as the lender of last resort (or comprehensive and credible deposit insurance) is necessary to prevent solvent but illiquid banks from succumbing to a bank run (see Kopf (2011)). The truth of this proposition has been underlined several times since 2010 in the case of the euro area (EA) where a single central bank, the Eurosystem, faced first seventeen and now nineteen sovereigns and is committed, through Article 123 of the Treaty on the Functioning of the European Union, to abstain from acting as lender of last resort to the sovereigns in its jurisdiction. The euro area is the only example we know of undoubted monetary dominance. If push came to shove, the US sovereign would, in our view, be able to force the Fed to monetize its debt and deficit. This is because when a single sovereign faces its central bank, political legitimacy ensures that fiscal dominance is the rule. For there to be a US sovereign default, there would either have to be an extreme, and politically implausible, case of monetary dominance (see also de Grauwe (2011) and Gros and Mayer (2010)) or parliamentary paralysis would have to stop the US Congress from raising the debt ceiling when this threatens to become a binding constraint on the ability of the federal government to service its debt. Such a sovereign debt default "own goal" is highly unlikely but not impossible.

The economic logic of the intertemporal budget constraints implies that the Treasury is solvent if and only if its comprehensive net worth is nonnegative, $\hat{W}_t^g \geq 0$. Likewise, the central bank is solvent if and only if its comprehensive net worth is nonnegative, $\hat{W}_t^{cb} \geq 0$. These solvency conditions are, of course, quite consistent with the conventionally defined financial net worth of the Treasury, W^g, and/or the conventionally defined financial net worth of the central bank, W^{cb}, being negative. This can be seen by noting that:

$$\hat{W}^g \equiv W^g + V(\{T^p, I\}) + V(\{T^{cb}, I\}) - V(\{S^g, I\}) - V(\{PC^g, I\})$$

$$(2.18)$$

and that

$$\hat{W}^{cb} \equiv W^{cb} + V(\{\Omega^2, I\}) + V_t(\lim_{j \to \infty} M_j, I)$$
$$-V(\{PC^{cb}, I\}) - V(\{T^{cb}, I\}) - V(\{H, I\}) - V(\{S^{cb}, I\}) \tag{2.19}$$

In the case of the central bank, for instance, even if its conventional financial net worth (regulatory net worth or regulatory capital) were negative, comprehensive net worth could be positive if the net present value of future interest saved because of the central bank's monopoly of the issuance of domestic base money, exceeds the net present value of its future running costs, $V(\{PC^{cb}, I\})$, its future payments to the Treasury, $V(\{T^{cb}, I\})$, its transfer payments to the private sector, $V(\{H, I\})$, and the future quasi-fiscal subsidies on its lending and other assets, $V(\{S^{cb}, I\})$.

Finally, Table 2.6 presents the conventional balance sheet of the consolidated general government (Treasury) and central bank, and

Table 2.6 *Conventional balance sheet of consolidated Treasury and central bank*

Assets	Liabilities	
$P_t^K K_t$ Market value of land, real estate, structures, mineral assets and other real assets, equity in public enterprises and other financial assets	Base money	M_t
	Nonmonetary liabilities of the central bank	M_t
	Marketable and nonmarketable Treasury debt held by public	B_t^p
	Consolidated Treasury and central bank conventional or financial net worth	$W_t^s = W_t^g + W_t^{cb}$

Table 2.7 *Comprehensive balance sheet of consolidated Treasury and central bank*

Assets		Liabilities	
$P_t^K K_t - V_t(\{S^s, I\})$	Fair value of land, real estate, structures, mineral assets and other real assets, equity in public enterprises and other financial assets under public ownership in period t	Nonmonetary liabilities of the central bank	N_t
$V_t(\{T^p, I\})$	Present value of taxes, levies and social security contributions	Marketable and nonmarketable general government debt	B_t^p
$V_t(\{\Omega^1, I\})$	Present value of future base money issuance	Present value of consolidated Treasury and central bank primary current expenditure	$V_t(\{PC^s, I\})$
		Present value of transfer payments by the central bank to the private sector	$V_t(\{H, I\})$
		Present value of implicit subsidies paid by the central bank on the financial assets it holds.	$V_t(\{S^{cb}, I\})$
		Comprehensive consolidated Treasury and central bank net worth	$\hat{W}_t^s$

Table 2.8 *Alternative but equivalent comprehensive balance sheet of consolidated Treasury and central bank*

Assets		Liabilities	
$P_t^K K_t - V_t(\{S^s, I\})$	Fair value of land, real estate, structures, mineral assets and other real assets, equity in public enterprises and other financial assets under public ownership in period t	Base money	M_t
$V_t(\{T^p, I\})$	Present value of taxes, levies and social security contributions	Nonmonetary liabilities of the central bank	N_t
$V_t(\{\Omega^2, I\})$	Present value of future interest saved by issuing base money	Marketable and nonmarketable general government debt	B_t^p
$V_t(\lim_{j \to \infty} M_j, I)$	Present value of terminal monetary base	Present value of consolidated Treasury and central bank primary current expenditure	$V_t(\{PC^s, I\})$
		Present value of transfer payments by the central bank to the private sector	$V_t(\{H, I\})$
		Present value of implicit subsidies paid by the central bank on the financial assets it holds	$V_t(\{S^{cb}, I\})$
		Comprehensive consolidated Treasury and central bank net worth	$\hat{W}_t^s$

Table 2.7 and 2.8 present two equivalent representations of the comprehensive budget constraint of the consolidated general government (Treasury) and central bank, corresponding to equation (2.16) and equation (2.17) respectively.

Note that the comprehensive net worth of the consolidated Treasury and central bank, $\hat{W}_t^s$, can be positive even when either the conventional financial net worth of the Treasury or the conventional financial net worth of the central bank, or both, are negative. This follows from

$$\hat{W}^s \equiv W^s + V(\{T^p, I\}) + V(\{\Omega^2, I\}) + V(\lim_{j \to \infty} M_j, I)$$
$$- V(\{PC^s, I\}) - V(\{H, I\}) - V(\{S^s, I\}) \tag{2.20}$$

where $W^s = W^g + W^{cb}$. The comprehensive balance sheet of the consolidated Treasury and central bank adds the intangible assets and the intangible liabilities of both the Treasury and the central bank to the conventional or financial balance sheet of the consolidated Treasury and central bank.

Of particular importance are the difference between the conventional and comprehensive balance sheets of the Treasury alone (Tables 2.1 and 2.3 respectively) and their consolidated counterparts, given in Tables 2.6 and 2.7 or 2.8 respectively. Contrast Tables 2.4 or 2.5 with 2.7 or 2.8. The additional PDV of the resources the central bank brings to the consolidated Treasury and central bank balance sheet is the PDV of current and future seigniorage – the PDV of interest saved by borrowing through the issuance of base money rather than through the issuance of nonmonetary debt instruments plus the PDV of the terminal base money stock. Since the central bank has the ability to issue this unquestionably liquid liability at will and at effectively zero marginal cost, the consolidated general government and central bank should never face a potential *domestic currency* illiquidity problem, nor a domestic currency debt default problem. Default is a matter of choice, never of necessity. This is one of the tenets of Modern Monetary Theory that is correct. If course, if the alternative to sovereign default (on domestic-currency-denominated debt) is highly inflationary monetization, a government may *choose* to default rather than risk the inflationary alternative.

The conventional general government without the central bank could face default risk even on its domestic-currency-denominated debt, B^p, if there are (political) limits on its ability to cut public spending and raise taxes, and its financial liabilities held by the public can become illiquid. We see this in the highly unusual government–central bank relationship in the Eurozone, discussed at length in Chapter 6.

2.2 EMPIRICAL DIMENSIONS OF THE CONSOLIDATION OF CENTRAL BANK AND TREASURY ACCOUNTS

2.2.a *The Arithmetic of Fiscal Sustainability*

The debt and deficit that are relevant to the analysis of fiscal sustainability are not the debt and deficit of the central or federal government, or even those of the general government (the consolidated central/federal, state/provincial and local/municipal governments). The reason is that the standard statistical definition of the central and general governments excludes the central bank. As we argued earlier, because the Treasury/ministry of finance is the beneficial owner of the central bank – regardless of the often esoteric formal ownership structures found, among others, in countries like the USA, Japan, Switzerland and Italy – the assets and liabilities and the flow of funds accounts of the central bank and the general government – should be consolidated in a single set of accounts, those of the 'State'.

The only ambiguity as regards the beneficial ownership of central banks concerns the ECB and the NCBs of the Eurosystem. The ECB is owned according to "capital key" shares by the nineteen national central banks (NCBs) of the EA member states.[4] These NCBs are each beneficially owned by their national Treasuries/

---

[4] Technically, the non-EA member states of the EU also have stock in the ECB. However, this does not entitle them to any material claim on the profits of the ECB nor does it commit them to a material contribution to any ECB losses. We can safely ignore this.

ministries of finance. The NCBs are supposed to share according to their capital keys in the profits and losses made by the entire Eurosystem (the ECB and the nineteen NCBs) in the conduct of the single monetary policy. There is an ambiguity because a growing, but hard to determine exactly, share of the assets and liabilities of the NCBs is devoted to "own risk" activities for which profit-and-loss sharing according to the capital key does not apply. This issue is addressed at length and in depth in Chapter 6.

The debt accumulation dynamics of the State are given in equation (2.21). We use the notation of the earlier Chapters and introduce some new compact notation: d_t is the contractual value of the net stock of nonmonetary liabilities (bonds) of the State at the beginning of period t, as a share of period $t–1$ GDP; g_t is public spending (of the consolidated State) on real goods and services (current and capital) during period t as a share of period t GDP; τ_t is tax revenues and other current revenues net of transfers by the State as a share of period t GDP; S_t is the period t (conventional) primary surplus of the State as a share of period t GDP; ω_t^1 is, as before, seigniorage (the net revenue from base money issuance) in period t as a share of period t GDP; $\hat{s}_t$ is the augmented primary surplus of the State as a share of GDP.

$$d_{t+1} = \left(\frac{1 + r_{t,t-1}}{1 + \gamma_{t,t-1}}\right) d_t - \hat{s}_t$$
or
$$\Delta d_{t+1} = \left(\frac{r_{t,t-1} - \gamma_{t,t-1}}{1 + \gamma_{t,t-1}}\right) d_t - \hat{s}_t$$

(2.21)

The augmented primary surplus (as a share of GDP) is the sum of the conventional primary surplus (as a share of GDP) and seigniorage (as a share of GDP): $\hat{s}_t = s_t + \omega_t^1$; the primary surplus is the financial surplus net of any interest income or payments. The primary surplus is therefore equal to recurrent revenues (taxes net of transfers) minus public spending on real goods and services: $s_t = \tau_t - g_t$.

Equation (2.21) shows that the (positive) ratio of public nonmonetary debt to GDP is boosted when the real interest rate on the debt exceeds the growth rate of real GDP and when there is an augmented primary deficit – the augmented primary surplus is negative. The term $\left(\frac{r_{t,t-1}-\gamma_{t,t-1}}{1+\gamma_{t,t-1}}\right)d_t$ – the differential between the real interest rate and the growth rate of real GDP times the initial debt-to-GDP ratio – is sometimes referred to as the "*snowball effect*" in the debt accumulation process. As we saw in Section 2.1, the period budget constraint of the State and the requirement that the State cannot run a Ponzi scheme forever (i.e. the growth rate of its debt cannot always be equal to or greater than the interest rate on the debt) imply the intertemporal budget constraint (IBC) of the State.

$$d_t \leq \sum_{j=t}^{\infty} \overline{R}_{j,t-1}\hat{s}_j = \sum_{j=t}^{\infty} \prod_{\ell=t}^{j}\left(\frac{1+\gamma_{\ell,\ell-1}}{1+r_{\ell,\ell-1}}\right)\hat{s}_j$$

This equation states that the contractual value of the outstanding stock of nonmonetary public debt cannot exceed the PDV of current and (expected) future augmented primary surpluses. The contractual value of the sovereign debt is its market value stripped of any credit risk discount.

This present value relationship is not operational. We can operationalize it by asking: what is the current value of the augmented primary surplus as a share of GDP that stabilizes the net debt-to-GDP ratio, denoted $\hat{s}_t^R$. We refer to this as the short-run required augmented primary surplus ratio. From equation (2.21) this is given by:

$$\hat{s}_t^R = \left(\frac{r_{t,t-1}-\gamma_{t,t-1}}{1+\gamma_{t,t-1}}\right)d_t \tag{2.22}$$

This measure, while easy to compute, is rather myopic. It could give a misleading answer if the current values of the growth rate of real GDP and of the real interest rate are unrepresentative of their expected future values.

We therefore also consider an alternative measure of the minimum fiscal effort required for fiscal sustainability: the smallest constant augmented primary surplus as a share of GDP that permits the IBC of the State to be satisfied. We shall call this the (minimum) permanent required augmented primary surplus ratio, denoted $\hat{s}_t^{\infty,R}$. Let $\bar{\gamma}$ be the long-run growth rate of real GDP and the long-run real interest rate on nonmonetary public debt.[5] It follows that

$$\hat{s}_t^{\infty,R} = \left(\frac{\bar{r} - \bar{\gamma}}{1 + \bar{\gamma}}\right) d_t \tag{2.23}$$

We could also, in principle, calculate the constant value of the augmented primary surplus as a share of GDP whose PDV is the same as the PDV of the augmented primary surplus actually projected for the infinite future. We shall call this the actual permanent primary surplus ratio, denoted $\hat{s}_t^{\infty,A}$.[6] A comparison of $\hat{s}_t^{\infty,R}$ and $\hat{s}_t^{\infty,A}$ would be a useful measure of the "permanent" fiscal tightening required to ensure solvency. Making such infinite-horizon predictions is, however, beyond the scope of this Chapter.

We can compare the value of $\hat{s}_t^{\infty,R}$ with the actual augmented primary surplus ratio in period $t, \hat{s}_t$, and with the maximum (politically and economically) feasible permanent augmented primary surplus ratio (MAPS), denoted $\hat{s}_t^{\max}$, to get two metrics of the amount of long-run fiscal space for the economy. The MAPS will be determined by economic, institutional and political factors. If positive, $\hat{s}_t^{\infty,R} - \hat{s}_t$ is a measure of the permanent adjustment required (relative to the current value of the augmented primary surplus ratio) if the State is to remain solvent. If $\hat{s}^{\infty,R} > \hat{s}^{\max}$, the State is insolvent. The gap, $\hat{s}^{\infty,R} - \hat{s}^{\max}$ measures the minimum percentage write-down required of the outstanding stock of debt for solvency to be restored.

This exercise should, ideally, be conducted in a setting that explicitly allows for uncertainty: what is the likelihood the State is insolvent; that is, what is the likelihood that $\hat{s}^{\infty,R} > \hat{s}^{\max}$? An example of such an approach can be found in Lukkezen and Rogas-Romagosa (2016). Stochastic simulations of interest rates and growth rates are combined with an empirically calibrated fiscal

---

[5] $\bar{\gamma}$ is solved from $\lim\limits_{i \to \infty} \dfrac{\prod\limits_{j=t}^{i}(1 + \gamma_{j,j-1})}{(1+\bar{\gamma})^{i-t}} = 1$ and $\bar{r}$ from $\lim\limits_{i \to \infty} \dfrac{\prod\limits_{j=t}^{i}(1 + r_{j,j-1})}{(1+\bar{r})^{i-t}} = 1.$

[6]   It is calculated by solving: $\hat{s}_t^{\infty} = \left(\sum\limits_{i=t}^{\infty} \prod\limits_{j=t}^{i} \dfrac{1}{1 + r_{j,j-1}}\right)^{-1} \sum\limits_{i=t}^{\infty} \prod\limits_{j=t}^{i} \left(\dfrac{1}{1 + r_{j,j-1}}\right) \hat{s}_j.$

response (reaction function) to the state of the economy to determine the likelihood of explosive public debt growth. Unfortunately, the Lukkezen and Rogas-Romagosa paper uses the general government (net) debt and the primary surplus of the general government for their fiscal metrics rather than the net nonmonetary debt of the consolidated general government and central bank (the State) and the augmented primary surplus of the State. Our approach can be viewed as a quick, simple shortcut, using the correct fiscal metrics, to the more comprehensive approach adopted by Lukkezen and Rogas-Romagosa (2016).

In what follows, we do not capitalize future social security benefit payments and contributions or their difference (the unfunded social security liability) and treat them as debt (defined as contractual liabilities). The reason is that we believe it is important to distinguish between, on the one hand, legal contractual obligations (e.g. debt contracts), where nonperformance can trigger default and insolvency procedures involving courts and arbitration, and often financial disruption and, on the other hand, hopes, expectations and political promises that can be and are broken routinely with at most political consequences for those deemed to have been in breach of the "social contract." Future expected social security contributions and benefits are included in future taxes net of transfers, that is, in the future augmented primary surpluses, not in the current outstanding net debt stock. They would therefore be included in $\hat{s}_t^{\infty,R}$.

2.2.b   The Data

The General Government Primary Surplus

Data on the primary surpluses of the consolidated general government and central bank (the State) are not routinely collected. Fortunately, central banks are intermediaries that can and do vary the size of their balance sheets, sometimes in major ways, without running large financial deficits and surpluses. We will use the primary surplus of the general government as a proxy for the primary surplus of the consolidated general government and central bank, effectively

Table 2.9 *General government primary balance (% of GDP)*

	USA	Japan	UK	EA	Germany	France	Italy
2007	−0.8	−2.7	−1.1	1.9	2.6	−0.1	3.0
2008	−4.6	−3.8	−3.7	0.4	2.2	−0.5	2.0
2009	−11.2	−9.3	−8.7	−3.8	−0.8	−4.9	−1.0
2010	−8.9	−8.6	−7.0	−3.7	−2.1	−4.5	−0.1
2011	−7.3	−8.3	−4.8	−1.6	1.1	−2.6	0.8
2012	−5.7	−7.5	−5.4	−1.0	1.8	−2.4	2.1
2013	−2.4	−7.0	−4.2	−0.5	1.5	−1.9	1.7
2014	−2.0	−4.9	−3.8	−0.2	1.7	−1.9	1.4
2015	−1.6	−3.1	−2.9	0.0	1.8	−1.7	1.3
2016	−2.3	−3.0	−1.3	0.4	2.1	−1.8	1.2
2017	−2.5	−2.7	−0.1	0.8	2.1.7	−1.1	1.2

Source: IMF

assuming central banks run balanced budgets. The data for the general government primary surplus as a percentage of GDP of the United States, Japan, the United Kingdom, the EA, Germany, France and Italy are shown in Table 2.9.

One point to note is that while the EA, Germany and Italy are running primary surpluses in the most recent years, the United States, Japan, the United Kingdom and France are running primary deficits. Since the recovery is mature now (mid-2018) in all of these countries except France and Italy, these actual primary surpluses are close to full-employment, cyclically adjusted or structural primary surpluses (see Table 2.10). Of the seven regions, the USA is in pretty bad shape according to this metric (and likely to get worse when the demand boost to growth provided by the fiscal stimulus wears off) and Japan is in seriously bad shape.

A second point to note is just how large the increases in the primary deficits of the United States, Japan and the United Kingdom were during the three or four years following the GFC. The automatic fiscal stabilizers were reinforced by discretionary fiscal stimulus measures. The countercyclical increase in the primary deficit was much

Table 2.10 *General government cyclically adjusted primary surplus (% of GDP)*

	USA	Japan	EA	UK	Germany	France	Italy
2007	-2.0	-3.0	0.4	-3.0	1.5	-1.0	1.7
2008	-4.0	-3.3	-0.8	-4.7	1.1	-1.0	1.2
2009	-5.9	-5.8	-2.4	-6.5	1.2	-3.4	0.5
2010	-7.6	-6.9	-2.6	-4.4	-1.4	-3.4	0.5
2011	-6.0	-6.8	-1.3	-2.7	0.6	-2.0	1.0
2012	-4.2	-6.3	0.0	-3.4	1.6	-1.4	3.4
2013	-2.4	-6.4	1.1	-2.5	1.6	-0.7	3.7
2014	-1.9	-4.6	1.0	-3.0	1.6	-0.6	3.3
2015	-1.7	-3.5	1.0	-2.6	1.8	-0.5	2.9
2016	-2.0	-3.6	1.0	-1.2	1.6	-0.6	2.7
2017	-2.3	-3.8	0.8	-1.0	1.2	-0.5	2.2

Source: IMF

smaller in the EA. A key question is whether, when the next deep recession hits, the United States, Japan and the United Kingdom will be able to relax the fiscal reins to the same extent they did in 2008–12 and whether the Eurozone will remain as fiscally unresponsive as it was following the GFC.

Seigniorage

The primary surplus that matters is the augmented primary surplus of the State, which adds seigniorage to the conventional primary surplus. As noted before, seigniorage during a given period is the change in the monetary base of that period minus any interest paid on the outstanding monetary base. For the three EA member states, we provided two measures. The first is the change in the monetary base of each country's national central bank minus interest paid on the outstanding stock of that NCB's base money. The data for seigniorage as a share of GDP are shown in Table 2.11.

The conventional seigniorage metrics are not strictly applicable to the NCBs of the Eurosystem. As noted earlier, in the conduct

Table 2.11 *Seigniorage (% of GDP)*

	EA	Germany	France	Italy	Japan	UK	USA
2007	0.5	0.4	#N/A	#N/A	0.0	0.2	−0.1
2008	2.3	3.2	#N/A	#N/A	0.3	1.5	3.9
2009	−0.2	−1.2	#N/A	#N/A	0.8	6.7	4.0
2010	0.0	−0.2	#N/A	#N/A	1.3	−0.1	−0.1
2011	1.9	1.5	1.2	#N/A	3.3	0.6	4.1
2012	4.0	6.3	4.9	#N/A	2.2	7.7	0.1
2013	−4.7	−6.1	−4.9	0.0	12.3	1.4	6.1
2014	−0.3	−0.8	−0.3	−0.2	13.9	0.2	1.4
2015	4.8	4.9	5.1	1.0	15.6	0.7	0.2
2016	5.7	5.9	7.3	2.4	14.4	2.4	−2.2
2017	7.1	7.8	7.5	5.7	10.1	5.3	1.2

Source: National central banks

of the common monetary policy, the nineteen NCBs of the Eurosystem are supposed to be profit-and-loss sharing. Profits and losses of each NCB were supposed to equal that NCB's share of the ECB's equity (its capital key share) times the total profits and losses of the consolidated ECB and nineteen NCBs. That would suggest a definition of seigniorage for, say, Italy, given by its capital key share, σ_I, times EA seigniorage as a share of EA GDP, $\frac{\Delta M_{EA} - i^{M^{EA}} M_{EA}}{P_{EA} Y_{EA}}$, times the ratio of EA GDP to Italian GDP, $\frac{P_{EA} Y_{EA}}{P_I Y_I}$. We show this series for Germany (capital key 25.57 percent), France (capital key 20.14 percent) and Italy (capital key 17.49 percent) as well. Of course, own-risk activities (ANFA [now including ELA], NCB-specific collateral, most of the PSPP) are riding roughshod over what were supposed to be capital key-weighted or shared-risk activities. The precise breakdown of the balance sheets of the NCBs between own-risk and shared-risk activities is rather opaque and will be discussed at greater length in Chapter 6. Euro area NCB seigniorage based on the capital key is shown in Table 2.12. The true number will be a convex combination of the number in Table 2.11 and the

Table 2.12 *Euro area seigniorage (capital key based)* *(% of GDP)*

	EA	Germany	France	Italy
2007	0.5	0.4	0.4	0.5
2008	2.3	2.2	2.2	2.3
2009	–0.2	–0.1	–0.1	–0.2
2010	0.0	0.0	0.0	0.0
2011	1.9	1.8	1.9	2.0
2012	4.0	3.6	3.8	4.2
2013	–4.7	–4.2	–4.4	–5.1
2014	–0.3	–0.2	–0.3	–0.3
2015	4.8	4.3	4.6	5.4
2016	5.7	5.0	5.6	6.4
2017	7.1	6.2	6.9	8.0

Source: National central banks and own calculations

corresponding one in Table 2.12, with weights that are, unfortunately, unknown.

The seigniorage data look pretty impressive, well into double digits as a share of GDP for Japan, up to 6 percent of GDP for the USA in 2013 and 7 percent of GDP for the EA in 2017. Adding the primary surplus figures of Table 2.9 to the seigniorage data of Table 2.11 yields the augmented primary surpluses as a percentage of GDP of the seven economies, as shown in Table 2.13:

These very large realized augmented primary surpluses mainly reflect the very high realized seigniorage figures of recent years. These historical seigniorage figures should not, however, be viewed as the amount of real resources that can be appropriated by running the printing presses during normal times, when inflation is a constraint, as discussed in Chapter 1. The high figures were all achieved when the economies in question were at the effective lower bound (ELB), that is, in a liquidity trap. Neither actual nor expected inflation responded significantly as the monetary liabilities of the central banks (and the size of their balance sheets) exploded.

Table 2.13 *Augmented primary surplus of the State (% of GDP)*

	USA	Japan	UK	EA	Germany	France	Italy
2007	−0.9	−2.7	−0.9	2.4	3.0	#N/A	#N/A
2008	−0.7	−3.5	−2.2	2.7	5.4	#N/A	#N/A
2009	−7.2	−8.5	−2.0	−4.0	−2.0	#N/A	#N/A
2010	−9	−7.3	−7.1	−3.7	−2.3	#N/A	#N/A
2011	−3.2	−5.0	−4.2	0.3	2.6	−1.4	#N/A
2012	−5.6	−5.3	2.3	3.0	8.1	2.5	#N/A
2013	3.7	5.3	−2.8	−5.2	−4.6	−6.8	1.7
2014	−0.6	9.0	−3.6	−0.5	0.9	−2.2	1.2
2015	−1.4	12.5	−2.2	4.8	6.7	3.4	2.3
2016	−4.5	10.4	1.1	6.1	7.8	5.6	3.8
2017	−1.0	6.1	4.2	7.7	9.5	6.1	7.2

Source: IMF and own calculations

Once out of the liquidity trap, with output at its potential level and with expected inflation, on average, close to actual inflation, the amount of real resources that can be extracted by monetary issuance dwindles very rapidly (as shown in Chapter 1). The numbers for the years prior to 2008 outside Japan (which was in a liquidity trap throughout the period covered in Table 2.11) are probably quite indicative of the amount of resources, as a share of GDP, that can be extracted with both actual and expected inflation at the inflation target and the economy operating at close to capacity. That would be no more than 0.5 percent of GDP. The EA ran slightly above that level during the period 2003–6, possibly because the euro was then beginning to establish itself as an aspiring global currency.[7] The large denominations of the euro notes (a maximum denomination of €500 as compared to a measly $100 for the US dollar) also likely made the euro an attractive store of value and medium of exchange for those engaged in illegal activities, both inside and outside the Eurozone.

[7]   The introduction of euro notes and coins started in January 2002.

We can also calculate, if we have a demand function for the monetary base, what the maximum amount of seigniorage is that can be extracted at any constant rate of inflation. We assume that doing better than that amount by entering hyperinflation territory would not be of interest to policy makers. We considered such estimates in Chapter 1.

General Government Gross Debt

It is easy to overstate the fragility of the fiscal position of most advanced economy governments by focusing on general government gross debt. Table 2.14 shows the gross general government debt-to-GDP ratios for the EA and six advanced economies.

General Government Net Debt

Subtracting the general government's financial assets from its financial liabilities yields the general government net debt to GDP ratio in

Table 2.14 *General government gross debt (EoP, % of GDP)*

	Euro Area	France	Germany	Italy	Japan	United Kingdom	United States
2007	65.0	64.5	63.7	99.8	175.4	41.7	64.8
2008	68.7	68.8	65.2	102.4	183.4	49.7	73.8
2009	79.2	83.0	72.6	112.5	201.0	63.7	86.9
2010	84.5	85.3	80.9	115.4	207.9	75.2	95.5
2011	86.6	87.8	78.6	116.5	222.1	80.8	99.9
2012	89.6	90.6	79.8	123.4	229.0	84.1	103.3
2013	91.5	93.4	77.5	129.0	232.5	85.2	104.9
2014	91.7	94.9	74.6	131.8	236.1	87.0	104.6
2015	89.8	95.6	70.9	131.5	231.3	87.9	104.8
2016	88.8	96.6	67.9	132.0	235.6	87.9	106.8
2017	86.6	96.8	63.9	131.8	237.6	87.5	105.2
2018	84.4	96.7	59.8	130.3	238.2	87.4	106.1

Source: IMF

Table 2.15 below. In the case of Japan, the net debt is more than 80 percentage points of GDP lower than the gross debt. For all countries the picture is less alarming than the gross debt picture.

Net Nonmonetary Debt of the Consolidated General Government and Central Bank

For fiscal sustainability, what matters is not the *net* debt of the general government, but the net nonmonetary debt of the State – the consolidated general government and central bank. As shown in Table 2.16, Japan, at the end of 2017, had a net nonmonetary debt to GDP ratio of 67.4 percent, a far cry from the 237.6 percent gross general government debt to GDP ratio for that same year, shown in Table 2.14.

Real Commercial Assets of the Public Sector

In most advanced economies, the State owns a very large amount of real commercial assets, mostly real estate and infrastructure, but also other real assets (public transport, airports, ports, utilities etc.). Detter

Table 2.15 *General government net debt (EoP, % of GDP)*

	USA	Japan	EA	UK	Germany	France	Italy
2007	44.9	97.6	52.4	36.6	52.9	58.1	92.1
2008	51.7	108.5	53.8	43.9	52.6	59.8	94.1
2009	62.7	122.7	61.9	57.0	59.4	69.7	102.8
2010	70.0	131.1	65.9	68.1	60.9	73.6	104.7
2011	76.5	142.4	68.4	72.5	59.2	76.4	106.8
2012	80.3	146.7	72.1	75.5	58.4	80.0	111.6
2013	80.8	146.4	74.6	76.8	57.6	83.0	116.7
2014	80.4	148.5	74.8	78.8	54.1	85.5	118.8
2015	80.1	147.6	73.8	79.3	51.1	86.4	119.5
2016	81.2	152.8	73.7	78.8	48.2	87.5	119.5
2017	78.8	154.9	71.8	77.9	44.9	87.5	119.5
2018	77.7	155.7	69.5	78.0	41.5	87.4	118.3

Source: IMF

Table 2.16 *Net consolidated general government and central bank non-monetary debt (EoP, % of GDP)*

	USA	Japan	Euro area	UK	Germany	France	Italy
2007	39.2	79.4	41.2	31.9	40.7	47.1	80.5
2008	39.8	89.2	39.0	37.5	36.6	45.4	78.7
2009	49.0	101.8	47.4	44.1	43.6	55.6	87.6
2010	56.6	109.1	50.4	55.8	46.1	59.2	88.9
2011	59.1	117.4	49.9	58.9	41.7	59.1	87.5
2012	63.5	118.8	50.3	56.1	39.1	60.8	89.5
2013	58.7	106.9	59.0	56.5	43.1	68.4	99.7
2014	57.8	95.6	58.9	59.0	39.5	70.3	101.2
2015	60.1	81.2	53.1	59.2	36.8	70.6	101.4
2016	62.8	72.4	47.1	56.3	34.4	71.9	101.6
2017	59.3	67.4	39.3	51.7	30.4	71.2	100.6

Source: IMF and own calculations

and Fölster (2015, 2017) argue convincingly that, properly managed, the fair value of these real commercial assets (measured by the PDV of current and anticipated future profits) likely exceeds the net debt of the general government sector in most advanced economies. This is confirmed in a recent IMF (2018) study. Unfortunately, these assets tend to be managed appallingly badly – in many cases we don't even have a complete inventory or listing of these assets, let alone an attempt at a valuation and a balance sheet.

The bad news is that, until these assets are properly managed (for instance through Urban Wealth Funds, as proposed in Detter and Fölster (2017) for the real commercial assets owned by local authorities), their fair value may well be negligible or even negative. The good news is that professional, transparent, accountable, profit-oriented management of these assets, at arms' length from the political leadership of the authorities, could transform the balance sheet of federal, state and local governments and thus meaningfully increase fiscal space. Pursuing this professionalization of commercial public asset management is not only desirable because it would increase the productive capacity (potential output) of the neighborhoods, regions or nations where these assets are located, it would also permit a larger countercyclical fiscal stimulus, should this make sense from a macroeconomic stabilization perspective.

Real GDP Growth Rates

The recent historical growth rates of real GDP are given in Table 2.17.

Effective Interest Rates on the Public Debt

We calculate the effective interest rate on the public debt in Table 2.18 as net interest payments on general government net debt as a percentage of the face value of the net debt.

We see how extraordinarily low these numbers have become in recent years as maturing public debt was replaced with new issues at significantly lower nominal rates and new net borrowing likewise benefited from the pervasive and persistent low interest rate environment.

Table 2.17 *Growth rate of real GDP (%YY)*

	Euro Area	Germany	France	Italy	Japan	United Kingdom	United States
2007	3.0	3.4	2.4	1.3	1.6	2.4	1.8
2008	0.3	0.8	0.1	−1.0	−1.1	−0.5	−0.3
2009	−4.5	−5.6	−2.9	−5.5	−5.4	−4.2	−2.8
2010	2.0	3.9	1.9	1.6	4.2	1.7	2.5
2011	1.7	3.7	2.1	0.7	−0.1	1.5	1.6
2012	−0.8	0.7	0.2	−2.9	1.5	1.5	2.2
2013	−0.2	0.6	0.6	−1.7	2.0	2.1	1.7
2014	1.4	1.9	1.0	0.2	0.3	3.1	2.6
2015	2.0	1.5	1.0	0.9	1.4	2.3	2.9
2016	1.8	1.9	1.1	1.1	0.9	1.9	1.5
2017	2.5	2.5	1.9	1.5	1.6	1.8	2.3

Source: IMF

Table 2.18 *Effective interest rate on general government net debt (%)*

	Germany	France	Italy	Japan	United Kingdom	United States	Euro Area
2007	4.6	4.1	4.9	0.0	4.3	4.7	4.8
2008	4.6	4.5	5.0	0.4	3.4	4.1	4.8
2009	4.1	3.3	4.2	0.5	2.4	3.0	4.0
2010	3.5	3.1	3.9	0.7	3.5	2.8	3.8
2011	3.6	3.3	4.2	0.7	3.7	3.0	3.8
2012	3.1	3.0	4.5	0.7	3.0	2.7	3.7
2013	2.8	2.5	3.9	0.7	1.8	2.5	3.4
2014	2.6	2.4	3.7	0.5	2.3	2.5	3.2
2015	2.6	2.2	3.3	0.3	1.7	2.5	3.0
2016	2.3	2.1	3.2	0.0	2.1	2.5	2.6
2017	1.7	1.7	3.0	−0.2	2.2	2.3	2.4

Source: IMF and own calculations

Table 2.19 *Inflation forecasts for 2018 (% YoY)*

	Germany	France	Italy	Japan	United Kingdom	United States	Euro Area
2018	1.8	2.1	1.3	1.2	2.5	2.1	1.8

Source: Citi Research

The current year real GDP growth numbers we use are Citi's September 2018 forecasts for 2018. The potential output growth estimates come from a variety of sources, in the case of the USA from the CBO. The CBO estimates that the growth rate of potential output of the USA will rise from 1.6 percent SAAR to 1.8 percent in 2020 and 1.9 percent in 2027.[8] Our inflation forecasts for 2018 are given in Table 2.19.

We subtract these inflation rates from the 2017 effective nominal interest rates (Table 2.18) to get $r_{t+1,t}$. The long-term real interest

---

[8] Congressional Budget Office, Budget and Economic Data, www.cbo.gov/about/products/budget-economic-data#6. The then-year projections data are from June 2017.

rates are estimates based in part on long-term index-linked debt yields or on the real rates implied by long-term nominal yields and inflation swaps. These were then reviewed upwards to allow for the expected slow upward drifts of both the actual and the neutral long-term real rates as the global output gap closes and which are not, in our view, priced in. The differences in the regional estimates of $\bar{r}$ are assumed to reflect differences in sovereign default risk rather than expectations of real exchange rate depreciation or appreciation.

The Fiscal Space Numbers

The current values of the augmented primary surplus, $\hat{s}_t$, tell us little more than that in the USA the balance sheet of the Fed is contracting while in the EA and in Japan the balance sheet of the central bank continues to expand, albeit at a diminishing rate. This is clear when we compare the augmented primary surpluses with the regular primary surpluses, sans seigniorage, s_t. From Chapter 1, sustainable seigniorage, away from the ELB, at a rate of inflation equal to the target (2 percent) is at most 0.5 percent of GDP in all the countries

Table 2.20 *Fiscal space in selected advanced economies 2017 (% or % of GDP)*

	USA	EA	Italy	Germany	Japan	UK	France
$r_{t+1,t}$	2.9	1.9	1.0	1.9	1.0	1.3	1.7
$\bar{y}$	1.9	1.5	0.5/1.0	1.5	0.9	1.9	1.7
$r_{t+1,t}$	0.2	0.6	1.7	−0.1	−1.4	−0.3	−0.4
$\bar{r}$	1.1	1.3	1.7	1.0	1.0	1.2	1.3
d_t	59.3	39.3	100.6	30.4	67.4	51.7	71.2
s_t	−2.2	0.6	1.5	1.7	−4.0	−1.1	−1.4
$\hat{s}_t$	−1.0	7.7	7.2	9.5	6.1	4.2	6.1
$\hat{s}_t^{max}$	2.5	2.5	2.5	2.5	2.5	2.5	2.5
$\hat{s}_t^{R}$	−1.55	−0.51	0.70	−0.60	−1.59	−0.82	−1.47
$\hat{s}_t^{\infty,R}$	−0.47	−0.19	1.40/0.90	−0.15	0.07	−0.35	−0.28

Source: own calculations

concerned. This is the assumption built into our guestimate as to the maximum sustainable primary surplus as a share of GDP, $\hat{s}_t^{max}$.

It is clear from Table 2.20, comparing $\hat{s}_t^R$ to $\hat{s}_t$, that the stabilization of the net nonmonetary public debt as a share of GDP for the current year does not require any fiscal sacrifice: in all countries except the United Kingdom, the cyclical recovery has boosted growth above potential. In addition, real interest rates are extraordinarily low and in all except the USA, seigniorage revenues last year were massive. A more realistic appreciation of the fiscal effort required is obtained by comparing $\hat{s}_t^R$ with the augmented primary surplus that would have been achieved last year with seigniorage as a share of GDP at a realistically sustainable noninflationary level of, say, 0.5 percent. We assume this in the remainder of the discussion.

The long-run sustainability calculus is, with the initial debt burden given, entirely driven by the difference between the long-run effective real interest rate on the public debt and the long-run growth rate of real GDP. Even with the benign real interest rate assumption we make, the USA would have to tighten fiscally by 1.23 percent of GDP rather than engaging in a procyclical fiscal stimulus. Japan has a persistent "flow problem"; the primary deficit of the general government is 4 percent of GDP. Even though the maximum long-run share of seigniorage in GDP for Japan is as high as 3.4 percent (see Table 1.1), that level of seigniorage would, once the country escapes the ELB, come with an inflation rate of 49 percent, which does not look politically sustainable. If Italy can keep its sovereign risk premium under control (as we assume with only a 70 bps sovereign risk spread over Germany) and can manage to raise its growth rate of potential output to 1.0 percent (which would require material structural reforms), fiscal tightening is not required for that country, which already runs a general government primary surplus of 1.5 percent of GDP. Without meaningful structural reforms, Italy's growth rate of potential output is unlikely to exceed 0.0 percent. This would raise the permanent required augmented primary surplus to 1.7 percent of GDP. In addition, we have had the end of the PSPP (which occurred in December 2018), and the departure of Mario Draghi from the Presidency of the ECB (on October 31, 2019) and his replacement with a President less wedded to minimizing the spread of the Italian sovereign debt yield over Bunds. Those two factors, combined with the election of a Liga-5 Star coalition government whose commitment to fiscal responsibility and continued membership of the Eurozone are not trusted by the public and the markets, and despite the resumption of QE in November 2019 and the announcement of the 750 bn euro Pandemic Emergency Purchase Programme in March 2020, can easily raise the sovereign risk premium by another 150 basis points, in which case the permanent required augmented primary surplus would rise to 3.2 percent of GDP.

Readers can make their own assumptions and plug them into equations (2.22) and (2.23) to derive alternative scenarios.

The bad news is that future real interest rates are likely to be somewhat higher than current real interest rates while real GDP growth is flattered by the cyclical upswing. Another sobering message is that the ample seigniorage revenues extracted in recent years cannot be a sustained phenomenon without risking hyperinflation, unless the economy remains in a (permanent) liquidity trap, which is possible, but, outside Japan, unlikely. The good news is that, provided long-term fiscal solvency is assured, seigniorage can be boosted massively if temporarily during the next cyclical downswing. A temporary monetized fiscal stimulus will always be effective in stimulating nominal aggregate demand, even when interest rates are at the ELB, as we show in the next Chapter.

3   Helicopter Money Drops

In this Chapter, we use the consolidated accounts of the State to study the effectiveness, as regards its ability to boost nominal aggregate demand, of a helicopter money drop, aka a monetized fiscal stimulus (tax cut or public spending increase). Before we can get to the substantive issues of helicopter money drops in this Chapter, and for the discussion of the fiscal theory of the price level (FTPL) in Chapter 4, and the economics of life at the ELB in Chapter 5, some investment in a very simple flexible price level general equilibrium model is necessary.

3.1   ADDING THE HOUSEHOLD SECTOR

In this Section, we add a private sector consisting of two types of competitive households, permanent income consumers and Keynesian consumers. The total population is represented as a continuum on a unit interval. There are no firms. Each household of either type receives each period an exogenous endowment, $Y_t > 0$, of a single perishable commodity. The asset menu of the previous chapter is also radically simplified. There is no durable capital: $K_t = 0$; there is no nonmonetary central bank liability: $N_t = 0$; there are no central bank loans to the private sector: $L_t = 0$; and the economy is closed: $R_t^f = 0$.

Permanent income households are a share η, $0 < \eta \leq 1$ of the total population. The representative permanent income household receives a share η of the economy-wide endowment and pays a share η of the taxes. It maximizes the utility function in equation (3.1), subject to its period budget constraint equation (3.2) and its solvency constraint equation (3.3). C_t^f is real household consumption by permanent income households in period t, C_t^k is real household consumption by Keynesian households in period t and M_{t+1}/P_t the end-of-period stock of real money balances in period t. We assume $M_t > 0$, $P_t > 0$ and $i_{t,t-1} \geq i_{t,t-1}^M$

$$E_t \sum_{j=t}^{\infty} \left(\frac{1}{1+\theta} \right)^j \left(\ln C_j^f + \phi \ln \left(\frac{M_{j+1}}{P_j} \right) \right); \quad \theta, \ \phi > 0 \tag{3.1}$$

$$M_{t+1} + B_{t+1}^{cb} \equiv \eta(P_t Y_t - T_t^s) - P_t C_t^f + (1 + i_{t,t-1}^M) M_t \\ + (1 + i_{t,t-1}) B_t^{cb} \tag{3.2}$$

$$E_t \lim_{j \to \infty} I_{j,t-1}(M_{j+1} + B_{j+1}^p) \geq 0 \tag{3.3}$$

Note the asymmetry between the treatment of terminal money balances in the permanent income household solvency constraint equation (3.3) and the solvency constraints of the central bank in equation (2.4) and by implication the solvency constraint of the State – the consolidated central bank and Treasury. To permanent income households, money is an asset, even in the long run.

We can combine the forward solution of equation (3.2) with equation (3.3) to obtain the intertemporal budget constraint of the permanent income household:

$$M_t + B_t^p \geq E_t \sum_{j=t}^{\infty} I_{j,t-1}[P_j C_j^f + \eta T_j^s - \eta P_j Y_j \\ + (i_{j,j-1} - i_{j,j-1}^M) M_j] \tag{3.4}$$

or, equivalently,

$$\frac{M_t}{P_t} + \frac{B_t^p}{P_t} \geq E_t \sum_{j=t}^{\infty} R_{j,t-1} \left[C_j^f + \eta \frac{T_j^s}{P_j} - \eta Y_j \\ + (i_{j,j-1} - i_{j,j-1}^M) \frac{M_j}{P_j} \right] \tag{3.5}$$

The optimality conditions are, for $t \geq 0$:

$$\frac{1/C_t^f}{E_t(1/C_{t+1}^f)} = \frac{1 + r_{t+1,t}}{1+\theta} \tag{3.6}$$

$$\frac{M_{t+1}}{P_t} = \frac{\phi(1 + i_{t+1,t})}{i_{t+1,t} - i_{t+1,t}^M} C_t^f \tag{3.7}$$

$$\frac{M_0}{P_0} + \frac{B_0^p}{P_0} = E_0 \sum_{j=0}^{\infty} R_{j,-1}$$

$$\left[C_j^f + \eta \frac{T_j^s}{P_j} - \eta Y_j + (i_{j,j-1} - i_{j,j-1}^M) \frac{M_j}{P_j} \right] \tag{3.8}$$

Because the period utility functions are increasing both in consumption and in real money balances (there is no satiation in either), the permanent income household intertemporal budget constraint will always hold with equality: no wealth is wasted, as is clear from equation (3.8), which can be viewed as the boundary condition for the first-order stochastic difference equation (3.6), together with (3.7). Equation (3.8) is the mathematical implication of the fact that the Lagrange multiplier on the household intertemporal budget constraint is strictly positive because of nonsatiation in consumption and real money balances, which implies that the household IBC holds with equality. We return to this issue in our discussion of the fiscal theory of the price level in Chapter 4.

Keynesian households consume their entire disposable income. They never hold any assets. Their consumption is given by:

$$C_t^k = (1 - \eta) \left(Y_t - (T_t^s / P_t) \right) \tag{3.9}$$

We now add the IBC of the State for this simple model from equation (2.12) or equation (2.11):

$$\frac{M_t + B_t^p}{P_t} \leq E_t \sum_{j=t}^{\infty} R_{j,t-1} \left(\frac{T_j^s}{P_j} + (i_{j,j-1} - i_{j,j-1}^M) \frac{M_j}{P_j} - C_j^s \right)$$

$$+ \frac{1}{P_t} \lim_{j \to \infty} E_t I_{j,t-1} M_{j+1} \tag{3.10}$$

or, equivalently, using the intertemporal seigniorage identity

$$B_t^p \leq E_t \sum_{j=t}^{\infty} R_{j,t-1} \left(\frac{T_j^s}{P_j} - C_j^s + \left(\frac{M_{j+1} - (1 + i_{j,j-1}^M) M_j}{P_j} \right) \right) \tag{3.11}$$

3.2 EQUILIBRIUM

Output market equilibrium in this endowment economy with a single perishable commodity is given by:

$$Y_t = C_t^f + C_t^k + C_t^s \tag{3.12}$$

Assume both the endowment and real public consumption spending are constant. The output equilibrium condition or real resource constraint now simplifies to:[1]

$$\overline{Y} = \overline{C}^s + C_t^f + C_t^k \tag{3.13}$$

Assume total real net taxes are constant. We define $\tau_t^s = T_t^s/P_t$. This means Keynesian consumption will be constant and given by $C_t^k = C^k = (1-\eta)(\overline{Y} - \overline{\tau}^s)$. Permanent income household consumption is therefore also constant in equilibrium with $C_t^f = \overline{C}^f = \eta\overline{Y} - \overline{C}^s + (1-\eta)\overline{\tau}^s$. With permanent income household consumption constant, the real interest rate is, from equation (3.6), given by the rate of time preference:

$$r_{t+1,t} = \theta \tag{3.14}$$

Earlier we assumed that the own interest rate on money is constant and less than or equal to the risk-free nominal interest rate on public debt. We will specify policy rules that support such an outcome.

Monetary equilibrium is given by:

$$\frac{M_{t+1}}{P_t} = \frac{\phi(1+i_{t+1,t})}{i_{t+1,t} - i^M}\left(\eta\overline{Y} - \overline{C}^s + (1-\eta)\overline{\tau}^s\right) \tag{3.15}$$

3.3 THE JOYS OF A HELICOPTER MONEY DROP

If we ignore uncertainty, we can obtain the following closed-form solution for permanent income household consumption:

$$C_t^f = \frac{\theta(1+r_{t,t-1})}{(1+\phi)(1+\theta)}\left[\left(\frac{M_t + B_t^p}{P_t}\right) + \sum_{j=t}^{\infty} R_{j,t-1}\eta(Y_j - \overline{\tau}_t^s)\right] \tag{3.16}$$

Substituting the IBC of the State (equation (3.10)), holding with equality and using equation (3.9) gives:

[1]   We assume $\overline{Y} > \overline{C}^s \geq 0$.

$$C_t^f = \frac{\theta(1 + r_{t,t-1})}{(1+\phi)(1+\theta)} \left[\sum_{j=t}^{\infty} R_{j,t-1} \left(Y_j - C_j^s - C_j^k + (i_{j,j-1} - i_{j,j-1}^M)\frac{M_j}{P_j} \right) \right.$$

$$\left. + \frac{1}{P_t} \lim_{j \to \infty} E_t I_{j,t-1} M_{j+1} \right] \tag{3.17}$$

Or, equivalently,

$$C_t^f = \frac{\theta(1 + r_{t,t-1})}{(1+\phi)(1+\theta)} \left[\frac{M_t}{P_t} + \sum_{j=t}^{\infty} R_{j,t-1} \right.$$

$$\left. \left(Y_j - C_j^s - C_j^k + \frac{M_{j+1} - (1 + i_{j,j-1}^M)M_j}{P_j} \right) \right] \tag{3.18}$$

Equation (3.18) says that – holding constant current and future interest rates (nominal and real), real income and real consumption spending by the State and by Keynesian consumers – it is possible to boost either public and/or private consumption demand by boosting the PDV of current and future monetary issuance (minus the PDV of the interest paid on current and future money stocks). This increases fiscal space and permits taxes to be cut. The equivalent equation (3.17) says that there are two sources of seigniorage: first, the PDV of profits earned from investing the existing money stock in assets yielding more than the interest rate on money; second, the PDV of the terminal stock of money.

Note that this contradicts the assertion by Borio et al. (2016), that a helicopter money drop – say a one-period tax cut funded by a permanent increase in the money stock – is only more expansionary than a bond-financed tax cut of the same magnitude and duration if the policy rate is permanently zero. All that is required is that the policy rate (interpreted here as the interest rate on money) be less than the interest rate on the central bank's assets. And this is only sufficient. Even if there are no interest rate profits for the central bank (we are in a permanent liquidity trap with $i_{t,t-1} = i_{t,t-1}^M$ for all t), helicopter money will boost aggregate demand as long as the growth rate of the nominal money stock is equal or greater than the interest rate (which at the ELB equals the interest rate on money), in the long run.

Substituting the IBC of the State (equation (3.10)) into equation (3.16) and adding the consumption of the Keynesian households yields

$$C_t^f + C_t^k = \frac{\theta}{(1+\phi)(1+\theta)} \left[\sum_{j=t}^{\infty} R_{j,t} \left(Y_j - C_j^k - C_j^s + (i_{j,j-1} - i_{j,j-1}^M) \frac{M_j}{P_j} \right) \right.$$
$$\left. + \frac{1}{P_t} \lim_{j \to \infty} I_{j,t} M_{j+1} \right] + (1-\eta)(Y_t - \tau_t^s) \qquad (3.19)$$

or, equivalently,

$$C_t^f + C_t^k = \frac{\theta}{(1+\phi)(1+\theta)} \left[\frac{M_t}{P_t} + \sum_{j=t}^{\infty} R_{j,t} \left(Y_j - C_j^k - C_j^s \right. \right.$$
$$\left. \left. + \left(\frac{M_{j+1} - (1+i_{j,j-1}^M)M_j}{P_j} \right) \right) \right] + (1-\eta)(Y_t - \tau_t^s)$$

$$(3.20)$$

A current period tax cut will, holding constant aggregate output and the general price level, boost demand by Keynesian consumers by their share of the tax cut, $-(1-\eta)\Delta\tau_t^s$. If the fiscal stimulus is monetized, the government can, *cet. par.*, continue to satisfy its IBC without ever raising future taxes (or cutting future public spending). This is the case even if there are no Keynesian consumers ($\eta = 1$).

A tax cut today will, other things being equal, including real current and future public spending *and monetary issuance*, require higher future taxes equal in PDV to the current tax cut. This would result in lower spending today by permanent income consumers, although not by enough, in the current period, to stop aggregate (Keynesian plus permanent income) private consumption from rising. If there were only permanent income consumers, aggregate private consumption would be unchanged. Higher monetary issuance can, however, offset the effect of a tax cut today on future taxes and thus on the comprehensive wealth of permanent income consumers:

$$M_t + \sum_{j=t}^{\infty} R_{j,t} \left(Y_j - C_j^k - C_j^s + \left(\frac{M_{j+1} - (1+i_{j,j-1}^M)M_j}{P_j} \right) \right)$$
$$= \sum_{j=t}^{\infty} R_{j,t} \left(Y_j - C_j^k - C_j^s + (i_{j,j-1} - i_{j,j-1}^M) \frac{M_j}{P_j} \right) + \frac{1}{P_t} \lim_{j \to \infty} I_{j,t} M_{j+1}.$$

Note again that the boost to household consumption demand (or government consumption demand) provided by a monetized tax cut (public spending increase) is present even if the economy were forever stuck at the ELB with $i_{t,t-1} = i_{t,t-1}^M$ for all t. In equation (3.19), the term $\frac{1}{P_t} \lim_{j \to \infty} I_{j,t} M_{j+1}$ can be increased by any desired amount if the long-run growth rate of the nominal stock is equal to or greater than the long-run nominal rate of interest.

There is only a small miracle involved in the ability of a helicopter money drop to increase fiscal space. Note that the additional fiscal space created by any excess of the interest rate on the central bank's assets and the interest rate on central bank money is "at the expense of" the private sector, which holds central bank money despite the positive pecuniary opportunity cost involved. Consider the IBC of the State, (equation (3.10)), and the IBC of the consolidated Keynesian and permanent income consumers (from equations (3.8) and (3.9)).

The consolidated IBC of the State and the private sector is:

$$E_t \sum_{j=t}^{\infty} R_{j,t-1}(C_j^p + C_j^k + C_j^s) \leq E_t \sum_{j=t}^{\infty} R_{j,t-1} Y_j$$

$$+ \frac{1}{P_t} \lim_{j \to \infty} E_t I_{j,t-1} M_{j+1} \tag{3.21}$$

So the term $E_t \sum_{j=t}^{\infty} R_{j,t-1}(i_{j,j-1} - i_{j,j-1}^M) \frac{M_j}{P_j}$ is absent from the consolidated IBC of the State and the private sector. The only perceived net addition to the "budgetary space" of the consolidated private and public sector is the term $\frac{1}{P_t} \lim_{j \to \infty} E_t I_{j,t-1} M_{j+1}$. This term is there because of the asymmetric treatment of the PDV of the terminal money stock in the IBCs of the private sector (the holders of central bank money) and the State (the issuer of central bank money). Money is treated as an asset by its holders but not as a liability by its issuer because of the irredeemability of central bank money. This makes central bank money, in a very precise way – that is, $\frac{1}{P_t} \lim_{j \to \infty} E_t I_{j,t-1} M_{j+1}$ can be positive – into an *outside* asset – an asset, that is, for which there is no meaningful offsetting liability somewhere in the system. This makes central bank money (or rather the PDV of the terminal stock of central bank money) into something akin to commodity moneys like gold, the stones of the Isle of Yap, Bitcoin and other cryptocurrencies.

However, the fact that, in PDV terms, the increased fiscal space of the State represented by the term $E_t \sum_{j=t}^{\infty} R_{j,t-1}(i_{j,j-1} - i_{j,j-1}^M) \frac{M_j}{P_j}$ comes at the expense of a reduced budgetary space of the private sector, does not make it irrelevant from the perspective of aggregate demand management. In a demand-constrained Keynesian equilibrium with involuntarily idle resources, helicopter money drops targeted at, say, Keynesian consumers or a monetized increase in real public spending on goods and services can boost aggregate demand and thus employment, output and income of both Keynesian and permanent income consumers. It is not necessary that there is an equal reduction (in PDV terms) in current and future demand from permanent income consumers who "pay for"' the increased opportunity cost of holding money balances, $E_t \sum_{j=t}^{\infty} R_{j,t-1}(i_{j,j-1} - i_{j,j-1}^M) \frac{M_j}{P_j}$, because the PDV of current and future GDP and income has been boosted. The term $\frac{1}{P_t} \lim_{j \to \infty} E_t I_{j,t-1} M_{j+1}$ is the "miraculous" little bit extra that will cause helicopter money to increase fiscal space without reducing private budget space even in a permanent liquidity trap, but which can be expected to equal zero under normal circumstances.

A Helicopter Money Drop Does Not Have to Be Permanent to Be Effective

There is a common misconception that an increase in the money stock associated with a monetized fiscal stimulus has to be permanent for it to be effective. By effective I mean that it has a larger effect on nominal aggregate demand than the same fiscal stimulus financed through borrowing with no increase in the path of the current and (anticipated) future money stock. From equation (3.18), it is clear that the fiscal space created by increasing the stock of money is the PDV of current and future increases in the monetary base, net of any interest paid on the outstanding current and future monetary base stocks:

$\sum_{j=t}^{\infty} R_{j,t-1} \left(\dfrac{M_{j+1} - (1 + i_{j,j-1}^{M})M_{j}}{P_{j}} \right)$. Even if the monetary expansion that

funds a current period tax cut, transfer payment or increase in exhaustive public spending is temporary, that is, it is reversed in the future, the PDV of current and future monetary issuance will still be boosted, because the future reversal of the monetary stimulus is discounted.

3.4 SEVEN PROPOSITIONS

The accounting framework of Chapters 1 and 2 and our simple model of consumer behavior of Chapter 3 can be used, with a bit of additional analysis that I shall skip here, (but see Buiter (2010, 2014a, b)) to establish a number of propositions, some of which have already been stated in a formal manner, but are restated here in a nontechnical manner to make this Chapter more self-contained. The only substantive assumptions I need are that the Treasury is the beneficial owner of the central bank and that financial markets are reasonably efficient, or at least orderly, so PDV calculations make sense. Many of these propositions can also be found in the work of Adair Turner, for example, Turner (2016).

Proposition 1: A central bank can be solvent with negative conventional equity or net worth.

Provided the PDV of future seigniorage is sufficiently large – relative to the PDV of the central bank's operating costs, the PDV of the future net payments it makes to the Treasury, the PDV of any future helicopter money drops it bestows on the private sector and the PDV of the quasi-fiscal subsidies it pays out – a central bank can have negative conventional net worth, capital or equity, as is clear from equation (2.19). It may make tradition-steeped accountants, financial market operators, analysts and central bankers uncomfortable to have a (conventional) net worth, equity or capital that is negative, but that is no reason for not making use of this option, should it turn out to be desirable for the conduct of monetary policy or the pursuit of financial stability. The Czech National Bank had negative conventional net worth during 2017 and the early part of 2018, and was none the worse for it.[2]

The objection that a central bank with negative net worth would immediately have to fill the hole in its balance sheet with base money issuance equal in magnitude to the hole in its balance sheet is incorrect. All that is required is that the PDV of future base money issuance be sufficient to fill the hole. In the short run, the central bank could issue nonmonetary liabilities "against the security of the PDV of current and future base money issuance," to finance their commitments, servicing them in the future through more gradual new base money issuance.

Proposition 2: Central bank current and future resources are "tax payers' money," regardless of whether the central bank is fully dependent, operationally independent or operationally and goal independent.

All that is required for this is the assumption that the Treasury is the beneficial owner of the central bank. Formal ownership structures of central banks are often peculiar. The United Kingdom is a notable exception, where beneficial and formal ownership coincide. In the United Kingdom, the Treasury has owned the stock of the Bank of England (technically a joint stock company) since 1946. The ECB is owned by the central banks of the member states of the euro area and these national central banks are in turn owned beneficially by their national Treasuries, but with formal ownership structures that vary country by country.

The Federal Reserve System is a federal institution consisting of a central, governmental agency, the Board of Governors and twelve regional Federal Reserve Banks. The twelve regional Federal Reserve Banks – the operating arms of the Federal Reserve system – are owned by their member banks. Reserve Bank stock may not be sold, traded, or

---

[2] See www.cnb.cz/en/about_cnb/performance/ten_day_balance_sheet/ten_day_balan ce_sheet_archives/.

pledged as security for a loan. Reserve Bank stockholders with $10 billion or less in total consolidated assets receive a 6 percent dividend on paid-in capital stock, while stockholders with more than $10 billion in total consolidated assets receive a dividend on paid-in capital stock equal to the *lesser* of 6 percent and the rate equal to the high yield of the ten-year Treasury note auctioned at the last auction held prior to the payment of such dividend. The 6 percent dividend makes this "stock" look rather like a fixed-rate perpetuity. The rate equal to the ten-year Treasury note makes this "stock" look like a variable-rate perpetuity, indexed to the ten-year yield. The Board of Governors and the Federal Reserve System as a whole aren't "owned" by anyone. The Federal Reserve System describes itself as an independent entity within the government (see Board of Governors of the Federal Reserve System (2017)). Since the US Treasury gets the profits of the Federal Reserve System, it would minimize confusion if the private "ownership" of the Federal Reserve Banks were abolished and the entire system (Board and Regional Reserve Banks) were explicitly owned by the US Treasury.

The Banca d'Italia is owned by banks, insurance companies and social security institutions (see Banca d'Italia (2013)). Although these shareholders are not supposed to influence the policies of the Banca d'Italia, this pseudo-private ownership structure is by no means innocuous. By revaluing its equity from a notional amount of euro 156,000 to euro 7.5 bn, the Banca d'Italia made a large quasi-fiscal capital transfer to its shareholders in 2014 – boosting their capital from 2015 on.

The Bank of Japan is capitalized at 100 mn yen and about 45 percent of the stock is held privately (see Bank of Japan (2020)). The stock trades in the over-the-counter market. For privately held stocks, there are no voting rights. If the BoJ were to be liquidated, all capital would be returned to the government. "Dividends" are paid at a rate of 5 percent of the "invested price" of the stock, which is JPY100. Again, this "stock" is a fixed-consol perpetuity.

For practical purposes, it makes sense to ignore the formal ownership structures of central banks and to focus on the reality of beneficial ownership of the central bank by the central government – the Treasury.

As beneficial owner of the central bank, the Treasury can appropriate, through the term T^{cb}, anything up to the comprehensive net worth of the central bank. Thus, to the extent that the current and future citizens/residents of the jurisdiction covered by the central bank are – as tax payers and beneficiaries of public spending – the beneficial owners of the Treasury, central bank resources are, through the Treasury's beneficial ownership of the central bank, indirectly beneficially owned by the tax payers and the beneficiaries of public spending.

Proposition 3: Consider the purchase of additional Treasury debt by the central bank funded by the permanent/irreversible issuance of additional base money equal in PDV to the purchase of Treasury debt. The cancellation (wiping out/forgiving) of that additional Treasury debt purchased by the central bank is equivalent to the central bank holding that additional Treasury debt forever (rolling it over as it matures). Both actions improve the solvency of the central bank and the consolidated State by the same amount.

Proposition 4: A permanent increase in the monetary base used by the central bank to purchase additional private domestic or foreign assets is equivalent, from the perspective of the IBC of the State, to an equal size permanent increase in the monetary base used by the central bank to purchase Treasury debt.[3]

Because the Treasury is the beneficial owner of the central bank, the Treasury can receive, up front, the PDV of the stream of current and future profits from monetary base issuance by the central bank as follows: (1) either the central bank repays the Treasury, today, the

---

[3] We assume the rate of return on private domestic and foreign assets is the same as that on Treasury debt.

PDV of the current and future interest the central bank earns on its holdings of Treasury debt, or the central bank cancels the Treasury debt and (2) the Treasury receives, today, from the central bank the PDV of current and future returns on the central bank's investments in private or foreign assets.

So why do some economists recommend Treasury debt forgiveness by the central bank as a unique way of boosting the resources of the Treasury and why are sovereigns often happier to sell their debt to the central bank than having the central bank invest in the same amount of private domestic and foreign assets? One possibility is that these economists and politicians don't understand the logic of the equivalence argument. Another answer is that the logic fails because financial markets are not sufficiently liquid and orderly. Liquidity constraints on the Treasury may make an actual up-front bird in the hand today worth more than the same PDV of future birds in the bush, when the PDV is calculated using the central bank's discount rate, which, because the central bank is not liquidity-constrained (when it comes to domestic currency financing), is potentially lower than that of the Treasury.

Politically, also, getting the free funding up front may be more attractive to a myopic government than having to wait to accrue the same PDV of interest costs saved. Borrowing from the market by the Treasury against the "security" of the future stream of profits to be transmitted to the Treasury by the central bank may also be less straightforward than the Treasury borrowing the same amount from the central bank and having the central bank cancel the debt or credibly promise to hang on to it forever.

Proposition 5: Permanent/irreversible QE in PDV terms creates fiscal space for a deferred helicopter money drop.

By permanent QE I mean an irreversible PDV increase in the monetary base (net of interest payments on the monetary base) used to purchase sovereign debt or private domestic or foreign securities. A helicopter money drop is an up-front temporary tax cut or increase in public spending financed through an immediate permanent increase in the monetary base. Permanent QE is a permanent increase in the PDV of the stock of base money brought about through an up-front increase in asset purchases by the central bank.[4] The profits generated by this operation (equal to the present discounted value of the interest saved plus the present discounted value of the increase in the terminal monetary base stock) relax the intertemporal budget constraint of the State and thus permit *future* tax cuts, increases in transfer payments or increases in public spending on goods and services. The helicopter money drop is deferred in the sense that the monetized balance sheet expansion by the central bank occurs first and the fiscal stimulus permitted because of the increase in State revenues generated by the monetized balance sheet expansion of the central bank follows later – is deferred.

Whether the increase in the base money stock is brought about through a purchase of Treasury bonds, through a purchase of private securities, with the increase in public spending or the tax cut occurring in later periods (deferred helicopter money drops) or through a contemporaneous tax cut, transfer payment increase or increase in exhaustive spending (helicopter money drops) makes no difference from the perspective of the intertemporal budget constraint of the State (holding constant all other arguments in the IBC of the State. For the general equilibrium impact on economic activity, of course, an immediate fiscal stimulus (which boosts demand in normal circumstances) can be very different from the anticipation today of a future fiscal stimulus, which could depress demand today by raising future interest rates and thus today's long yields.

---

[4]   Defining QE as a *permanent* increase in the monetary base through central bank asset purchases and helicopter money drops as a temporary fiscal stimulus funded through a *permanent* increase in base money, is more restrictive than is strictly necessary and I use the *"permanent"* restriction only for expositional simplicity. As noted in section 3.3, even a temporary (reversible) increase in the stock of base money will result in a positive PDV of interest saved.

Proposition 6: Assume the interest rate on base money is zero. A helicopter money drop today boosts demand even in a permanent liquidity trap, when the nominal interest rate is at the *zero lower bound* (ZLB) forever. It relaxes the intertemporal budget constraint of the state by an amount equal to the permanent increase in the stock of base money.

Because of the irredeemability of base money, the State can use the (discounted) increase in the value of the terminal base money stock to fund tax cuts or public spending increases, even in a permanent liquidity trap. Consider the case where base money is interest-bearing, and the safe nominal interest rate is forever at the *effective lower bound* (ELB) given by the interest rate on base money minus the carry cost of base money. In such a world, the proposition that, in a currency-only world, a permanent increase in the monetary base today (no matter how it is brought about) relaxes the intertemporal budget constraint of the state by an amount equal to the up-front increase in the monetary base and is therefore equivalent to a helicopter money drop, generalizes easily. When the monetary base is interest-bearing, an increase in the base money stock today, at the ELB, no matter how it is brought about, with the base money stock subsequently growing at a proportional rate equal to the "own" interest rate on base money, relaxes the intertemporal budget constraint of the State by an amount equal in present discounted value to the increase in the base money stock today.

What this means is that, in an economy with fiat base money, the fiscal channel of monetary policy always works. This is worth restating as a proposition:

Proposition 7: Lack of effective demand is a policy choice or the result of a failure of cooperation and coordination between the central bank and the Treasury, not an unavoidable fate, even for an economy apparently stuck at the ELB. The same holds for "secular stagnation" caused by persistent lack of effective demand. A sufficiently large helicopter money drop will always boost nominal aggregate demand. Even if the private sector were suffering from spending paralysis, aggregate demand can be boosted by government purchases of real goods and services. Whether the higher nominal aggregate demand manifests itself as higher real aggregate demand or higher inflation depends on the amount of excess capacity in the economy.

4 The Fallacy of the Fiscal Theory of the Price Level – and Why It Matters

In this chapter, we show how inappropriate use of the intertemporal budget constraint of the State can result in a theoretical framework for the determination of the general price level whose logic is fatally flawed. This matters not only because it undermines respect for economics as a serious social science but also because it can lead fiscal policy badly astray, with potentially materially adverse real-world consequences.

4.1 THE HISTORY OF THE FTPL

The fiscal theory of the price level (FTPL) was developed in the 1990s and early 2000s by a number of distinguished economists, among them Leeper (1991), Sims (1994, 1999a), Woodford (1994, 1995, 1996, 1998a, b, c, 1999, 2001) and Cochrane (1999, 2001, 2005). It was further discussed and developed by many others, for example, Cushing (1999), Loyo (1999), Kocherlakota and Phelan (1999), Christiano and Fitzgerald (2000), Schmitt-Grohe and Uribe (2000) and McCallum (2001). The FTPL was quite popular for a number of years, with extensions to open-economy settings (see e.g. Sims (1999b, 2001), Bergin (2000), Dupor (2000) and Daniel (2001)), although there were few, if any, attempts at empirical verification of its observable implications.

The original FTPL proposed an alternative theory of the determination of the general price level in a dynamic monetary general equilibrium model with freely flexible nominal prices in which there is a continuum of solutions for the general price level and the nominal money stock. This version of the FTPL was shown to be a fallacy by Buiter (1998, 1999, 2001, 2002, 2005), Niepelt (2004) and Daniel (2007). We shall focus here on Buiter's arguments.

The original FTPL was based on an elementary but fatal error: it confused a budget constraint with an equilibrium condition. Specifically, it confused the intertemporal budget constraint (IBC) of the State (the consolidated general government and central bank), with a mis-specified equilibrium sovereign nominal bond pricing equation. It then applied this sovereign bond pricing equation as an additional equilibrium condition, thus apparently both resolving the price level indeterminacy problem and the sovereign solvency problem: the equilibrium price level is the one that ensures that, given the stock of nominal government bonds outstanding, sovereign solvency is assured: the PDV of current and future augmented primary surpluses of the State equals the real value of the nonmonetary nominal debt outstanding, that is, the IBC of the State holds with equality. Unfortunately, the IBC of the State holding with equality is not a valid additional equilibrium condition because, in equilibrium, it is implied by the IBC of the household sector, holding with equality, which characterizes optimal consumption behavior as shown in Chapter 3.

Before getting to the substance of the fiscal theory of the price level, we define two key concepts. A *Ricardian* fiscal-financial-monetary program (budgetary rule) is a set of values or rules for current and future public spending, taxation, monetary issuance, borrowing and policy interest rates that ensure that the intertemporal budget constraint of the State is always (or identically) satisfied, that is, for all feasible values of the exogenous and endogenous variables that enter into the IBC of the State. A *non-Ricardian* budgetary rule is set of instrument values or rules for which the IBC of the State is not necessarily satisfied. It may be satisfied in equilibrium, that is, for some values of the exogenous and endogenous variables that enter into the IBC of the State, but it need not be. Effectively, non-Ricardian rules are arbitrary rules for public spending, taxation, monetary issuance, borrowing and interest rates that may or may not satisfy the IBC of the State, in or out of equilibrium.

The *contractual* value of a security (a government bond, say) is its value if all contractual obligations (interest payments, repayment of principal) are certain to be met exactly, now and in the future. If there is default risk, the current and future interest and principal payments would be discounted using interest rates that reflect a default risk premium. The *market value* of the bond in that case would be less than the contractual value, which can be viewed as the present discounted value (PDV) of current and future interest and principal payments discounted using interest rates that do not incorporate any default risk. There can of course be other sources of risk that cause future interest rates to be uncertain and that can result in variations over time of the contractual value of bonds of a given *face value* (contractual value when issued). In the deterministic model considered next, there is no risk or uncertainty, so the contractual value of a bond is the PDV of its contractual interest and principal repayment obligations discounted using risk-free interest rates.

The original FTPL asserted that the IBC of the State, holding with equality and with government bonds priced at their *contractual* (i.e. free of default risk) values, determines the general price level. The equilibrium value of the general price level equates the real value of the outstanding stock(s) of nominal government bonds (priced at their contractual values) to the present discounted value of anticipated future augmented primary surpluses of the State. The authors of the original FTPL did not recognize that this "additional" equilibrium condition – that the IBC of the State holds with equality, with sovereign bonds priced at their contractual values – had already been used elsewhere in the model: it is an implication of the equilibrium real resource constraint and the IBC of the representative consumer, holding with equality and with bonds priced at their contractual values. This IBC holds with equality when household consumption and money demand are derived from the optimizing behavior of forward-looking households with rational expectations, when there is nonsatiation in real money balances and/or consumption.

The aforementioned fatal fallacy was compounded with another confusion: the identification of the FTPL with "fiscal dominance" or "active fiscal policy and passive monetary policy" in a game-theoretic view of the interaction of monetary and fiscal authorities (see e.g. Leeper (1991), Bassetto (2002) and Minford (2017)). This is discussed in Section 4.4.b. The perfectly coherent (and conventional) view of the determination of the price level and the interaction of fiscal and monetary policy in the famous "Unpleasant Monetarist Arithmetic" model of Sargent and Wallace (1981) has sometimes been misinterpreted as an example of the FTPL because that model has a "second policy regime" – "fiscal dominance" – when the public debt-to-GDP ratio and real public spending and real net taxes as a share of GDP are kept constant and base money issuance is endogenously determined to satisfy the budget constraint of the State.[1] Clearly, the issue of monetary vs. fiscal dominance is an important one both theoretically and empirically. Both policy regimes should, however, be analyzed in conventional, non-FTPL models, in which the IBC of the State, holding with equality and with all financial instruments priced at their contractual values, is imposed only once.

Kocherlakota and Phelan (1999) investigated whether it might be possible to salvage the FTPL by interpreting it as an equilibrium selection mechanism when there are multiple equilibria. They reject this interpretation because the FTPL as an equilibrium selection mechanism can select unacceptable equilibria. We discuss this in Section 4.6 and in the Appendix to this Chapter and confirm the conclusions of Kocherlakota and Phelan. Buiter (1998, 1999, 2001, 2002, 2005 and Buiter and Sibert (2018)) showed that the original flexible price level FTPL produces a handful of anomalies and two logical inconsistencies or contradictions.

The FTPL is a fallacy regardless of whether the model of the economy is deterministic or stochastic. It is a fallacy when expectations are forward-looking, forward-looking and rational or backward-looking. Note that neither inconsistency with the empirical evidence

---

[1] Sargent and Wallace (1981) and Sargent (1987) also show that in the "game of chicken" between the monetary and fiscal authorities, both the monetary dominance and the fiscal dominance equilibrium produce outcomes for the general price level that are perfectly consistent with conventional monetary theory. In addition, since all nonmonetary government debt in the "Unpleasant Monetarist Arithmetic" model is index-linked or real, the FTPL cannot even get to first base in this model.

nor the lack of realism of its assumptions were reasons for the refutation of the FTPL by Buiter, Niepelt and Daniel. A logically inconsistent theory has no empirical implications, and the realism of its assumptions is irrelevant.

4.2 THE ATTEMPTED RESURRECTION OF THE FTPL

The refutations of the original FTPL by Buiter, Niepelt and Daniel were never disputed, let alone shown to be incorrect, in scholarly publications or other scientifically reputable media or fora. It is therefore surprising indeed that a theory exposed as a fallacy made a comeback. This resurrection has both a scholarly and an economic policy dimension.

4.2.a *The Scholarly Revival of the FTPL*

As regards the scholarly revival, on April 1, 2016, a conference with as its theme "Next Steps for the Fiscal Theory of the Price Level" was held at the Becker Friedman Institute for Research on Economics at the University of Chicago.[2] Three of the four originators of the FTPL, Christopher Sims, John Cochrane and Eric Leeper, participated and asserted its continued validity and relevance (see e.g. Sims (2016b), Cochrane (2016b, c) and Leeper (2015), Jacobson, Leeper and Preston (2016)).

The attempted scholarly revival takes two forms. One is an unreconstructed restatement of the original FTPL in a world with flexible prices. No new arguments are offered and because repeated assertion is not yet accepted in scholarly circles as an alternative mode of proof to induction and deduction, we dismiss it in what follows using the familiar earlier arguments of Buiter and Niepelt.

4.2.b *Sims's New FTPL: The FTLEA*

The second attempted scholarly resurrection of the FTPL, due to Sims (2011, 2013, 2016a, b, c) uses dynamic monetary general equilibrium

---

[2]   For the program and links to the presentations see https://bfi.uchicago.edu/events/next-steps-fiscal-theory-price-level. The only critical noise at the conference came from Harald Uhlig (2016).

models with sticky nominal prices. There is both a New-Keynesian and an Old-Keynesian variant. Sims now accepts that the Old-Keynesian variant is not an example of his "new" FTPL; we deal with it in Section 4.8 and in the Appendix to this Chapter. The New-Keynesian variant also turns out to be quite unlike the traditional FTPL in that it does not use the IBC of the State twice (holding with equality and with sovereign bonds priced at their contractual values). However, it also does not produce the result, insisted on by Sims (2011, 2013), that sovereign solvency is guaranteed, in equilibrium, by the appropriate response of consumption and of nominal and real discount factors to the introduction of a "non-Ricardian" budgetary policy. This New-Keynesian FTPL (or FTLEA – for fiscal theory of the level of economic activity) turns out to be a perfectly conventional macroeconomic model for which non-Ricardian budgetary rules may be, but are not guaranteed to be, consistent with government solvency in equilibrium.

4.3 WHY THE FALLACY OF THE FTPL MATTERS IN THE REAL WORLD

The main reason we are worried about this attempted resurrection of the FTPL is that in 2017 and 2018, the FTPL cropped up three times in the economic policy arena. In Japan, Katsushiko Aiba and Kiichi Murashima noted – referring to the "new" FTPL (in the version developed by Christopher Sims (2011, 2013, 2016a, b, c)) – that "the Nikkei and other media have recently reported his prescription for achieving the inflation target based on the FTPL. We should keep a close eye on this theory because PM Abe's economic advisor Koichi Hamada is a believer, meaning that it might be adopted in Japan's future macroeconomic policies" (Aiba and Murashima (2017, page 1)).

In Brazil, André Lara Resende (2017) argued in a contribution to *Valor Econômico*, a Brazilian financial newspaper, that high real interest rates in Brazil are simply the result of high nominal interest rates. His analysis is based on the analysis of John Cochrane in Cochrane (2016a), which has the FTPL as one of its key building blocks.

In Turkey, a senior economic advisor to President Erdogan, Professor Cemil Ertem, is a believer in the FTPL who cites John Cochrane's work. It is quite likely that President Erdogan's view that high nominal interest rates are the cause of high inflation is at least in part a reflection of "FTPLitis."[3] It may also reflect a mistaken application of the Fisher equation, reproduced here with the expectations operator added explicitly and any inflation risk premium omitted:

$$E_t\Big((1 + \pi_{t+1,t})(1 + r_{t+1,t})\Big) = 1 + i_{t,t+1}$$

We take the nominal interest rate to be the exogenous policy instrument here. An increase in the nominal interest rate with the real interest rate exogenous and constant is translated one-for-one into higher (expected) inflation. Except that the assumption of an unchanged real interest rate is incorrect, at least for a significant interval following an (unexpected) increase in the nominal policy rate. An alternative scenario is that an unexpected increase in the nominal policy interest rate increases the expected real interest rate on impact by more than the increase in the nominal interest rate and thus produces a lower rate of inflation. The higher real and nominal rates sustain a disinflationary process (through the output gap). Actual and expected inflation fall and this permits, in due course, the nominal interest rate to be lowered again. If the long-run (neutral) real interest rate is constant (say fixed by the time preference rate, the trend growth rate of productivity and the other drivers of ex-ante saving and investment propensities), the real interest settles down again to its old equilibrium value after contributing to a cyclical downturn to bring down the rate of inflation.

There are material real-world policy risks associated with the FTPL: policy disasters could happen if fiscal and monetary policy makers were to become convinced that the FTPL is the appropriate

---

[3] See e.g. http://newmonetarism.blogspot.com/2018/05/inflation-interest-rates-and -neo.html.

way to consider the interaction of monetary and fiscal policy in driving inflation, aggregate demand, real economic activity and sovereign default risk.

The key assertion of the FTPL is that, no matter how large the outstanding stock of domestic-currency-denominated public debt and the public sector deficits that have to be financed, now and in the future, there is no need to worry about the budgetary rule of the State becoming unsustainable. Debt sustainability analysis will always produce the answer that the public debt is indeed sustainable. This miracle happens because, no matter how large the nominal value of the debt stock, there always exists a value of the general price level high enough to make the real value of the outstanding stock of public debt small enough for the budgetary rule to be sustainable. And, somehow, the actual price level always takes on this unique value that ensures the sustainability of the public finances. In the more recent alternative version of the FTPL proposed by Sims, the role of the general price level is taken over by the level of real economic activity – real GDP, say, through the endogeneity of private consumption.

An implication of the FTPL is that monetary and fiscal policy makers – either acting in a cooperative and coordinated manner or acting in an independent and uncoordinated manner – can choose just about any paths or rules for real public spending on goods and services, real taxes net of transfers, policy interest rates and/or monetary issuance, now and in the future, without having to be concerned about meeting their contractual debt obligations. Somehow, the general price level (in the classic FTPL) or real aggregate demand (in the FTLEA version of Sims) is guaranteed to take on the value required to ensure that the real contractual value of the outstanding stock of nominal nonmonetary public debt outstanding is always equal to the present discounted value of the current and future real augmented primary surpluses of the State, even if the budgetary, monetary and interest rate policy rules are designed in ways that ignore the need to satisfy the IBC of the State.

Because this is manifestly incorrect (as shown in Sections 4.6, 4.7 and 4.8 and in the Appendix to this Chapter) it could be extremely dangerous if taken seriously and acted upon by monetary and fiscal policy makers, as pointed out in Buiter (2017a, b, c) and in Buiter and Sibert (2018). After all, what could be more appealing to a politician anxious to curry favor with the electorate through public spending increases and tax cuts, than the reassurance provided by the FTPL, that solvency of the State is never a problem? Regardless of the outstanding stocks of State assets and liabilities, the State can specify arbitrary paths or (contingent) rules for public spending, taxation, monetary issuance and/or nominal policy interest rates. Explosive sovereign bond trajectories will never threaten sovereign solvency. The general price level (or in Sims's FTLEA real economic activity, working through the nominal and real discount factors), will do whatever it takes to make the real contractual value of the outstanding stock of nominal government bonds consistent with solvency of the State for arbitrary, non-Ricardian budgetary rules. If some misguided government were to take this delusional theory seriously and were to act upon it, the result, when reality belatedly dawns, could be some combination of painful fiscal tightening, government default, excessive recourse to inflationary financing or even hyperinflation.

4.4 WHAT THE FTPL IS NOT

4.4.a Unanticipated Inflation and/or Financial Repression Can Reduce the Real Value of Nominal Public Debt and Unbridled Monetary Expansion May Prevent Sovereign Default

In standard/conventional monetary economics, a change in the general price level changes the real value of the outstanding stock of nominal bonds. Indeed, when faced with imminent default on its debt, a government may opt for monetary financing of its deficits. Inflation that was unanticipated at the time that fixed-rate nominal debt was issued can cause the realized real interest rate to be lower than was expected when the debt was issued. Financial repression (keeping nominal interest rates artificially low) can result in a reduction in the real value of current and future nominal debt service even if the inflation is anticipated, because it stops nominal interest rates from rising with expected inflation. This accounted for a sizeable part of the reduction in debt-to-GDP ratios after World War II in the United Kingdom, the United States and in many other countries. But this has nothing to do with the FTPL.

In Japan today, the monetary authorities *target the yield curve* – they set a minus 0.1 percent interest rate on Policy-Rate Balances in financial institutions' deposit accounts at the Bank of Japan and target the yield on ten-year government bonds at near zero percent. The ten-year government bond market is one of the most liquid markets in Japan and assuming that term premia and other risk premia are relatively small, the ten-year rate should be close to the average expected short-term policy rate over the next ten years. Thus, the overnight rate is expected to average near zero over the next ten years. If the markets expect a successful attainment of the two percent inflation target starting, say, two years from now, this would mean the average term premium over the next ten years is expected to be about *minus* 1.7 percent or the real interest rate is expected to be around minus 1.7 percent for the next ten years. It seems unlikely that term premia in liquid markets can be manipulated in such a significant and persistent manner just by varying the net supplies, say. Indeed, in Sims (2011) the strict expectations hypothesis of the term structure of interest rates links the price of a nominal perpetuity to the expected future path of the instantaneous policy rate. A decade of real interest rates averaging –1.7 percent in Japan is possible but not likely. This looks like classic financial repression.

The key point is that the FTPL is *not* about monetizing deficits (endogenously) to ensure that the PDV of current and anticipated future seigniorage satisfies the IBC of the State in equilibrium when taxes and public spending are exogenously determined. That instead would be a reasonable interpretation of the policy prescriptions and expectations of Modern Monetary Theory. Instead the FTPL asserts that the general price level always assumes the value required to ensure that the real contractual value of the stock of nominal government debt satisfies the IBC of the State with equality.

That these are two different theories is clear from the fact that most of the original contributors to the FTPL have applied this theory explicitly to models in which money exists only as a numeraire, and not as an asset/store of value, that is, models without any seigniorage or monetary issuance. Sims's original FTPL contribution (Sims (1994, pp. 396–399)) contains a Section IX titled "Equilibrium prices and interest rates without money"; Sims (2011) analyses cashless models in Sections III2 and III3; and despite its title ("Active fiscal, passive monetary equilibrium in a purely backward-looking model"), the Sims (2016a) model does not contain money as a store of value but only uses something called money as the numeraire. Woodford (1998a, 2001) considers price level determination in an FTPL world "in the cashless limit," when seigniorage becomes negligible and therefore incapable of satisfying the IBC of the State. Cochrane's "Frictionless View of U.S. Inflation" (Cochrane (1999)) is an FTPL approach to price level determination in a world in which money does not exist, except as the numeraire. One of our reasons for rejecting the FTPL is precisely that it permits the determination of the general price level (the reciprocal of the price of money) in a model in which there is no demand for or supply of money – a feature it shares with a number of non-FTPL DSGE models.

4.4.b The Original FTPL and Fiscal Dominance

The FTPL (and non-Ricardian policies) are sometimes identified with fiscal dominance or active fiscal policy and passive monetary policy, while the conventional approach (and Ricardian policies) are identified with monetary dominance or active monetary policy and passive fiscal policy. For instance, Patrick Minford (2017), in a comment on Buiter and Sibert (2018, n.p.) states: "The difference between the Ricardian and the FTPL descriptions is a difference in what processes are 'exogenous.' Under FTPL both fiscal variables -spending and tax – are exogenous stochastic processes, while money is endogenous; whereas under the 'Ricardian' description the monetary policy process is exogenous and only one fiscal variable, say spending, can be exogenous."

While there is no point in having arguments about semantics, when we (and the FTPL originators) refer to Ricardian budgetary rules what is meant are rules for (real) taxes (net of transfers), (real) public spending on goods and services, monetary issuance, the own interest rate on central bank money, and the short, risk-free nominal rate of interest (the "policy rate"), that ensure that the IBC of the State is always satisfied, in equilibrium and out of equilibrium, with all securities priced at their contractual values. Such Ricardian rules can have either monetary or fiscal dominance, as the famous "Unpleasant Monetarist Arithmetic" paper by Sargent and Wallace (1981) shows. In that paper, before the (index-linked) public debt reaches the (exogenously given) upper bound, monetary policy is active – the growth rate of the nominal money stock is exogenous. Government borrowing is passive. Once the (exogenous) government bond debt ceiling is reached, monetary growth passively finances the public-sector deficit (real public spending and real taxes don't change).

More generally, we can have a Ricardian policy rule for which the path of the nominal money stock is specified exogenously ("monetary dominance"), as well as the path of one of the fiscal policy instruments, real public spending, say, with the other fiscal policy instrument, real net taxes in this case, adjusting endogenously to ensure that the IBC of the State is always satisfied.[4] Minford's endogenous money supply rule (both public spending and net taxes are exogenous) may not actually be Ricardian. That is because it is not certain that the *real* value of the resulting government deficit (net of

---

[4]   We assume that the path of real exhaustive public spending is feasible. In the exogenous endowment model considered below, this requires that real public spending does not exceed the real value of the endowment.

any government bond issuance that is consistent with solvency of the State) can be financed through an increase in the nominal money supply, however large, or, if it can be financed through monetary issuance, this will result in a permanent hyperinflationary "equilibrium" – something we don't consider a sensible equilibrium.

The fiscal dimension of monetary policy (and specifically of central bank monetized balance sheet expansion) exists even if the central bank is operationally independent and even if there is "monetary dominance" (or active monetary policy and passive fiscal policy) rather than the "fiscal dominance" (or active fiscal policy and passive monetary policy), that characterizes the "Unpleasant Monetarist Arithmetic" model after the ceiling on the government debt-to-GDP ratio is reached. The key insight is that, given the outstanding stocks of State assets and liabilities, if you want to ensure the State remains solvent (if you want a Ricardian budgetary rule), you cannot specify monetary policy (base money issuance) and fiscal policy (public spending and taxes) independently. Either there is a cooperative solution, or there is fiscal dominance and monetary issuance becomes endogenously determined (the residual), or there is monetary dominance and public spending and/or taxation have to adjust (becomes the residual) to maintain sovereign solvency.[5]

The outline of the rest of the Chapter is as follows. Sections 4.5 through 4.8 contain a nontechnical exposition of the main issues. The Appendix to the Chapter provides a rigorous technical analysis of the original FTPL, which addressed a world with flexible nominal prices and its extension to a world with nominal price rigidities. We identify two inconsistencies and six unacceptable anomalies. We also address the merits of treating the FTPL as an equilibrium selection mechanism when there are multiple equilibria. In Section 4.8 and in the Appendix (Section A4.2), we review recent attempts by Sims to make the case for non-Ricardian budgetary rules in a world with nominal price rigidities.

---

[5] We have to assume that, in the fiscal dominance case, the model can generate sufficient real seigniorage to finance the exogenous real budget deficit of the State.

4.5 THE FTPL: A NONTECHNICAL PRESENTATION

4.5.a Key Concepts and Relationships

Consider a very simple closed endowment economy with two sectors: the household sector (represented by a representative household) and the State. As before, the State (or the sovereign) is the consolidated general government and central bank. Again we will refer to the general government sector as the *Treasury* or the fiscal authority. There are no firms, because of the simple endowment technology, and no financial institutions other than the central bank. There are four financial instruments: central bank money, which can only be issued by the State, a short (one-period) nominal bond, a nominal consol (perpetuity) and a short index-linked bond. The formal model assumes there is no default and no default risk for both households and the State, so the bonds of the State and the bonds issued by the households are perfect substitutes.

Formally we deal with a deterministic model without any risk or uncertainty. We do, however, adopt the common approach of considering a completely unexpected shock to one or more policy instruments. From the initial date, $t = t_0 = 0$, say, households expect the State to follow a fiscal-financial-monetary and interest rate program (henceforth a *budgetary rule*) under which solvency of the State is always guaranteed, in and out of equilibrium. This rule can, in principle, have time-varying parameters. Households hold their expectations concerning this rule with complete certainty and expect the budgetary rule to be followed forever. Then, at some later date, $t = t_1 > 0$, there is a completely unexpected change to another budgetary rule. Households immediately expect that this new budgetary rule will be implemented forever. All endogenous variables in the economy will adjust to reflect the unexpected, permanent introduction of the new budgetary rule and the matching new set of firmly held beliefs of the households.

The condition for State bonds to be priced at their contractual value is that the present discounted value (using default-risk-free discount factors) of its current and future real primary surpluses, plus the PDV of the real value of its current and future monetary issuance (net of any interest paid on money) is greater than or equal to the real value of its net bond debt, when bonds are priced at their contractual values. The real augmented primary surplus of the State, $\hat{s}_t = \tau_t^s - C_t^s + \frac{M_{t+1} - (1 + i_{t,t-1}^M) M_t}{P_t}$, is the sum of the (noninterest) primary surplus and monetary issuance minus interest paid on the outstanding stock of money.

Any budgetary rule that does not ensure that the State always satisfies its IBC with sovereign bonds priced at their contractual values is called a *non-Ricardian* budgetary rule. It is of course possible that a non-Ricardian budgetary rule (or arbitrary budgetary rule) allows the State to satisfy its IBC, with sovereign bonds priced at their contractual values, *in equilibrium,* or for some other *subset* of the possible values that can be assumed by the exogenous, predetermined and endogenous variables that enter into the IBC of the State. Ricardian budgetary rules are *always* consistent with the State satisfying its IBC with its bonds priced at their contractual values, in and out of equilibrium. It is, however, easy to come up with examples of non-Ricardian budgetary rules that, for certain values of the parameters of the model and exogenous and the predetermined variables of the model, are consistent with the State satisfying its IBC in equilibrium, with State bonds priced at their contractual values. We don't, however, have a set of necessary and sufficient conditions for a budgetary rule to satisfy the IBC of the State *in equilibrium.* It is *sufficient* for the State to always satisfy its IBC in equilibrium, that the budgetary rule be Ricardian, because Ricardian rules ensure the solvency of the State both in and out of equilibrium. It is not necessary, however.

Any model that prices sovereign debt at its contractual value but imposes a non-Ricardian budgetary rule should be subjected to a consistency check in the form of a *counterfactual analysis*: assuming that current and future discount factors are free of default risk, is the IBC of the State indeed satisfied *in equilibrium* with the sovereign debt priced at its equilibrium value? If the answer is "yes," the analysis can proceed. If the answer is "no," the bonds of the State cannot be priced at their contractual values and the assumption that default-risk-free discount factors can be used is falsified. The model is not fit for purpose. Sovereign default risk and sovereign insolvency have to be considered and modeled explicitly. The terms on which a sovereign that is in default or at risk of default has access to the bond markets have to be made explicit etc.

The consistency check for any non-Ricardian rule is performed by using the IBC of the State as a counterfactual sovereign bond pricing equilibrium condition. Let $\hat{s}(t)$ be the real value of the augmented primary surplus of the State at time t (as defined previously). As before $V_t(\{X, I\})$ is the present discounted value at time t of a nominal variable X over an infinite horizon when default-risk-free nominal discount factors are used, $V_t(\{\frac{X}{P}, R\})$ denotes the present discounted value, at time t, of all current and future values of a real variable X/P over an infinite horizon when default-risk-free real discount factors are used to discount the future values of X/P and B_t^p is the number of one-period nominal government bonds outstanding (held by the private sector) at the beginning of period t. The contractual value of such an instantaneous nominal bond is 1 unit of money. B_t^L is the number of nominal consols (perpetuities) outstanding at the beginning of period t; it is a promise to pay 1 unit of money in each period forever. Its nominal contractual value at time t, denoted P_t^L, is given by $P^L(t) = V_t(\{1, I\})$; b_t is the number of one-period index-linked government bonds outstanding at the beginning of period t: its nominal contractual value at time t is P_t, the general price level in period t – the reciprocal of the price of money in terms of the endowment commodity.

The intertemporal budget constraint of the State at time t is the requirement that the PDV of current and future augmented primary surpluses of the State is equal to or greater than the contractual value of the outstanding nonmonetary debt of the State. It can be written as follows:

$$\frac{B_t^p + V_t(\{1,I\})B_t^L}{P_t} + b_t \leq V_t(\{\hat{s}, R\}) \tag{4.1}$$

A *budgetary rule* at time t is a set of current and future values for, or a set of functions determining the current and future values for, the augmented primary surplus, the interest rate on money and either the short nominal interest rate on bonds or the nominal money stock, that is in effect at time t and is believed with complete certainty by households to be in effect in period t and for all future periods; we denote it $\{\hat{s}, \ i^M, \ i \text{ or } M; \ t\}$. Assume the authorities have followed a Ricardian budgetary rule, $\{\hat{s}_{Ric}, \ i^M_{Ric}, \ i_{Ric} \text{ or } M_{Ric}; \ t < t_1\}$ until period t_1 and that the private sector have, right up to period t_1, believed with complete certainty that this Ricardian rule would always continue to be implemented. In period t_1 there is a "black swan" event: unexpectedly the State changes its budgetary rule to a non-Ricardian rule, denoted $\{\hat{s}_N, \ i^M_N, \ i_N \text{ or } M_N; \ t \geq t_1\}$. This new non-Ricardian rule is again expected by the private sector, with complete confidence, to be implemented for all future time.

Under the old, Ricardian budgetary rule, it is true, by the definition of a Ricardian rule, that equation (4.1) is satisfied: $\frac{B_t^p + V_t(\{1,I_{Ric}\})B_t^L}{P_t} + b_t \leq V_t(\{\hat{s}_{Ric}, R\})$ for $t < t_1$. The conventional or standard (non-FTPL) approach would check whether the assumption that the State remains solvent and there is no default risk under the new, non-Ricardian policy rule is indeed satisfied in the new equilibrium by verifying whether $\frac{B_{t_1}^p + V_{t_1}(\{1,I_N\})B_{t_1}^L}{P_{t_1}} + b_{t_1} \leq V_{t_1}(\{\hat{s}_N, R\})$. This can be done by treating the IBC of the State, holding with equality, as an equilibrium government bond pricing equation, determining the counterfactual market value of the bonds. If this counterfactual market value is equal to or greater than the contractual value of outstanding bond debt of the State, the maintained assumption of the model, that sovereign bonds are priced at their contractual values, is verified and the analysis can proceed. If it is falsified, a different model is required. A simple way of representing the counterfactual government bond pricing equilibrium condition is to write it as:

$$D_{t_1} \left(\frac{B_{t_1}^p + V_{t_1}(\{1, I_N\})B_{t_1}^L}{P_{t_1}} + b_{t_1} \right) = V_{t_1}(\{\hat{s}_N, R\}) \tag{4.2}$$

where D_{t_1} is the "bond revaluation factor" at time t, or the ratio of the (counterfactual) market value of the bonds to their contractual values. For simplicity, we assume all three bonds share a common revaluation factor. The market price of a bond obviously cannot be higher than its contractual value; government debt trades at its contractual value if the government is "super-solvent," that is, if $\frac{B_{t_1}^p + V_{t_1}(\{1, I_N\})B_{t_1}^L}{P_{t_1}} + b_{t_1} < V_{t_1}(\{\hat{s}_N, R\})$. In this case, the government is wasting "fiscal space." Nor can the market value of a bond be negative, so, if $V_{t_1}(\{\hat{s}_N, R\}) < 0$ and there is a positive net amount of government debt outstanding, the creditors of the sovereign get nothing – they cannot lose more than the entire contractual value of the government debt they hold. Therefore, if the net contractual value of the outstanding bonds is positive, we must have $0 \le D \le 1$.

Note for future reference that this counterfactual equilibrium bond pricing equation (4.2), works perfectly well if all government debt is index-linked or, in an open economy extension of the model, denominated in foreign currency. When all government bonds are index-linked, the counterfactual equilibrium government bond pricing equation simplifies to:

$$D_{t_1} b_{t_1} = V_{t_1}(\{\hat{s}_N, R\}) \tag{4.3}$$

The FTPL introduces the intertemporal budget constraint of the State, holding with equality and with sovereign debt priced at its contractual value, as an additional equilibrium condition, but without adding the bond revaluation factor. So, it replaces equation (4.2) with

$$\frac{B_{t_1}^p + V_{t_1}(\{1, I_N\})B_{t_1}^L}{P_{t_1}} + b_{t_1} = V_{t_1}(\{\hat{s}_N, R\}) \tag{4.4}$$

The FTPL then assumes that the general price level, P_{t_1} can do the job of the bond revaluation factor. With all sovereign debt priced at its contractual value, the general price level takes on the value required to ensure that the IBC of the State, holding with equality and with sovereign debt priced at its contractual value, is satisfied. Because a negative price level is not considered acceptable, if there is a nonzero stock of net nominal government bonds outstanding, the FTPL requires:

$$\text{sgn}\{B_{t_1}^p + V_{t_1}(\{1, I_N\})B_{t_1}^L\} = \text{sgn}\{V_{t_1}(\{\hat{s}_N, R\}) - b_{t_1}\} \tag{4.5}$$

Consider the empirically most interesting case where there is positive net nominal public debt outstanding: $B_{t_1}^p + V_{t_1}(\{1, I_N\})B_{t_1}^L > 0$. In that case, the PDV of the augmented real primary surpluses has to be larger than or equal to the real value of the outstanding stock of index-linked public debt, if a negative price level is to be avoided.

The starting point in showing that the FTPL is a fallacy is quite independent of whether equation (4.4) solves for a positive value of the general price level. Equation (4.4), the IBC of the State holding with equality and with sovereign debt priced at its contractual value, *cannot* be imposed by the FTPL as an additional or independent equilibrium condition in a general equilibrium model that includes household consumption behavior derived from the optimizing behavior of forward-looking households. That is because this same IBC of the State (holding with equality and with sovereign debt priced at its contractual value), or its mirror image, the IBC of the optimizing household (holding with equality and with debt priced at its contractual value), has already been used to derive the optimal consumption rule. The only qualification of this "don't use the same equilibrium condition twice" requirement is to interpret the second application to be an equilibrium selection device in a model with multiple equilibria. We will show that this qualification cannot salvage the FTPL.

The following distinction is key to understanding the fallacy underlying the FTPL and why Cochrane's attempted rehabilitation of the FTPL (see Cochrane (2005)) is no more than a lengthy restatement of the original fallacy. It is the distinction between (1) the intertemporal budget constraint of the government, with all government liabilities priced at their contractual values (that is, assuming no default and no default risk), holding as a weak inequality (given in equation (4.1)), and (2) the equilibrium government bond pricing equation, with government debt priced as the lesser of (a) its contractual value and (b) the PDV of the actual current and (expected) future augmented primary surpluses (given in equation (4.2)).

In this second interpretation, the IBC of the State, holding with equality, is viewed as an equilibrium bond pricing equation although sovereign debt is constrained to be valued at its contractual value and policy rules are arbitrary or non-Ricardian. The FTPL asserts that the general price level can, if there is a positive stock of nominal government bonds outstanding, assume the role of D_t, the sovereign debt revaluation factor. Our refutation of the FTPL is the demonstration that this leads to logical inconsistencies and/or anomalies (i.e. economic nonsense).

With Ricardian policy rules, the assumption, made in equation (4.1), that government debt is valued at its contractual value is, by construction, always valid. With arbitrary, non-Ricardian policy rules, equation (4.1) is not always satisfied. It may be satisfied in equilibrium, but that has to be verified for each non-Ricardian rule by solving the model under the assumption that equation (4.1) is satisfied and then verifying whether it is indeed satisfied, that is, whether it solves equation (4.2) with $D_t \geq 1, t \geq 0$. If this condition holds, then this particular non-Ricardian rule is consistent with the absence of sovereign default and sovereign default risk. If this condition does not hold (that is, if $D_t < 1$ for some $t \geq 0$), there is sovereign default risk and the government may default. We have to specify rules that are not part of the conventional model – rules on how default is handled (seniority, *pari passu*, hold-outs, CACs, aggregation etc.) and how private sector behavior is affected by default risk and the way default is handled. The management of default and the impact of default risk and default are not part of the model as specified.

The FTPL tries to have it both ways. It wants to consider non-Ricardian rules, yet it imposes the constraint that the IBC of the State must be satisfied *in equilibrium*, with equality, and with sovereign debt priced at its contractual value, that is, it imposes $D_t = 1, t \geq 0$. This may work for specific non-Ricardian rules. It does not work for all non-Ricardian rules. We provide simple counterexamples in the Appendix to this Chapter.

4.5.b The FTPL Is Invalid because It Uses the Same Equilibrium Condition Twice

It is intuitively obvious, and we show this rigorously in the formal model in the Appendix to this Chapter, that, if the household utility function exhibits nonsatiation (more is better) in consumption and/or real money balances, the IBC of the household will hold with equality: no resources that could be devoted to additional consumption or to accumulating additional real money balances are wasted.

The IBC of the household, holding with equality and with debt priced at its contractual value can, in equilibrium, be written as:

$$\frac{B_t^p + V_t(\{1, I\})B_t^L}{P_t} + b_t$$
$$= V_t\left(\left\{C_t^p + \tau_t^s - Y_t + \frac{M_{t+1} - (1 + i_{t,t-1}^M)M_t}{P_t}, R\right\}\right) \tag{4.6}$$

Equation (4.6) states that the real value of the net nonmonetary financial assets held by the household equals the PDV of the augmented primary deficits of the household – its conventional primary deficit, $C_t^p + \tau_t^s - Y_t$, plus the real value of its accumulation of money balances net of interest received on money.

In equilibrium (if an equilibrium exists), the economy-wide real resource constraint holds: real output (the real endowment) equals real household consumption plus real public spending on goods and services: $Y_t = C_t^p + C_t^s$. Substituting the economy-wide real resource constraint into the household IBC, holding with equality and with debt valued at its contractual value, turns the IBC of the household (equation (4.6)) into the IBC of the State, holding with equality and with the public debt priced at its contractual value – that is, it turns equation (4.6) into equation (4.1), holding with equality. It is a basic rule of sound general equilibrium economics that you cannot use the same equilibrium condition more than once. The FTPL therefore cannot impose the IBC of the State, holding with equality and with sovereign debt priced at its contractual value as an additional equilibrium condition when this "additional" equilibrium condition is implied, in equilibrium, by other equilibrium conditions: the IBC of the household, holding with equality and with debt priced at its contractual value, that has already been used in the derivation of the optimal household consumption rule, and the real resource constraint. This fatal flaw invalidates the entire FTPL literature except for the New-Keynesian model developed in Sims (2011), which only uses the IBC of the State (or the household sector) once and is therefore not really part of the FTPL approach.

4.5.c The Original FTPL, Overdetermined Systems, Other Inconsistencies and Anomalies

Because the FTPL introduces an additional equilibrium condition (the IBC of the State, holding with equality and with sovereign bonds priced at their contractual values) without adding another endogenous variable (such as D_t in the standard approach of equation (4.2)), it should lead to an overdetermined system (more equations than unknowns) in any model where the conventional approach yields a determinate equilibrium. And indeed, this is the case in many commonly used models, as we show in our formal model in the Appendix to this Chapter. There is, however, one class of models for which the standard approach results in indeterminacy of all nominal variables – the general price level and the nominal money stock – although all real variables (including the stock of real money balances, the real interest rate, the rate of inflation, and the pecuniary opportunity cost of holding central bank money) are well determined. This is the class of models that has a freely flexible price level and a pegged risk-free (short) nominal interest rate on bonds.[6]

---

[6]   The own (nominal) interest rate on money will be treated as exogenous throughout and plays no role in our rejection of the FTPL as a false theory.

4.6   A FLEXIBLE PRICE LEVEL AND A PEGGED NOMINAL INTEREST RATE

When the short (instantaneous) nominal interest rate is pegged (set as an exogenous policy instrument or driven by a rule that does not make it a function of current and anticipated future nominal variables), the nominal money stock is endogenously determined. The monetary equilibrium condition in most standard models typically specifies the stock of real money balances demanded as an increasing function of some scale variable like real consumption, real output, real wealth or real transactions volumes, and a decreasing function of the difference between the short risk-free nominal interest rate on bonds and the nominal interest rate on money. In our formal model in the Appendix to this Chapter, real household consumption is the scale variable. The monetary equilibrium condition can be written as $\frac{M_{t+1}}{P_t} = \frac{\phi(1+i_{t+1,t})}{i_{t+1,t}-i_{t+1,t}^M} C_t^f$; $i > i^M$; $\phi > 0$.

In equilibrium, in the flexible price model, real household consumption equals the exogenous level of real output, $\overline{Y}$, minus the level of real public spending on goods and services (also treated as exogenous and constant for simplicity) $\overline{C}^s$. With both the nominal interest rate on bonds and the nominal interest rate on money pegged (and assuming we are away from the effective lower bound with the safe nominal interest rate on bonds higher than the own interest rate on money), the equilibrium stock of real money balances is uniquely determined:

$$\frac{M_{t+1}}{P_t} = \frac{\phi(1+\overline{i})}{\overline{i}-\overline{i}^M}(\overline{Y}-\overline{C}^s), \quad i > i^M \tag{4.7}$$

But neither the price level nor the nominal money stock is determined. This flexible price level, pegged nominal interest rate world is one where imposing the IBC of the State, holding with equality and with the sovereign debt priced at its contractual value, does not lead to a mathematically overdetermined system. We still have the problem that the same equilibrium condition is imposed twice, but we don't have the problem of mathematical overdeterminacy.

The suggestion of Kocherlakota and Phelan (1999) that the FPTL might be viewed as an equilibrium selection device to resolve the indeterminacy of the price level and the nominal money stock in the flexible price level model under a nominal interest rate rule is, in our view, the only conceivable rationalization for using the same equilibrium condition twice. We agree with Kocherlakota and Phelan that (as shown in the Appendix to this Chapter) the equilibrium selection device rationalization of the FTPL fails because it will select unacceptable equilibria when the nominal money stock rather than the nominal interest rate is exogenous. In games or general equilibrium models with multiple equilibria, the selection mechanisms that are favored in the literature are those that select "natural focal points." Using the IBC of the State twice (holding with equality and with sovereign debt priced at its contractual value) does not, in our (admittedly subjective) view meet the "natural focal point" criterion. More importantly, it does not cure the following six anomalies associated with the "equilibria" that can be selected in this manner:

(1) The price level can be negative unless the condition given in equation (4.5), is satisfied.
(2) The theory ceases to function when all government debt is index-linked (or, in an open economy, denominated in foreign currency).
(3) The FTPL determines the price of money even in a world where there is no money except as an abstract numeraire, like phlogiston, the (imaginary) substance believed, in the pre-scientific world, to cause combustion in materials. The ability to price phlogiston, and to determine an equilibrium price without an associated quantity is a bridge too far, in our view. Note that a phlogiston-denominated bond in this model is the ultimate *nondeliverable* forward contract. A one-period phlogiston-denominated bond cannot promise to pay $1 + i_{t+1,t}$ units of phlogiston in period $t+1$ for every unit of that bond purchased in period t. The reason is that there is no phlogiston – it doesn't exist except as a name. So the bond can only promise to pay something *worth* $1 + i_{t+1,t}$ units of phlogiston. We are of course familiar with nondeliverable forward contracts, but not, to the best of my knowledge, with nondeliverable forward contracts for which there is no deliverable benchmark contract and market.

(4) The logic of the FTPL can be applied to the IBC of the household sector or indeed to the IBC of an individual household, Mrs. Jones, say, as long as the household has positive nominal debt outstanding, follows a non-Ricardian rule for consumption and money accumulation, and the analogue of condition in equation (4.5) is satisfied. The household theory of the price level (HTPL) or the Mrs. Jones theory of the price level (MJTPL) have equal standing (none, that is, in our view) with the FTPL.

(5) When the (counterfactual) equilibrium bond pricing equation is specified properly, say by introducing an addition endogenous variable like the bond revaluation factor D in equation (4.2) (thus introducing the market value of the bonds as a counterfactual separate variable from its contractual value), there is no FTPL. If there is positive net nominal sovereign debt outstanding, equation (4.2) determines the real market value of the outstanding public debt, $D_{t_1}\left(\frac{B^p_{t_1}+V_{t_1}(\{1,I\})B^L_{t_1}}{P_{t_1}}+b_{t_1}\right)$, but not D_{t_1} and P_{t_1} separately (nor the nominal money stock). When there is only index-linked debt, equation (4.2) determines D_{t_1} but not the price level or the nominal money stock, which are indeterminate.

Finally, if we were to accept the IBC of the State, holding with equality and with sovereign bonds priced at their contractual values, as the equilibrium selection device in the flexible price level model when the nominal interest rate is exogenous, it would surely make sense to also use it as the equilibrium selection device in the flexible price level model when the nominal money stock is exogenous. This model too has, as pointed out in Section (A.4.1.c), a continuum of price level equilibria for a given path of the current and future nominal money stock. The problem is that, in this case, the use of the FTPL equilibrium selection criterion would, almost surely, lead to the selection of a bubble equilibrium, with the real stock of money balances either exploding or imploding to zero. We summarize this as the sixth anomaly:

(6) When viewed as an equilibrium selection criterion, the FTPL in general produces explosive or implosive solutions for the inflation rate when the nominal money stock is exogenous.

4.7   A FLEXIBLE GENERAL PRICE LEVEL AND A MONETARY RULE

Consider the case where the nominal money supply is exogenous or driven by a rule that does not depend on the general price level (current or future anticipated values) or anticipated future values of the nominal money stock. It is well-known that flexible price level models of the kind analyzed in the FTPL literature have infinitely many equilibria under an exogenous rule for the nominal money stock. With a constant nominal money stock, the behavior of the general price level is driven by

$$\frac{\overline{M}}{P_t} = \frac{\phi(1+\theta)P_{t+1}/P_t}{\left(1 + \phi(1+\theta)P_{t+1}/P_t\right) - (1+\bar{\imath}^M)}(\overline{Y} - \overline{C}^s). \tag{4.8}$$

In the standard approach (without double use of the IBC of the State as a bond pricing equilibrium condition) such an economy has a barter equilibrium with $\frac{1}{P_t} = 0$ for all time. It has one "fundamental" equilibrium, which will have a constant price level (and a nominal interest rate equal to the real interest rate). And it has infinitely many sunspot or bubble equilibria, which can either be inflationary or deflationary (see Buiter and Sibert (2007)). In equation (4.8), even with a constant nominal money stock, the price level can rise without bound, reducing the real money stock to zero and pushing the nominal interest rate towards infinity or it can fall without bound, raising the real money stock to infinity and driving the nominal interest rate down to the ELB value of $\bar{\imath}^M$.

Note that this multiplicity of equilibria is different from the indeterminacy in the conventional approach under an interest rate rule. Under the interest rate rule, neither the price level nor the nominal money stock are determined. Under the monetary rule, the nominal money stock is (by construction) determined but there is a continuum of equilibria for the price level and the nominal interest rate. Our preferred approach to equilibrium selection in this model is the standard one: to select among this continuum of possible solutions for the current and future price level using the equilibrium selection criterion that stationary exogenous variables support stationary endogenous variables. We view this "fundamental" solution as the "natural focal point."

Choosing the fundamental equilibrium, the monetary equilibrium condition becomes

$$\frac{\overline{M}}{P_t} = \frac{\phi(1+\theta)}{\theta - \overline{i}^M} (\overline{Y} - \overline{C}^s) \tag{4.9}$$

which determines a constant price level. If we select this fundamental solution, adding the IBC of the State, holding with equality and with sovereign debt priced at its contractual value, given in equation (4.1) holding with equality, as another equilibrium condition, the model is overdetermined.

Can we *instead* of using the fundamental equilibrium selection criterion use the IBC of the State as an equilibrium selection device when there is this continuum of equilibria for the price level and the rate of inflation under a monetary rule? In principle, yes, because in the absence of a generally agreed upon "theory of equilibrium selection rules" anything can be an equilibrium selection rule. The FTPL equilibrium selection criterion appears highly unusual, however. Why would an equilibrium condition that has already been used to construct the equilibria of a model be used again to select among the multiple equilibria of the model? In the case where the nominal money stock is constant, unless the IBC of the State picks the stationary, "fundamental" solution by happenstance, the FTPL solution will be an inflationary or deflationary bubble with the nominal interest rate rising without bound or falling to the level of the interest rate on money.

4.8   THE FTPL AND STICKY NOMINAL PRICES

When the price level is predetermined (and updated, say, through an Old-Keynesian or New-Keynesian Phillips curve), it obviously cannot jump endogenously at $t = t_1$ to the level required to make the IBC of the State hold with equality, with the sovereign debt priced at its contractual value. If we impose the IBC of the State as an equilibrium condition *and* have also used the equilibrium mirror image of the IBC of the State – the IBC of the household, holding with equality and with household debt priced at its contractual value – to determine the optimal consumption rule, the system is overdetermined. There is no "equilibrium selection mechanism" escape valve.

Sims's New FTPL – the FTLEA

Sims (2011) does not fall into the overdeterminacy trap. In his analytical and numerical models, household consumption behavior is characterized by the Euler equation for consumption (growth) – a first-order differential equation (Sims uses a continuous time model). The IBC of the household, holding with equality and with household and sovereign debt priced at its equilibrium value – the boundary condition which, together with the Euler equation, permits one to solve for optimal consumption behavior – is *replaced*, as an equilibrium condition, with the IBC of the State holding with equality and with sovereign debt priced at its contractual value. This, however, does not mean that all is well with the conclusions of the Sims (2011) model. Why would arbitrary non-Ricardian budgetary rules be consistent with government solvency if the price level cannot jump to the level necessary to satisfy equation (4.4) or, equivalently in equilibrium, equation (4.6)?

Sims argues that the default-risk-free real and nominal discount factors in equation (4.4), represented by I and R can do the job of ensuring sovereign solvency. According to Sims, these discount factors (current and anticipated future default-risk-free nominal and real interest rates) will jump in the desired manner – to ensure sovereign solvency – when a non-Ricardian rule is unexpectedly introduced at t_1. These discount factors can indeed jump when a surprise hits the system, because household consumption, which is chosen by forward-looking optimizing households, can jump when the non-Ricardian rule is introduced unexpectedly at t_1. Because it is not the price level that jumps but consumption, and with it the demand-determined level of real economic activity, we call the Sims (2011) New-Keynesian model the fiscal theory of the level of economic activity (FTLEA).

Can a jump in consumption (and presumably, in a richer model, consumption and real capital expenditure) really do the job of setting the nominal and real discount factors at values that ensure government solvency? They could for certain non-Ricardian rules and for certain values of the exogenous variables, parameters and initial values of the predetermined state variables, but it is trivial to come up with examples of non-Ricardian rules that cannot do the job and will violate the IBC of the State with sovereign debt priced at its contractual value. We provide a couple of examples in the Appendix to this Chapter.

Note that, in the flexible price level model too, nominal and real discount factors can, in principle, jump, because there also, household consumption is nonpredetermind, driven by optimizing, forward-looking households. Household consumption therefore can, in principle, jump in response to news; it is a nonpredetermined state variable. Of course, with real government spending and real output constant, *equilibrium* consumption will not jump in the classical model of the original FTPL unless the endowment or public spending jump. Because of that, real interest rates too will not change in equilibrium. If the nominal interest rate is pegged at the same level in both the Ricardian regime (pre-t_1) and the non-Ricardian regime, following the unexpected regime change at t_1, the nominal discount factors also would not change in the flexible price level model.

Because we have no way of determining a priori whether an arbitrary, non-Ricardian budgetary rule is consistent with government solvency when the economic model is specified properly – that is, without double use of the IBC of the State – one always should do a counterfactual analysis, using equation (4.2), to determine whether the budgetary rule in question does indeed satisfy the IBC of the State in equilibrium, holding with equality and with sovereign debt priced at its contractual value, for a robust range of initial conditions and values of the exogenous variables and parameters. If it does, all is well. If the PDV of current and future real augmented primary surpluses exceeds the real contractual value of the outstanding sovereign debt, the sovereign is wasting fiscal space. If the PDV of current and future real augmented primary surpluses falls short of the real contractual value of the outstanding sovereign debt, there is at the very least default risk and possibly actual sovereign default and sovereign insolvency. An assumption on which the model is based – default-risk-free bond pricing – is then falsified. The household cannot satisfy its IBC with equality and with its holdings of sovereign bonds valued at their contractual values, because the market value of that sovereign debt will be less than its contractual value. Depending on the procedures for dealing with sovereign default (including the seniority of old and new creditors of the government) the terms of access of the State to the bond markets will be different. The maintained assumption of no sovereign default risk and no sovereign default have been falsified. The model is not fit for purpose.

Appendix to Chapter 4: A Formal Approach to the FTPL

A4.1 THE FTPL IN THE FLEXIBLE PRICE LEVEL MODEL

We summarize a model without uncertainty, without Keynesian consumers and with the interest rate on money constant. The real augmented primary surplus and real public spending are exogenous: $\hat{\sigma}_t = \overline{\hat{\sigma}}_t$ and $C_t^s = \overline{C}_t^s$. Each period, t, the State also chooses the end-of-period stock of short nominal government bonds, B_{t+1}^p. Real money balances and therefore also real seigniorage revenue $\frac{M_{t+1}}{P_t} - (1 + \bar{i}^M)\frac{M_t}{P_t}$ are determined endogenously by the model and real taxes, τ_t^s, adjust endogenously to ensure the government's budgetary program adds up and satisfies the period budget constraint. The nominal consols and the index-linked bond will be added when required. Absent uncertainty, note that $R_{j,t} = \prod\limits_{\ell=t+1}^{j} \frac{1}{1+r_{\ell,\ell-1}}$ for $j > t$, $R_{t,t} = \frac{1}{1+r_{t,t}} = 1$, and likewise $I_{j,t} = \prod\limits_{\ell=t+1}^{j} \frac{1}{1+i_{\ell,\ell-1}}$ for $j > t$, $I_{t,t} = \frac{1}{1+i_{t,t}} = 1$.

The model can be summarized as follows:

For $t \geq 0$:

$$\frac{C_{t+1}^f}{C_t^f} = \frac{1 + r_{t+1,t}}{1 + \theta}$$

$$\frac{B_{t+1}^p}{P_t} \equiv C_t^s - \tau_t^s - \left(\frac{M_{t+1} - (1 + i_{t,t-1}^M)M_t}{P_t}\right) + (1 + i_{t,t-1})\frac{B_t^p}{P_t}$$

$$\frac{M_{t+1}}{P_t} = \frac{\phi(1 + i_{t+1,t})}{i_{t+1,t} - \bar{i}^M} C_t^f$$

$$Y_t = \overline{C}_t^s + C_t^f$$

$$Y_t = \overline{Y}$$

$$\frac{B_0^p}{P_0} = \sum_{j=0}^{\infty} \prod_{\ell=0}^{j} \left(\frac{1}{1+r_{\ell,\ell-1}}\right) \left[C_j^f + \tau_j^s - Y_j + \left(\frac{M_{j+1} - (1+i^M)M_j}{P_j}\right)\right]$$

$$B_0^p = \overline{B}_0^p$$

A4.1.a An Exogenous Nominal Interest Rate

Consider the case where the nominal interest rate is exogenous and constant, $i_{t,t-1} = \overline{i} > \overline{i}^M$ (so we are not at the ELB). The eight equations (4.1) to (4.8), together with the four boundary conditions (4.9) to (4.12), are supposed to determine for $t \geq 0$ the equilibrium values of the four state variables, $C_t^f, \pi_{t+1,t}, M_{t+1}/P_t$ and B_t^p/P_t and the four endogenous variables that are not state variables $r_{t+1,t}, \tau_t^s, P_{t+1}/P_t$ and Y_t.

For $t \geq 0$:

$$\frac{C_{t+1}^f}{C_t^f} = \frac{1+r_{t+1,t}}{1+\theta} \tag{4.1}$$

$$\frac{B_{t+1}^p(1+\pi_{t+1,t})}{P_{t+1}} \equiv \overline{C}_t^s - \tau_t^s - \left(\frac{M_{t+1}}{P_t} - (1+\overline{i}^M)\frac{M_t}{P_{t-1}(1+\pi_{t,t-1})}\right)$$
$$+ (1+\overline{i})\frac{B_t^p}{P_t} \tag{4.2}$$

$$\frac{M_{t+1}}{P_t} = \frac{\phi(1+\overline{i})}{\overline{i} - \overline{i}^M} C_t^f \tag{4.3}$$

$$\overline{\sigma}_t = \tau_t^s - \overline{C}_t^s + \frac{M_{j+1}}{P_j} - (1+\overline{i}^M)\frac{M_j}{P_{j-1}(1+\pi_{j,j-1})} \tag{4.4}$$

$$Y_t = \overline{C}_t^s + C_t^f \tag{4.5}$$

$$1+\overline{i} = (1+r_{t+1,t})(1+\pi_{t+1,t}) \tag{4.6}$$

$$1+\pi_{t+1,t} = \frac{P_{t+1}}{P_t} \tag{4.7}$$

$$Y_t = \overline{Y} > 0 \tag{4.8}$$

$$\frac{B_0^p}{P_0} = \sum_{j=0}^{\infty} \prod_{\ell=0}^{j} \left(\frac{1}{1+r_{\ell,\ell-1}}\right)$$
$$\left[C_j^f + \tau_j^s - Y_j + \frac{M_{j+1}}{P_j} - (1+\overline{i}^M)\frac{M_j}{P_{j-1}(1+\pi_{j,j-1})}\right] \tag{4.9}$$

$$B_0^p = \overline{B}_0^p \tag{4.10}$$

$$M_0/P_{-1} = \overline{M}_0/\overline{P}_{-1} \tag{4.11}$$

$$\pi_{0,-1} = \overline{\pi}_{0,-1} \tag{4.12}$$

The boundary condition for the nonpredetermined state variable, C^f, given in equation (4.9) states that the IBC of the household holds with equality: no current assets or current and anticipated future after-tax income flows are wasted. We don't, however, have a boundary condition for the *real* stock of government nonmonetary debt (bonds), B^p/P, but only for the nominal stock of government bonds, B^p given by the initial condition equation (4.10). The model therefore determines $C_t^f, r_{t+1,t}, \tau_t^s, M_{t+1}/P_t, \pi_{t+1,t}, \ P_{t+1}/P_t$ and Y_t but not $\frac{B_t^p}{P_t}, P_t$ and M_t. Real money balances and the rate of inflation are determined, but the price level and the nominal money stock are not, and neither is the real value of the stock of nominal government bonds.

The FTPL "solves" this nonuniqueness or nominal indeterminacy problem by adding another equation: the IBC of the State, holding with equality and with government bonds valued *at their contractual value*: a price of one unit of money for each government bond.

$$\frac{B_0^p}{P_0} = \sum_{j=0}^{\infty} \prod_{\ell=0}^{j} \left(\frac{1}{1+r_{\ell,\ell-1}}\right) \left[\tau_j^s - \overline{C}_j^s + \frac{M_{j+1}}{P_j} - (1+\overline{i}^M)\frac{M_j}{P_j(1+\pi_{j,j-1})}\right]$$

$$= \sum_{j=0}^{\infty} \prod_{\ell=0}^{j} \left(\frac{1}{1+r_{\ell,\ell-1}}\right) \overline{\sigma}_j \tag{4.13}$$

Given the initial value of the nominal stock of public debt, B_0^p, the price level assumes the value required to equate the real contractual value of the public debt to the PDV of current and future augmented primary surpluses.

The first problem with this "solution" is that equation (4.13) has been used already. Substituting the output market equilibrium condition (called real resource constraint by Sims) equation (4.5) into the IBC of the household equation (4.9), yields the IBC of the State, holding with equality and with government debt priced at its contractual value.

To make the key results more transparent, we assume in what follows that all exogenous variables are constant. The model then simplifies to:

$$r = \theta \tag{4.14}$$

$$\frac{B_{t+1}^p (1 + \pi_{t+1,t})}{P_{t+1}} \equiv -\bar{\sigma} + (1 + \bar{i}) \frac{B_t^p}{P_t} \tag{4.15}$$

$$\frac{M_{t+1}}{P_t} = \frac{M}{P} = \frac{\phi(1 + \bar{i})}{\bar{i} - \bar{i}^M} (\bar{Y} - \bar{C}^s) \tag{4.16}$$

$$\bar{\sigma} = \tau^s - \bar{C}^s + \frac{M}{P} \left(\frac{\pi - \bar{i}^M}{1 + \pi} \right) \tag{4.17}$$

$$\bar{Y} = \bar{C}^s + C^f \tag{4.18}$$

$$1 + \bar{i} = (1 + r)(1 + \pi) \tag{4.19}$$

$$1 + \pi = \frac{P_{t+1}}{P_t} \tag{4.20}$$

$$\frac{B_0^p}{P_0} = \left(\frac{1 + \theta}{\theta} \right) \left(C^f + \bar{\tau}^s - \bar{Y} + \frac{M}{P} \left(\frac{\pi - \bar{i}^M}{1 + \pi} \right) \right) \tag{4.21}$$

$$B_0^p = \bar{B}_0^p \tag{4.22}$$

We now add the IBC of the State, holding with equality and with government bonds valued at their contractual value, although this condition is implied already by equations (4.17), (4.18) and (4.21).

$$\frac{B_t^p}{P_t} = \left(\frac{1 + \theta}{\theta} \right) \bar{\sigma} \tag{4.23}$$

Note that equation (4.23) determines the initial price level, given the initial stock of nominal bonds outstanding, and, in subsequent periods, all future price levels, given the future nominal bond stocks. Equation (4.15) updates the nominal stock of bonds given the current and future price levels. Is the indeterminacy problem solved? Unfortunately not. A number of anomalies arise.

Anomaly 1: The price level can be negative

From (4.23), unless $\text{sgn}(B_0^p/P_0) = \text{sgn}(\bar{\sigma})$ the price level will be negative. This is not considered a desirable property of a macroeconomic model.

Anomaly 2: If the public debt is index-linked and/or denominated in foreign currency, there is no FTPL

Consider the case where instead of a one-period risk-free nominal bond paying a contractual one-period nominal interest rate i, with a contractual value in terms of money of 1, we have a one-period risk-free real (index-linked) bond paying a contractual real interest rate r, with a contractual value in terms of the real endowment of 1. The quantity of this real bond outstanding equals the real contractual value of these bonds, b^p. The IBC of the State, holding with equality and with bonds priced at their contractual value becomes:

$$b_0^p = \left(\frac{1+\theta}{\theta}\right)\bar{\sigma} \tag{4.24}$$

The initial stock of the real bond, b_0^p is determined by history (predetermined). Equation (4.24) contains only exogenous or predetermined variables and will therefore only hold by happenstance.

Anomaly 3: The FTPL can price phlogiston

The FTPL price level determination equation (4.23) can also hold in a model in which money does not exist as a store of value, medium of exchange or means of payment but only as an abstract, purely imaginary numeraire. We can see this by setting $\phi = 0$ and $M_t = 0, t \geq 0$ in the model. Money is now an abstract, imaginary object of which no quantity has ever been or ever will be outstanding – rather like phlogiston, the substance believed, by eighteenth-century chemists, to exist in all combustible bodies, and to be released in combustion. Do we really want to be associated with a model that can price phlogiston, through the simple expedient of issuing bonds denominated in phlogiston?

Anomaly 4: If the FTPL holds, there is also the Mrs. Jones Theory of the Price Level (MJPTL)

Consider the IBC of one of the continuum of households we have modeled – Mrs. Jones, say. Assume Mrs. Jones has a positive stock of nominally denominated personal debt outstanding. Assume that instead of pursuing forward-looking consumption and asset allocation plans that always respect her IBC (Ricardian consumption and asset allocation plans) she exogenously fixed her real augmented primary surplus:

$$Y_t - C_t^{Mrs\ Jones} - \overline{\tau}_t^s - \left(\frac{M_{t+1}^{Mrs\ Jones}}{P_t} - (1+\overline{i}^M) \frac{M_t^{Mrs\ Jones}}{P_{t-1}(1+\pi_{t,t-1})} \right) = \overline{\tilde{\sigma}}^{Mrs\ Jones} \text{ for all}$$

t≥0. Mrs. Jones's IBC, holding with equality and with Mrs. Jones's bonds priced at their contractual values, would determine the general price level:

$$\frac{B_t^{Mrs\ Jones}}{P_t} = \left(\frac{1+\theta}{\theta} \right) \overline{\tilde{\sigma}}^{Mrs\ Jones}$$

If there were more than one household following a non-Ricardian consumption and asset allocation rule (and each had nominally denominated debt outstanding), or if the State insisted on a non-Ricardian budgetary rule even though Mrs. Jones is also in a non-Ricardian mood, there would be an overdetermined price level. The logic supporting Mrs. Jones's TPL is as valid as the logic underlying the FTPL – completely invalid, that is.

A4.1.b   The IBC of the State as a Sovereign Bond Pricing Equation

Sovereign debt is indeed serviced out of the current and future augmented primary surpluses of the State. The *market value* of government bonds is indeed (subject to two obvious qualifications) equal to the PDV of current and future augmented primary surpluses of the State. The FTPL however, argues that it is the real *contractual value* of the outstanding stock of government bonds that is determined by the IBC of the State holding with equality. To make sense of this, we introduce the debt revaluation factor or debt default discount factor

D_t. Assume that the outstanding debt stocks are positive: $B_t^p, b_t^p > 0$. At any time the equilibrium bond pricing equation is:

$$D_t\left(\frac{B_t^p}{P_t} + b_t^p\right) = \sum_{j=0}^{\infty}\prod_{\ell=0}^{j}\left(\frac{1}{1+r_{\ell,\ell-1}}\right)\hat{\sigma}_j \tag{4.25}$$

$$0 \le D_t \le 1$$

$$D_t = 0 \quad \text{if} \quad \sum_{j=0}^{\infty}\prod_{\ell=0}^{j}\left(\frac{1}{1+r_{\ell,\ell-1}}\right)\hat{\sigma}_j < 0$$

$$D_t = 1 \quad \text{if} \quad \frac{B_t^p}{P_t} + b_t^p < \sum_{j=0}^{\infty}\prod_{\ell=0}^{j}\left(\frac{1}{1+r_{\ell,\ell-1}}\right)\hat{\sigma}_j \tag{4.26}$$

Government bonds are like equity in the PDV of future augmented primary surpluses with two qualifications. First, it is limited liability equity: you cannot lose more than the entire contractual value of the bonds (the first line of equation (4.26). Second, it has limited upside: the PDV of future augmented primary surpluses in excess of the contractual value of the bonds does not accrue to the bond holders (the second line of equation (4.26)). Instead fiscal space is being wasted.

Note that by introducing the debt revaluation factor, price level indeterminacy returns when the nominal interest rate is exogenous. Equation (4.25) determines the real market value of the debt, $D_t\left(\frac{B_t^p}{P_t} + b_t^p\right)$, but not, in general, either D_t or P_t separately. If there is only real (index-linked) debt (and/or foreign currency-denominated debt), equation (4.25) determines the debt revaluation factor, but not the price level. All real variables are determined, but not the nominal money stock or the price level. We summarize this as Anomaly 5:

> **Anomaly 5:** When the debt revaluation factor is introduced to turn the IBC of the State, holding with equality, into a proper equilibrium debt pricing equation, the FTPL vanishes.

A4.1.c An Exogenous Nominal Money Stock

Consider the case where the nominal money stock is exogenous and the nominal interest rate endogenous. We also assume

$\frac{M_{t+1}}{M_t} = 1 + \bar{\mu} > \frac{1+\bar{i}^M}{1+\theta}$, so again we are not at the ELB if we adopt the fundamental solution.

The model becomes:

$$r = \theta \tag{4.27}$$

$$\frac{B_{t+1}^p (1 + \pi_{t+1,t})}{P_{t+1}} \equiv -\bar{\sigma} + (1 + i_{t,t-1}) \frac{B_t^p}{P_t} \tag{4.28}$$

$$\frac{M_{t+1}}{P_t} = \frac{\phi(1 + i_{t+1,t})}{i_{t+1,t} - \bar{i}^M} (\bar{Y} - \bar{C}^s) \tag{4.29}$$

$$\bar{\sigma} = \tau^s - \bar{C}^s + \frac{M_{t+1}}{P_t} - (1 + \bar{i}^M) \frac{M_t}{P_{t-1}(1 + \pi_{t,t-1})} \tag{4.30}$$

$$\bar{Y} = \bar{C}^s + C^f \tag{4.31}$$

$$1 + i_{t+1,t} = (1 + r_{t+1,t})(1 + \pi_{t+1,t}) \tag{4.32}$$

$$1 + \pi_{t+1,t} = \frac{P_{t+1}}{P_t} \tag{4.33}$$

$$\frac{B_0^p}{P_0} = \left(\frac{1+\theta}{\theta}\right) \\ \left(C^f + \bar{\tau}^s - \bar{Y} + \frac{M_{t+1}}{P_t} - (1 + \bar{i}^M) \frac{M_t}{P_t(1 + \pi_{t,t-1})}\right) \tag{4.34}$$

$$B_0^p = \bar{B}_0^p \tag{4.35}$$

$$M_0/P_{-1} = \bar{M}_0/\bar{P}_{-1} \tag{4.36}$$

$$\pi_{0,-1} = \bar{\pi}_{0,-1} \tag{4.37}$$

Only the real interest rate and real private consumption are determinate. Even though the nominal money stock is exogenous, the nominal interest rate, the price level, the rate of inflation and the real public debt stock are indeterminate. There is a barter solution in which money has no value (the price level is infinite). There is one equilibrium that will produce a constant rate of inflation for a constant growth rate of the nominal money stock. This is the equilibrium normally chosen. This "fundamental" equilibrium selection criterion is what I will call the 'stationary input, stationary output' equilibrium selection criterion: if there exists an equilibrium with a positive value of money and with non-explosive or implosive behavior of the rate of inflation and/or the price level for a constant growth rate of the nominal money stock, then choose that equilibrium. This fundamental equilibrium selection criterion provides a natural and intuitive focal point.

The fundamental equilibrium is given by:

$$r = \theta \tag{4.38}$$

$$\frac{B^p_{t+1}(1+\bar{\mu})}{P_{t+1}} \equiv -\bar{\sigma} + (1+\theta)(1+\bar{\mu})\frac{B^p_t}{P_t} \tag{4.39}$$

$$\frac{M_{t+1}}{P_t} = \frac{\phi(1+\theta)(1+\bar{\mu})}{(1+\theta)(1+\bar{\mu}) - (1+\bar{i}^M)}(\bar{Y} - \overline{C}^s) \tag{4.40}$$

$$\bar{\sigma} = \tau^s - \overline{C}^s + \frac{M_{t+1}}{P_t} - (1+\bar{i}^M)\frac{M_t}{P_{t-1}(1+\pi_{t,t-1})} \tag{4.41}$$

$$\bar{Y} = \overline{C}^s + C^f \tag{4.42}$$

$$1 + i_{t+1,t} = (1 + r_{t+1,t})(1 + \pi_{t+1,t}) \tag{4.43}$$

$$1 + \pi_{t+1,t} = \frac{P_{t+1}}{P_t} \tag{4.44}$$

$$\frac{B^p_0}{P_0} = \left(\frac{1+\theta}{\theta}\right)$$
$$\left(C^f + \bar{\tau}^s - \bar{Y} + \frac{M_{t+1}}{P_t} - (1+\bar{i}^M)\frac{M_t}{P_{t-1}(1+\pi_{t,t-1})}\right) \tag{4.45}$$

$$B^p_0 = \overline{B}^p_0 \tag{4.46}$$

The unique initial value of the price level, P_0, that supports a solution with a constant rate of inflation equal to the growth rate of the nominal money stock, $1 + \pi_{t+1,t} = 1 + \bar{\mu}$, is given by:

$$\frac{M_0}{P_0} = \frac{\phi(1+\theta)}{(1+\theta)(1+\bar{\mu}) - (1+\bar{i}^M)}(\bar{Y} - \overline{C}^s) \tag{4.47}$$

This raises the question as to whether the FTPL can be viewed as an alternative equilibrium selection criterion in a monetary model with a continuum of equilibria. This issue was raised by Kocherlakota and Phelan (1999) who came to the same negative solution reached here. If, instead of using the fundamental "stationary input, stationary output" criterion for equilibrium selection, we were to use the IBC of the State, holding with equality and with public debt valued at its contractual value, given in equation (4.48), the initial price level would only by happenstance be the same as the initial price level supporting the "stationary input, stationary output" solution.

$$\frac{B_t^p}{P_t} = \left(\frac{1+\theta}{\theta}\right)\bar{\sigma} \tag{4.48}$$

It follows that, in general, the FTPL solution will support a rate of inflation that either explodes or implodes. In the implosive equilibrium, the inflation rate declines until the nominal interest rate on bonds equals the nominal interest rate on money, which happens when $1 + \pi_{t+1,t} = \frac{1+\bar{i}^M}{1+\theta} < 1 + \bar{\mu}$, at which point the demand for real money balances goes to infinity.

But isn't it a problem with the conventional, stationary input, stationary output solution that the IBC of the State need not be satisfied? It is not. One way to respond to this objection is that we require the authorities to follow Ricardian budgetary rules only, that is, programs for which the IBC is satisfied identically, that is, for all feasible values of income, consumption, price level, rate of inflation, interest rates and any other nonpolicy instrument variables that enter into the IBC of the State. After all, that's what households are assumed to do in the model (except possibly Mrs. Jones ...). The second approach is to permit non-Ricardian budgetary rules but to introduce the debt revaluation factor, that is, to replace equation (4.48) with:

$$D_0\frac{B_0^p}{P_0} = \left(\frac{1+\theta}{\theta}\right)\bar{\sigma} \tag{4.49}$$

With the initial price level determined by the monetary equilibrium condition (4.47) and B_0^p inherited from the past, equation (4.49) can be viewed as a counterfactual validity check on the model. If equation (4.49) solves for $D_0 \geq 1$, and if this is also the case for all future IBCs of the State, that is,

$$D_t \frac{B_t^p}{P_t} = \left(\frac{1 + \theta}{\theta} \right) \bar{\bar{\sigma}} \text{ solves for } D_t \geq 1 \text{ for } t \geq 0 \tag{4.50}$$

then there no default and no default risk now or in the future and the assumption made throughout the rest of the model, that public debt trades at its contractual value, is validated. The analysis can proceed. If, however, condition (4.50) is violated for any $t \geq 0$, there will be a sovereign default in some period. The maintained assumption in the rest of the model – that sovereign debt trades at its contractual value – is falsified. The model is therefore not fit for purpose and it is back to the drawing board for the model builder. A new model has to be constructed that allows explicitly for default and default risk and for the response of markets and other institutions to the presence of default risk, the occurrence of default and the resolution of default.

This suggests another anomaly:

Anomaly 6: When viewed as an equilibrium selection criterion, the FTPL in general produces explosive or implosive solutions for the inflation rate when the nominal money stock is exogenous.

If we adopt the fundamental solution *and* impose the FTPL, the model is, of course, overdetermined, with the price level determined twice, once by the monetary equilibrium condition (4.40) and once by the IBC of the State, holding with equality and with sovereign debt priced at its contractual value, equation (4.48). This is Inconsistency 1.

Inconsistency 1. If the FTPL is not viewed as an equilibrium selection rule but is imposed as another equilibrium condition when the nominal money stock is exogenous and the fundamental equilibrium is chosen (a constant growth rate of the nominal money stock supports a constant rate of inflation), then the model is overdetermined.

A4.2   THE FTPL IN A MODEL WITH A PREDETERMINED PRICE LEVEL

Let's now consider the case where the price level is not freely flexible. For concreteness and simplicity, assume both the price level and the rate of inflation are predetermined and that the inflation rate is updated through an accelerationist Phillips curve. The actual level of output is assumed to be demand-determined. We consider the constant nominal interest rate version. The model becomes:

$$\frac{C_{t+1}^f}{C_t^f} = \frac{1 + r_{t+1,t}}{1 + \theta} \tag{4.51}$$

$$\frac{B_{t+1}^p (1 + \pi_{t+1,t})}{P_{t+1}} \equiv \overline{C}_t^s - \tau_t^s - \left(\frac{M_{t+1}}{P_t} - (1 + \overline{i}^M) \frac{M_t}{P_{t-1}(1 + \pi_{t,t-1})} \right)$$
$$+ (1 + \overline{i}) \frac{B_t^p}{P_t} \tag{4.52}$$

$$1 + \pi_{t+1,t} = \frac{P_{t+1}}{P_t} \tag{4.53}$$

$$\pi_{t+1,t} = \alpha(Y_t - \overline{Y}) + \pi_{t,t-1}$$
$$\alpha > 0 \tag{4.54}$$

$$\frac{M_{t+1}}{P_t} = \frac{\phi(1 + \overline{i})}{\overline{i} - \overline{i}^M} C_t^f \tag{4.55}$$

$$\overline{\sigma}_t = \tau_t^s - \overline{C}_t^s + \frac{M_{t+1}}{P_t} - (1 + \overline{i}^M) \frac{M_t}{P_{t-1}(1 + \pi_{t,t-1})} \tag{4.56}$$

$$Y_t = \overline{C}_t^s + C_t^f \tag{4.57}$$

$$1 + \overline{i} = (1 + r_{t+1,t})(1 + \pi_{t+1,t}) \tag{4.58}$$

$$\frac{B_0^p}{P_0} = \sum_{j=0}^{\infty} \prod_{\ell=0}^{j} \left(\frac{1}{1 + r_{\ell,\ell-1}} \right)$$
$$\left[C_j^f + \tau_j^s - Y_j + \frac{M_{j+1}}{P_j} - (1 + \overline{i}^M) \frac{M_j}{P_{j-1}(1 + \pi_{j,j-1})} \right] \tag{4.59}$$

$$B_0^p = \overline{B}_0^p \tag{4.60}$$

$$P_0 = \overline{P}_0 \tag{4.61}$$

$$\pi_{0,-1} = \overline{\pi}_{0,-1} \tag{4.62}$$

This model has four state variables, three of them predetermined, B, P and π, and one non-predetermined, C^f. There are also four endogenous variables that are not state variables: M, Y, r and r^s. We have three initial conditions for the predetermined state variables (equations (4.60), (4.61) and (4.62)) and one other (terminal) boundary condition for the non-predetermined state variable (equation (4.59)). This model is fully determined with the right number of equations and unknowns and the right number and types of boundary conditions for the state variables. Adding the IBC of the State, holding with equality and with government bonds priced at their contractual values, would result in an overdetermined system. We summarize this as Inconsistency 2:

> **Inconsistency 2:** When the price level is predetermined, adding the IBC of the State, holding with equality and with sovereign bonds priced at their contractual values as an equilibrium condition, in addition to the IBC of the household sector, holding with equality, results in an overdetermined system, even when the nominal interest rate is exogenous.

Consider what would happen if one added to the asset menu in both the flexible price level model and the model with nominal price rigidity a nominal consol, that is, a security promising to pay 1 unit of money each period forever. This was done by Sims (2011, 2013). The fundamental contractual value of such a security would be $\sum_{j=t}^{\infty} \prod_{\ell=t}^{j} \frac{1}{1+i_{\ell,\ell-1}}$. Let's consider the IBC of the State, holding with equality and with all government bonds priced at their equilibrium values with the perpetual bond added (but without the index-linked bonds, which play no role here). The number of consols outstanding is B^L. The FTPL equation becomes:

$$\frac{1}{P_t}\left(B_t^p + \sum_{j=t}^{\infty}\prod_{\ell=t}^{j}\frac{B_t^L}{1+i_{\ell,\ell-1}}\right) = \sum_{j=0}^{\infty}\prod_{\ell=0}^{j}\left(\frac{1}{1+r_{\ell,\ell-1}}\right)\hat{\sigma}_j \qquad (4.63)$$

It is easily checked that all Anomalies and the Inconsistencies are unaffected by the addition of a long nominal bond to the asset menu. The same would hold for the addition of an index-linked consol to the asset menu.

As regards Sims's hope that the nominal and real discount factors in equation (4.63) can be relied upon to achieve sovereign solvency, it is clear that while this may be the case for specific non-Ricardian budgetary rules, it cannot be true in general. A simple counterexample suffices. Consider the non-Ricardian budgetary rule given in equation

$$1 + i_{\ell,\ell-1} = (1+\theta)(1+\pi_{\ell,\ell-1})$$
$$\hat{\sigma}_j = \bar{z} + \frac{B_t^L}{P_t}\prod_{\ell=t}^{j}\left(\frac{1}{1+\pi_{\ell,\ell-1}}\right) \qquad (4.64)$$

Under this budgetary rule, equation (4.63) becomes:

$$\frac{B_t^p}{P_t} = \left(\frac{1+\theta}{\theta}\right)\bar{z} \qquad (4.65)$$

Equation (4.65) will only hold by happenstance.

An even simpler counter example is:

$$1 + i_{\ell,\ell-1} = (1+\theta)(1+\pi_{\ell,\ell-1})$$
$$\hat{\sigma}_j < 0 \qquad (4.66)$$

with $B_t^p > 0$ and $B_t^L > 0$.

5 Life at the Zero Lower Bound and How to Escape from It

Thus far, the analysis has been conducted on the assumption that there is a zero lower bound, or rather an effective lower bound on the short risk-free nominal interest rate that is set by the interest rate on the monetary base. Once the interest rate reaches the ELB and if the own interest rate on the monetary base is not a policy instrument, conventional monetary policy is at the end of its tether and only (announcements about) the size and composition of the central bank's balance sheet, now and in the future, and announcements ('forward guidance') about future interest rates if and when the ELB ceases to be a binding constraint, are available as policy instruments.[1] The analysis that follows is based on earlier work by Buiter and Panigirtzoglou (2001, 2003), Goodfriend (2000), Buiter (2004, 2007b, 2009) and Rogoff (2016, 2017).

To be practically relevant, we need to distinguish between currency, J, and reserves, z (bank reserves with the central bank, both required and excess). Currency is a negotiable bearer bond with a fixed exchange rate (equal to 1) vis-à-vis reserves. Because the holder of currency is, in principle, anonymous, paying interest on currency, at a positive or negative rate is cumbersome – the currency must be stamped/marked when interest due has been paid/received, or some other way to establish verifiably that interest due has been paid or received has to be created. So for most of the analysis we set the interest rate on currency, i^J equal to zero. The interest rate on reserves is, as before, denoted i^z.[2] We only consider permanent income consumers in what follows, so $\eta = 1$, and uncertainty is ignored.

---

[1] In an open economy, foreign exchange market intervention would be an additional instrument.

[2] We don't distinguish between required and excess reserves.

The most general approach would be to assume that the monetary services (means of payment, transactions medium and store of value) in the utility function, equation (3.1), can be provided by either cash or reserves, say through a constant elasticity of substitution 'production function' of monetary services, where λ is the elasticity of substitution between cash and reserves:

$$\frac{M_{t+1}}{P_t} = \left(a\left(\frac{J_{t+1}}{P_t}\right)^{\frac{\lambda-1}{\lambda}} + (1-a)\left(\frac{Z_{t+1}}{P_t}\right)^{\frac{\lambda-1}{\lambda}} \right)^{\frac{\lambda}{\lambda-1}} \tag{5.1}$$

$$0 \le a \le 1, \quad \lambda \ge 0, \quad J_t \ge 0, \quad Z_t \ge 0$$

The household period budget constraint, equation (3.2), the no-Ponzi game condition, equation (3.3), and household IBC, equation (3.4), change to:

$$J_{t+1} + Z_{t+1} + B_{t+1}^{cb} \equiv P_t Y_t - T_t^s - P_t C_t^p + (1 + i_{t,t-1}^J)J_t$$
$$+ (1 + i_{t,t-1}^Z)Z_t + (1 + i_{t,t-1})B_t^{cb}$$

$$\lim_{j\to\infty} I_{j,t-1}(J_{j+1} + Z_{t+1} + B_{j+1}^p) \ge 0$$

$$J_t + Z_t + B_t^p \ge \sum_{j=t}^{\infty} I_{j,t-1}$$

$$[P_j C_j^p + T_j^s - P_j Y_j + (i_{j,j-1} - i_{j,j-1}^J)J_j + (i_{j,t-1} - i_{j,j-1}^Z)Z_j]$$

The desired ratio of cash to reserves in this economy is given by:

$$\frac{J_t}{Z_t} = \left[\left(\frac{a}{1-a}\right)\left(\frac{i_{t,t-1} - i_{t,t-1}^Z}{i_{t,t-1} - i_{t,t-1}^J}\right)\right]^{\lambda} \tag{5.2}$$

According to equation (5.2), the demand for cash is zero when $i = i^Z$ as long as $i > i^J$. The demand for reserves goes to infinity when its pecuniary opportunity cost, $i - i^Z$, equals zero. To make this ELB story applicable in the real world we have to recognize that cash has a real carry cost, $\varsigma > 0$ per unit of cash. This is the cost of storing, safekeeping and insuring cash and using it in time- and labor-intensive transactions. The –0.75 percent number that has been the real-world floor on the policy rate in Sweden, Denmark and Switzerland suggests that the carry costs of cash are around 0.75 percent. One would, however, expect there to be economies of scale in managing cash, and learning by doing could further lower the carry costs.

In what follows, we simplify the analysis further by assuming that only cash yields nonpecuniary services (medium of exchange, means of payment etc.), which means we set $a = 1$ in equation (5.1). Central bank excess reserves are a pure store of value and a perfect substitute for short risk-free sovereign debt, so $i^Z = i$.

It is clearly desirable to lower the ELB significantly – and preferably to abolish it altogether – if we are to prevent central banks from being deprived of the interest rate instrument in the next cyclical downturn. There are three ways to get rid of the ELB completely: (1) abolish cash, (2) tax cash sufficiently harshly and (3) introduce a variable exchange rate between cash and reserves. We consider them in turn.

5.1   ABOLISHING CASH

Setting $J_t = 0$ for all t would solve the problem of the ELB by abolishing it. Unless cash and reserves are perfect substitutes in transactions, there will be a utility/efficiency loss associated with the abolition of cash.

Abolishing cash would have the further advantage (not considered in our formal analysis) of ending the subsidy to criminal activity represented by the provision of anonymous bearer bonds with legal tender status. As is clear from Table 5.1, the stock of US dollar currency notes in circulation has more than doubled since the start of the GFC, from $810 bn at the end of June 2007 to $1,633 bn in April 2018. Much of this is likely to be used in the furtherance of criminal activity or in shielding the fruits of criminal activity – tax evasion, financing terrorism, money laundering and funding other forms of criminal activity. This is consistent with the fact that the vast majority by value of the currency outstanding – 79.7 percent – is

Table 5.1 *Composition of US$ currency notes in circulation, December 31, 2017, $bn*

Year	$1	$2	$5	$10	$20	$50	$100	$500 to $10,000	Total
2017	$12.1	$2.4	$14.8	$19.6	$183.8	$86.4	$1,251.7	$0.3	$1,571.1

Source: Federal Reserve Board

Table 5.2 *Composition of euro currency notes in circulation, June 2018, € bn*

Period	€5	€10	€20	€50	€100	€200	€500	Total
June 2018	9.3	24.9	75.9	495.2	269.0	50.0	257.2	1,181.5

Source: ECB

in $100 bills – the largest commonly available denomination. There is likely to be considerable chagrin in the criminal communities that notes in $500 to $10,000 denominations are no longer issued.

As regards the euro, notes and coins in circulation rose from €633 bn in June 2007 to €1,182 bn in June 2018. Some 90.7 percent by value of the notes outstanding were in denominations of €50 or higher (see Table 5.2).

There are a number of arguments against abolishing physical currency notes.

The first argument is that there is a significant population that still uses cash as its principal (retail) means of payment and a significant number of small transactions that are mostly conducted using cash as a means of payment. The solution to this problem is to abolish all denominations in excess of, say, $10 or €10. This would increase the cost of holding and using cash for (mostly illegitimate) large payments but permit the pre-electronic funds transfer and pre-Apple Pay generation to live out its days without undue discomfort.

By raising the carry cost of currency, it would lower the ELB without abolishing it.

The second argument applies to US dollar currency specifically rather than to paper currency in general. The US dollar is the world's leading currency and reserve currency. Many countries are badly managed from a monetary, financial and fiscal perspective, to the point that high inflation or even hyperinflation makes the domestic currency highly unattractive as a store of value. This creates a foreign demand for US dollars. Meeting this legitimate foreign demand for US dollar notes is providing a privately and socially valuable financial service indeed. Rogoff (2016, 2018) estimates that just under half of US dollar notes (by value) is held abroad (admittedly not all for legitimate purposes).

The third argument is that the alternative to cash is likely to be some web-based electronic payment mechanism(s) that will be vulnerable to cyber-attacks. Most legitimate large payments are already made electronically (say by wire transfer) and this vulnerability will not go away by retaining cash. It could be another argument for retaining small denominations, so people's immediate need for food etc. can be satisfied even if the Cloud is temporarily out of order.

The fourth argument is the libertarian one that the same anonymity of cash that makes it attractive to criminals also makes it attractive to those who don't trust the State or any large entity, private or public, that has the resources to track electronic payments. From this perspective, privacy when faced with the prying eyes of an intrusive and overbearing government is a private and public good that must be preserved, even at a cost.

5.2   TAXING CASH

Taxing (or subsidizing) cash, in the spirit of Gesell (1916) and Fisher (1933), is subject to the same problem as paying interest, positive or negative on cash: there has to be a verifiable record of taxes paid/ subsidies received for each and every currency note. Currency notes have to be marked, stamped or otherwise altered to allow a third party (the issuer in the case of interest payments, the tax administrator in the case of tax payments) to determine whether interest/taxes due have been paid (or received).

It is not enough to declare that unstamped currency will no longer be 'money' that is generally accepted as a means of payment or medium of exchange. At most, the authorities can withdraw legal-tender status from unstamped currency and refuse to accept it as means of payment/medium of exchange in transactions involving the State and its agencies, including the payment of taxes. But as regards transactions between private parties, anything that is generally viewed as money *is* money. The objects (including electronic bookkeeping entries) that are generally accepted as means of payment or medium of exchange are chosen through an uncoordinated, decentralized collective choice process.

So any decision to eliminate untaxed cash as money would have to be enforced through procedures that are bound to be viewed as intrusive and oppressive and would likely be costly. For instance, individuals could be accosted anywhere by currency tax enforcement officials to ascertain that any currency they have on their person is up to date as regards tax payments due.

Ways of taxing currency through mechanism like those mentioned by Mankiw (2009), who attributes it to one of his graduate students, appear to get around this monitoring and enforcement problem. Under this proposal, all currency notes have a serial number ending in an integer from 0 to 9. All currency notes also should have a year printed on them. Once a year, on a fixed date, the central bank randomly selects an integer from 0 to 9. All currency notes ending in that integer, printed in that year or earlier, lose their legal tender status and are no longer redeemable/exchangeable at the central bank or its agents for anything else. The expected nominal interest rate on currency is therefore -10 percent under this scheme. It can also be viewed as a lottery version of putting an expiration date on all currency notes and charging a 10 percent of face value tax on each note as it is redeemed.

However, the Mankiw scheme falls foul of the same problem that currency with an expiration date falls foul of, unless there is external enforcement. The value of fiat money is what people collectively think it is. If the central bank randomly selects 7 as the unlucky number this year and I own a € 100 note whose serial number ends in 7, I may still be able to purchase goods and services worth €100 with that note, provided other private agents are willing to accept it as being worth that much. Legal tender status or convertibility into other government notes at the central bank is not necessary for fiat money to have value. Some form of monitoring currency holdings and a penalty for those caught with expired currency (such as the threat of confiscation plus a fine) are likely to be necessary to make Mankiw's scheme work.

5.3 A VARIABLE EXCHANGE RATE BETWEEN CURRENCY AND RESERVES

Consider the case where we keep noninterest-bearing currency, but introduce a variable exchange rate between reserves and currency, as proposed by Eisler (1932). Assume, for concreteness, we introduce this change in the Eurozone. Reserves will be denominated in euro, but currency in terms of the wim, in honor of Wim Duisenberg, the first President of the ECB. Let S_t be the spot exchange rate between the wim and the euro, measured as number of wim per euro and $F_{t+1,t}$ the period t one-period forward exchange rate between the wim and the euro – the number of wim that have to be paid in period $t + 1$ in exchange for one euro in period t. Assume we wish to set a −10 percent euro short rate of interest. This is implemented by setting $i^Z_{t+1} = -0.10$ and using the covered interest parity condition $1 + i^Z_{t+1,t} = \frac{S_t}{F_{t,t+1}}$ to determine the forward discount on the wim, that is, $F_{t,t+1} = 1.111 S_t$. We can complete the exchange rate rule by setting the spot rate each period equal to last period's forward rate: $S_t = F_{t,t-1}$. By depreciating the wim at a rate of just over 11 percent vis-à-vis the euro, we avoid arbitrage opportunities between the wim and the euro even though euro reserves yield −10 percent (in terms of euro) and the wim yields 0 percent in terms of wim.

Is this 'problem solved' – the ELB abolished without eliminating currency? Only if the euro rather than the wim remains the numeraire in terms of which all price and wage contracts are denominated, and if it is the euro price level that remains the target of policy and the euro rate of inflation that is determined by the Phillips curve. We will emphasize the inflation measure that is targeted by adding a Taylor rule in equation (5.8) to the simple sticky price level dynamic model of Chapter 4, reproduced in equations (5.3) to (5.7); π^* is the target rate of inflation; θ can be interpreted as the neutral real interest rate. The wim currency has a zero nominal interest rate. When the ELB constraint is not binding, we assume that the exchange rate between the wim and the euro is kept constant. In what follows, variables denominated in wim have the superscript w. Variables denominated in euro don't have a superscript. The model is summarized in equations (5.3) to (5.13). The exchange rate rule, equation (5.9), ensures there are no arbitrage opportunities even if the Taylor rule generated a euro interest rate equal to or lower than the interest rate on wim currency – zero. There are also wim-denominated one-period bonds with a wim interest rate $i^w \geq 0$.

For $t \geq 0$

$$\frac{C^p_{t+1}}{C^p_t} = \frac{1 + r_{t+1,t}}{1 + \theta} \tag{5.3}$$

$$Y_t = \overline{C}^s_t + C^p_t \tag{5.4}$$

$$1 + i_{t+1,t} = (1 + r_{t+1,t})(1 + \pi_{t+1,t}) \tag{5.5}$$

$$\pi_{t+1,t} = \alpha(Y_t - \overline{Y}) + \pi_{t,t-1} \atop \alpha > 0 \tag{5.6}$$

$$\frac{M^w_{t+1}}{S_t P_t} = \frac{\phi(1 + i_{t+1,t})}{i_{t+1,t}} C^p_t \tag{5.7}$$

$$i_{t+1,t} = (1 + \theta)(1 + \pi^*) - 1 + \vartheta_1(\pi_{t+1,t} - \pi^*) + \vartheta_2(Y_t - \overline{Y}) \tag{5.8}$$
$$\vartheta_1 > 1; \quad \vartheta_2 > 0$$

$$\frac{F_{t+1,t}}{S_t} = 1 \qquad \text{if } i_{t+1,t} > 0$$

$$\frac{F_{t+1,t}}{S_t} = \frac{1}{1 + i_{t+1,t}} \qquad \text{if } i_{t+1,t} \leq 0 \tag{5.9}$$

$$S_{t+1} = F_{t+1,t}$$

$$C_0^p = \frac{\theta}{(1 + \phi)(1 + \theta)} \left[\frac{M_0^w / S_{-1}P_{-1}}{(1 + \pi_{0,-1}^w)} + \sum_{j=0}^{\infty} \prod_{\ell=0}^{j} \frac{1}{1 + r_{\ell,\ell-1}} \right.$$
$$\left. \left(Y_j - \overline{C}_j^s + \left(\frac{M_{j+1}^w}{S_j P_j} - \frac{M_j^w}{S_{j-1}P_{j-1}(1 + \pi_{j,j-1}^w)} \right) \right) \right] \tag{5.10}$$

$$P_t^w = S_t P_t \tag{5.11}$$

$$r_{t+1,t}^w = r_{t+1,t} \tag{5.12}$$

$$1 + i_{t+1,t}^w = (1 + r_{t+1,t}^w)(1 + \pi_{t+1,t}^w)$$

$$= (1 + r_{t+1,t})(1 + \pi_{t+1,t})F_{t+1,t}/S_t \tag{5.13}$$

$$P_{-1} = \overline{P}_{-1} \tag{5.14}$$

$$S_{-1} = \overline{S}_{-1} \tag{5.15}$$

$$\pi_{0,-1} = \overline{\pi}_{0,-1} \tag{5.16}$$

$$M_0^w = \overline{M}_0^w \tag{5.17}$$

Equation (5.11) is the law of one price – there are no arbitrage opportunities in the market for the single good. Equation (5.12) is an implication of equation (5.11) and covered (and uncovered) interest parity: the real euro interest rate equals the real wim interest rate.

The economy described by equations (5.3) to (5.13) cannot get stuck at the ELB. This is because although the currency (the wim) no longer has a fixed exchange rate with euro central bank reserves, the numeraire or unit of account for pricing decisions (as reflected in the Phillips curve) remains the euro and the inflation rate targeted by the authorities through the Taylor rule is the euro rate of inflation. If, by contrast, the numeraire/unit of account were to "follow the currency," we would replace the Phillips cure and the Taylor rule by equations (5.18) and (5.19) respectively, and the ELB would be reincarnated as a lower bound on the wim interest rate. We would be back where we started without the variable exchange rate between the wim currency and the euro central bank reserves.

$$\pi^w_{t+1,t} = \alpha(Y_t - \overline{Y}) + \pi^w_{t,t-1}$$
$$\alpha > 0 \tag{5.18}$$

$$i^w_{t+1,t} = (1 + \theta)(1 + \pi^{*,w}) - 1 + \vartheta_1(\pi^w_{t+1,t} - \pi^{*,w})$$
$$+ \vartheta_2(Y_t - \overline{Y}) \; \vartheta_1 > 1; \quad \vartheta_2 > 0 \tag{5.19}$$

$$i^w_{t+1} \geq 0 \tag{5.20}$$

We would have had a pure change in numeraire, like the change from the old French franc to the new French franc – something without any implications for the real economy, the rate of inflation, real and nominal interest rates or anything else that matters.

Unfortunately, we don't have a theory of how the numeraire is chosen and under what circumstances it is tied to the medium of exchange/means of payment. The only sure way to eliminate the ELB is therefore to abolish cash. A more palatable policy that could materially lower the ELB would be to eliminate all currency denominations larger than, say, $10 or €10.

The wim currency need not be a publicly provided currency. It could be a private currency, including cryptocurrencies like Bitcoin or Ether. A key difference between proof-of-work based cryptocurrencies like Bitcoin and fiat money provided by the state as currency (or potentially through an accessible-to-all wire transfer network operated through the web and backed by central bank–guaranteed individual accounts) is that public fiat money can be created at effectively zero marginal cost while creating additional Bitcoin requires costly mining which strictly limits the maximum number of Bitcoins that can be produced. Let the marginal real resource cost of mining a unit of Bitcoin be $\zeta(M) > 0$, then $\zeta' > 0$; $\zeta'' > 0$ and $\lim_{M \to \overline{M}} \zeta(M) = +\infty$ at some finite value of $\overline{M}$.[3] It will be profitable to mine additional Bitcoin (if the mining industry is competitive) as long as $\frac{P^B_t}{P_t} \geq \zeta$, where P^B is the price of a Bitcoin in terms of conventional money. The price of Bitcoin is, unlike the managed exchange rate of the wim currency, determined by asset markets of varying degrees of technical efficiency. Because of its history of extreme price variability, Bitcoin is unlikely ever to become the numeraire of a material set of wage and price contracts. Since the total potential supply of Bitcoin is capped at 21,000,000 (the quantity at which the marginal cost of mining becomes infinite),[4] it is useless as a ready source of additional liquidity for lender-of-last-resort and market-maker-of-last-resort operations. It's hard to identify a problem that Bitcoin (or other cryptocurrencies relying on proof-of-work), could be a socially efficient solution to.[5]

---

[3] Wikipedia defines a proof-of-work system as follows: A proof-of-work (PoW) system (or protocol, or function) is an economic measure to deter denial of service attacks and other service abuses such as spam on a network by requiring some work from the service requester, usually meaning processing time by a computer. https://en.wikipedia.org/wiki/Proof-of-work_system.

[4] That is, $\overline{M} = 21$ million.

[5] Note that although the overall quantity of Bitcoin is capped, the technology behind it is open source, so Bitcoin can be replicated ad infinitum. The explosion in the number of decentralized cryptocurrencies supports the view that "if it has value it will be replicated until it no longer has any value."

6   Why the Eurosystem Isn't a Proper Central Bank – and How to Make It One

6.1   INTRODUCTION

The main thesis of this Chapter is that there is a potentially fatal flaw in the design of the Eurosystem. The comprehensive balance sheet approach (or IBC approach) developed in Chapter 2 is essential for a proper understanding of just how flawed and vulnerable the Eurosystem is. The Chapter relies heavily on the material developed in the first three Chapters of this book.

The nineteen national central banks (NCBs) hold significant amounts of assets for their own risk rather than on a risk-sharing basis, and for some of these NCBs a significant share of these assets is subject to material credit risk. Because NCBs have no control over their issuance of central bank money – this is a collective decision taken by the Governing Council of the European Central Bank (ECB) – a central bank can go bankrupt – become insolvent. Effectively, all euro-denominated assets and liabilities of an NCB (and all euro-denominated Eurozone sovereign debt instruments) are foreign-currency-denominated financial instruments, both from the perspective of the issuers (including sovereigns) and from the perspective of the holders, including the NCBs.

The Eurosystem is not an operationally decentralized central bank like the Federal Reserve System; it is a system of currency boards (see Buiter (2015)). If the losses that drive an NCB into insolvency are due to a default by its sovereign, it is unlikely that this sovereign will be able to repair the NCB insolvency. This leaves three possible outcomes. First, the bankrupt NCB exits the Eurosystem and its member state leaves the euro area. Second, there is ex-post mutualization by the other NCBs of the losses on the bad assets of the insolvent NCB (ex-post risk sharing). This would create the risk of a breakup of the Eurozone through a voluntary exit of the fiscally sound creditor nations. Third, capital and foreign exchange controls are imposed while an emergency rescue program is mounted by the ECB, using the outright monetary transactions programme (OMT), and the European Stability Mechanism (ESM), including possible sovereign debt restructuring. In the future, a European Monetary Fund (an ESM with much-enhanced financial resources and the power to manage sovereign debt restructuring) might act as sovereign lender of last resort and market maker of last resort. Enhanced collective action clauses (CACs) for EA sovereign debt, including more robust "aggregation" features, could make a contribution here. Significant progress was made in 2018 when the finance ministers of the euro area agreed to introduce "single limb" CACs by 2022 and to include this commitment in the ESM Treaty.[1]

The third outcome amounts to a de facto temporary suspension of EA membership. It is a temporary fix, which either gives way to one of the first two outcomes or creates a window of opportunity for a restoration of the NCB's solvency – presumably through a restoration of the solvency of its sovereign.

There are three non–mutually exclusive approaches to addressing the problem of insolvency risk for individual Eurosystem NCBs. The first is for the Eurosystem to recognize a key off–balance sheet asset of each NCB – the present discounted value of its future seigniorage income – and to lend to a financially challenged NCB up to a limit that reflects the seigniorage asset of that NCB. There is, of course, no guarantee that the NCB's capital key share of the PDV of future Eurosystem profits will be large enough to restore it to solvency. The second is to replace the risky assets it holds with safer assets. This can be achieved through financial engineering and/or a

---

[1] A collective action clause (CAC) allows a supermajority of bondholders to agree to a debt restructuring. With "single-limb aggregation," a single restructuring decision encompasses all bonds. There is no need to obtain a supermajority for each individual bonds issue involved in the restructuring.

combination of risk sharing and risk reduction by the sovereigns and banking sectors of the EA member states. The third is to materially reduce (ideally to zero) the scope of own-risk activities undertaken by NCBs.

6.2   WHERE WE ARE TODAY

The Economic and Monetary Union (EMU) is an operationally decentralized common currency arrangement currently involving nineteen EU member states – henceforth the Eurozone member states.[2] The Eurosystem, consisting of the nineteen national central banks of the Eurozone member states and the European Central Bank (owned by the NCBs according to the capital key), manages the common currency and designs and implements the common monetary policy, credit policy (including lender-of-last-resort and market-maker-of-last-resort interventions) and (probably) exchange rate policy.[3] The

---

[2]   All EU member states other than the United Kingdom and Denmark, which have derogations, are in principle obliged to and committed to adopting the common currency. They can, however, choose to fail one or more of the accession criteria, so, in practice, joining the common currency is a choice for the nine (soon to be eight) EU member states that are not part of the Eurozone.

[3]   Although setting a number of short-term interest rates and determining the size and composition of the balance sheet of the Eurosystem are generally considered legitimate activities of the ECB, there is some disagreement about whether it can set, manage or target the exchange rate of the euro (should it wish to do so). This may seem surprising as Article 119–2 of the consolidated Treaties appears to assign exchange rate policy to the same entity to which monetary policy has been assigned: "as provided in the Treaties and in accordance with the procedures set out therein, these activities shall include a single currency, the euro, and the definition and conduct of a single monetary policy and exchange-rate policy the primary objective of both of which shall be to maintain price stability." Article 291 follows (appropriately in our view) the universal practice of qualifying the ability of the central bank to manage the exchange rate of the euro by granting the Council (of the European Union) the power to determine (by unanimity) the nature of the exchange rate system, regime or arrangement (e.g. a fixed exchange rate vis-à-vis some other currency or basket of currencies or a crawling peg). More surprisingly, it then goes on to also grant the Council the power to "formulate exchange rate orientations" even when the exchange rate is not pegged to some other currency or basket of currencies. There has been no attempt thus far by the Council to "formulate exchange rate orientations." The unanimity requirement for the Council would likely be an insurmountable obstacle. It is also not clear what an "orientation" is – other than a wonderful Gallicism. Its possible meanings range from "order" via directive and recommendation to preference and suggestion. Could it be

Governing Council, consisting of the six-member Board of the ECB and the nineteen NCB Governors, makes the policy decisions.[4]

The Eurosystem is not only operationally decentralized, it has twenty distinct and legally independent profit-and-loss centers: the ECB and the nineteen NCBs of the Eurosystem. This is the source of its unique vulnerability: an individual NCB can become insolvent even if the Eurosystem as a whole is solvent, if the Governing Council opposes a bailout of a financially troubled NCB.[5]

In principle, all EU member states contribute to the capital of the ECB, and share in the profits and losses of the "shared-risk" operations according to a capital key given by their shares of EU population and EU GDP. The subscribed capital key shares are given, for the Eurozone member states, in the second column of Table 6.1. However, the shares of the fully paid-up capital provided by the Eurozone member states are what matters for the distribution of profits and losses from the Eurosystem's shared-risk activities.[6] These shares are given in column 3 of Table 6.1. Henceforth

ignored? On balance, it seems reasonable to treat the exchange rate as another (potential) monetary policy instrument.

The EMU is not alone in casting doubt on who is responsible for exchange rate management. In the USA, the Exchange Stabilization Fund (ESF) is owned by the Treasury but managed by the Federal Reserve Bank of New York in its capacity as fiscal agent for the Treasury Department. On its website, the US Treasury states: "All operations of the ESF require the explicit authorization of the Secretary of the Treasury who is responsible for the formulation and implementation of U.S. international monetary and financial policy, including exchange market intervention policy." See US Department of the Treasury, www.treasury.gov/resource-center/international/ Pages/default.aspx. The implied distinction between international and domestic monetary policy makes no sense.

[4]   Only fifteen out of the nineteen NCB governments have voting rights at any one time. Germany, France, Italy, Spain and the Netherlands share four voting rights. The fourteen other governors share eleven voting rights. The Governors take turns using the rights on a monthly rotation. The six Board members have permanent voting rights.

[5]   A bailout of an NCB that has become insolvent because of a default by a sovereign whose debt it holds could be judged to be a form of "monetary financing" of the defaulted sovereign. This could be deemed to violate Article 123 of the Treaty on the Functioning of the European Union.

[6]   "The non-euro area NCBs are required to pay up to 3.75% of their subscribed capital as a contribution to the operational costs of the ECB. ... Non-euro area NCBs are not entitled to receive any share of the distributable profits of the ECB, nor are they liable to cover any loss of the ECB," ECB Annual Report 2017, p. A50.

Table 6.1 *Eurozone's NCBs' contributions to the ECB's capital*

National central bank	Eurozone subscribed capital key %	Eurozone fully paid up capital key %
Nationale Bank van België/ Banque Nationale de Belgique (Belgium)	2.4778	3.52
Deutsche Bundesbank (Germany)	17.9973	25.57
Eesti Pank (Estonia)	0.1928	0.27
Central Bank of Ireland (Ireland)	1.1607	1.65
Bank of Greece (Greece)	2.0332	2.89
Banco de España (Spain)	8.8409	12.56
Banque de France (France)	14.1792	20.14
Banca d'Italia (Italy)	12.3108	17.49
Central Bank of Cyprus (Cyprus)	0.1513	0.21
Latvijas Banka (Latvia)	0.2821	0.40
Lietuvos bankas (Lithuania)	0.4132	0.59
Banque centrale du Luxembourg (Luxembourg)	0.203	0.29
Central Bank of Malta (Malta)	0.0648	0.09
De Nederlandsche Bank (The Netherlands)	4.0035	5.69
Oesterreichische Nationalbank (Austria)	1.9631	2.79
Banco de Portugal (Portugal)	1.7434	2.48
Banka Slovenije (Slovenia)	0.3455	0.49
Národná banka Slovenska (Slovakia)	0.7725	1.10
Suomen Pankki – Finlands Bank (Finland)	1.2564	1.78
Total	70.3915	100.00

Source: ECB, www.ecb.europa.eu/ecb/orga/capital/html/index.en.html

"own-risk" assets held by and activities undertaken by an individual NCB mean that profits and losses associated with these assets and activities are for the account of the NCB alone. "Shared risk" means that profits and losses are shared according to the capital key shares in the paid-up capital of the ECB.

6.3 A POTENTIALLY FATAL FLAW IN THE DESIGN OF THE EUROSYSTEM

As noted earlier, the Eurosystem has twenty independent profit-and-loss centers: the ECB and the nineteen NCBs. Normal, unitary central banks (that is, central banks that have a single profit-and-loss center) cannot be forced into default or insolvency if they don't have a material amount of foreign-currency-denominated debt. This is because a unitary central bank can "print money" to pay its bills; that is, it can either literally print currency notes or create demand deposits or reserves held with the central bank that are legal tender or freely convertible into legal tender at a fixed exchange rate. This ability to create central bank money or base money at will at effectively zero marginal cost is, however, not part of the toolkit of an individual NCB in the Eurosystem. Central bank money creation is a collective decision. It requires a majority on the Governing Council (GC) of the ECB. It follows that, for an individual NCB, its euro-denominated liabilities are de facto like foreign currency liabilities. Unless all its assets are shared-risk, an individual NCBs can therefore go broke/become insolvent/go bankrupt if its *comprehensive net worth* becomes negative, even if the Eurosystem as a whole is solvent.

The problem of own-risk activities can be traced right to Protocol (No 4) of the Treaty on the Functioning of the European Union (TFEU) "On the Statute of the European System of Central Banks and of the European Central Bank." It first, and entirely appropriately, defines, in Article 3, the tasks of the European System of Central Banks (ESCB) to be "to define and implement the monetary policy of the Union" ... "to conduct foreign-exchange operations consistent with ... Article 219" ... "to hold and manage the official foreign reserves of the Member States"; ... "to promote the smooth operation of payment systems." and "to contribute to the smooth conduct of policies pursued by the competent authorities relating to the pruden-tial supervision of credit institutions and the stability of the financial system."[7] Unfortunately, Article 14.4 opens the door to own-risk activities: "National central banks may perform functions other than those specified in this Statute unless the Governing Council finds, by a majority of two thirds of the votes cast, that these interfere with the objectives and tasks of the ESCB. Such functions shall be performed on the responsibility and liability of national central banks and shall not be regarded as being part of the functions of the ESCB."

Note, however, that the Protocol also asserts that the sum of the "monetary incomes" of the NCBs, (where monetary income is defined as "the income accruing to the national central banks in the perfor-mance of the ESCB's monetary policy function"[8]) shall be allocated to the NCBs in proportion to their capital key shares in the capital of the ECB (Article 32.5). Likewise, the net profit of the ECB, after an appro-priate transfer to the general reserve fund, is to be distributed to the Eurosystem NCBs in proportion to their capital key shares (Article 33.1). This suggests that the own-risk provision applied to 80 percent of the purchases under the Public Sector Purchase Programme (PSPP) is in direct violation of the Treaty, as the expanded Asset Purchase Programme (APP) (which includes the PSPP), clearly is an integral part of the implementation of the monetary policy function.[9]

---

[7]   The ESCB would normally include the central banks of the EU member states that are not part of the EA. In the current context, it refers exclusively to the Eurosystem.

[8]   Protocol (No 4), Article 32.1.

[9]   Indeed, according to the ECB's website "The expanded asset purchase programme (APP) includes all purchase programmes under which private sector securities and public sector securities are purchased to address the risks of a too prolonged period of low inflation. It consists of the

- corporate sector purchase programme (CSPP)
- public sector purchase programme (PSPP)
- asset-backed securities purchase programme (ABSPP)
- third covered bond purchase programme (CBPP3)" www.ecb.europa/mopo/imple ment/omt/html/index.en.html.

The main own-risk assets and activities are the following:

(i) **Gross assets held under the Agreement on Net Financial Assets (ANFA).** In the words of the ECB: "The Agreement on Net Financial Assets (ANFA) is an agreement between the national central banks (NCBs) of the euro area and the European Central Bank (ECB), which together form the Eurosystem. The agreement sets rules and limits for holdings of financial assets which are related to national tasks of the NCBs. ... ANFA was established to set an overall limit to the total net amount of financial assets relating to national, nonmonetary policy tasks, such that they would not interfere with monetary policy."[10]

It would, of course, be helpful if we are to evaluate the amount of balance sheet risk an NCB takes on in the pursuit of its national tasks, to have data readily available on the individual NCBs' GFAs (gross financial assets) and GFLs (gross financial liabilities) whose difference equals the NFA (net financial assets). We now have to extract them laboriously from the Eurosystem's balance sheets. During 2015, the Eurosystem's aggregate NFA averaged €518 bn.[11] By 2017, Eurosystem NFA had come down to €105 bn and by 2018 it averaged –€108 bn. The numbers differ vastly across countries (Table 6.2). During 2018, Germany averaged NFA worth –€241 bn while Italy averaged €95bn.[12]

Now included in ANFA activities are Eurosystem lending operations under Emergency Liquidity Assistance (ELA). Although the lender-of-last-resort-operations conducted by a number of central banks under ELA would seem to fall squarely under the core competencies of the Eurosystem ("to contribute to the smooth conduct of policies pursued by the competent authorities relating to the prudential supervision of credit institutions and the stability of the financial system"), ELA operations have been designated own-risk. The ELA data appear as Asset Item 6 on the balance sheet of the Consolidated Eurosystem "Other claims on euro area credit institutions denominated in euro." It amounted to €48.3 bn on May 4, 2018.

---

[10]   www.ecb.europa.eu/explainers/tell-me-more/html/anfa_qa.en.html.
[11]   Source: ECB www.ecb.europa.eu/press/pr/date/2016/html/pr160205.en.html.
[12]   Annual average net financial assets according to ANFA (in EUR million; adjusted for the amount of securities lending against cash collateral carried out under the Asset Purchase Programme. Source: ECB www.ecb.europa.eu/explainers/tell-me-more/shared/data/annual_average_nfa.en.xlsx.

Table 6.2 *ANFA assets*

AT	7,769
BE	12,140
CY	−937
DE	−240,670
EE	−86
ES	25,211
FI	311
FR	3,515
GR	1,528
IE	7,091
IT	95,208
LT	2,262
LU	−3,393
LV	4,287
MT	764
NL	−11,587
PT	6,434
SI	−1,673
SK	−17,874
ECB	1,828
Eurosystem	−107,872

(ii) **Lending operations under the de facto resurrected tier-2 collateral system.** Here an NCB is responsible for any losses on collateral accepted (with the approval of the ECB) by that NCB but not generally accepted in the Eurosystem. The original two-tier collateral framework, in operation since the start of EMU to handle idiosyncratic legacy national collateral, was replaced on January 1, 2007, by a single collateral system. On October 15, 2008, the Governing Council decided to expand – initially until the end of 2009 – the list of eligible Eurosystem collateral on a temporary basis. This was the first of a sequence of collateral standards reductions.[13] Lending against this new, lower-grade collateral is at the own risk of the NCB providing the credit. There appear to be no publicly available data on

[13]   See Eberl and Weber (2014) and Bindseil et al. (2017)

how much of this "temporary" tier-2 collateral has been accepted by NCBs at their own risk and how much, if any, remains outstanding.

(iii) **Own-risk asset purchases under the PSPP.** Under the expanded asset purchase programme announced by the ECB on January 22, 2015, 80 percent of the additional asset purchases under the PSPP (consisting of bonds issued by EA central governments, agencies and European institutions) were own-risk. About €1.56 trillion worth of public debt purchased under the PSPP component of the ECB's QE program is therefore own-risk.[14]

The own-risk assets and activities matter because there is a lot of risk attached to some of them. Table 6.3 gives the sovereign risk ratings for the nineteen EA member states.

Only three of the nineteen sovereigns (Germany, Luxembourg and the Netherlands) are rated AAA by all four rating agencies. France is rated AAA by DBRS only. Greece and Cyprus are rated non–investment grade by all four rating agencies. Italy is rated lower medium grade by all four agencies.

6.4 CONVENTIONAL AND COMPREHENSIVE BALANCE SHEETS IN THE EUROSYSTEM

To gain greater precision about the financial vulnerability of an NCB, we construct the conventional and comprehensive balance sheets of the ECB and then the conventional and comprehensive balance sheets of the Banca d'Italia. The comprehensive balance sheet of the consolidated Eurosystem turns out to be an essential input into the construction of the comprehensive balance sheet of each individual NCB.

For the formal approach to the balance sheets we use the following notation: there are K national central banks (currently $K = 19$). A^*_{ECB} is the stock of foreign assets of the ECB, including gold and foreign exchange reserves held by the ECB; L^*_{ECB} is the stock of foreign liabilities of the ECB;[15] $D^{g_j}_{ECB}$ is the stock of debt of Eurozone member

---

[14] The cumulative monthly net purchases under the PSPP were €1.95 trillion on April 6, 2018. Source: ECB.

[15] Foreign assets and liabilities can be denominated either in euro or in foreign currency. The same holds for claims on EA entities.

Table 6.3 *Sovereign ratings for EA member states*

	S&P	Moody's	Fitch	DBRS
Belgium	AA	Aa3	AA–	AA (high)
Cyprus	BB+	Ba3	BB	BB (low)
Czech Rep.	AA–	A1	A+	
Estonia	AA–	A1	A+	AA (low)
Finland	AA+	Aa1	AA+	AA (high)
France	AA	Aa2	AA	AAA
Germany	AAA	Aaa	AAA	AAA
Greece	B	B3	B	CCC (high)
Ireland	A+	A2	A+	A (high)
Italy	BBB	Baa2	BBB	BBB (high)
Latvia	A–	A3	A–	A (low)
Lithuania	A	A3	A–	A (low)
Luxembourg	AAA	Aaa	AAA	AAA
Malta	A–	A3	A+	A (high)
Netherlands	AAA	Aaa	AAA	AAA
Portugal	BBB–	Ba1	BBB	BBB (low)
Slovakia	A+	A2	A+	A (high)
Slovenia	A+	Baa1	A–	A
Spain	A–	Baa2	A–	A

Source: Tradingeconomics.com, April 13, 2018, https://tradingeco
nomics.com/euro-area/rating

state government j held by the ECB; $D^{p_j}_{ECB}$ is the stock of private debt from Eurozone member state j held by the ECB; this includes both securities bought outright and collateralized loans; M_{ECB} is the monetary base issued by the ECB; N^j_{ECB} are the nonmonetary liabilities of the ECB owed to residents of Eurozone member state j; A^j_{ECB} are the gross (mostly Target2) liabilities of the ECB to the NCB of member state j; L^j_{ECB} are the gross (mostly Target2) claims of the ECB on the NCB of member state j and W_{ECB} is the conventional net worth, equity or capital of the ECB. All activities undertaken by the ECB are assumed to be shared-risk.

6.4.a Conventional and Comprehensive Balance Sheets of the ECB

The conventional balance sheet of the ECB is given in Table 6.4:

The gross assets and liabilities vis-à-vis the rest of the Eurozone of the ECB (mostly Target2) are large. In the ECB balance sheet of December 31, 2017, the claims on euro area NCBs in respect of Target2, (most of $\sum_{j=1}^{K} L_{ECB}^{j}$), were €1,047 bn; claims by euro area NCBs on the ECB in respect of Target2, (most of $\sum_{j=1}^{K} A_{ECB}^{j}$), were €1,264 bn, making for a net ECB liability in respect of Target2 of €217 bn.[16] In its

Table 6.4 *Conventional balance sheet of the ECB, December 31, 2017; € bn*

Assets			Liabilities		
A_{ECB}^{*}	Claims on foreigners	62.0	L_{ECB}^{*}	Foreign liabilities	19.5
$\sum_{j=1}^{K} D_{ECB}^{g_j}$	Claims on EA governments	258.5	M_{ECB}	Monetary base	93.6
$\sum_{j=1}^{K} D_{ECB}^{p_j}$	Claims on EA private sector		$\sum_{j=1}^{K} N_{ECB}^{j}$	Nonmonetary liabilities to EA	3.8
$\sum_{j=1}^{K} L_{ECB}^{j}$	Mostly Target2 claims on NCBs	1,140.9	$\sum_{j=1}^{K} A_{ECB}^{j}$	Mostly Target2 liabilities to NCBs	1,304.8
			W_{ECB}	Conventional net worth	38.7
Total Assets		1,461.4	Total Liabilities		1,460.4

Assets and liabilities don't necessarily add up because of rounding errors
Source: Annual Accounts of the ECB, 2017

---

[16] Source: ECB, Annual Accounts of the ECB, 2017, p. A44. The balance sheet in the ECB publication only shows the net Target2 liability of the ECB; figure 8.2 includes the gross Target2 assets and liabilities.

own accounts, the ECB nets out its Target2 assets against its Target2 liabilities, which shrinks its balance sheet by more than €1 trillion. We consider this netting operation undesirable, because it results in an understatement of the balance sheet risk of the ECB.

The conventional net worth of the ECB can be negative without this implying that the ECB is insolvent. As long as its financial commitments are denominated in euro, it can always meet them by creating additional base money and use this to pay any outstanding or future bills.

Formally, as noted in Chapter 2, the comprehensive balance sheet of any entity is its intertemporal budget constraint with a "no-Ponzi finance" terminal condition imposed. The comprehensive balance sheet of the ECB adds a "hidden asset" to the conventional balance sheet: the present discounted value of the future seigniorage profits of the ECB: $V\big(\{(i - i^M)M_{ECB}, I\}\big)$.[17] Because the rate of return on the assets of a central bank tends to exceed the interest rate on its monetary liabilities, monetary issuance is a profitable business. We also have to add an intangible liability – the present discounted value of current and future operating costs (salaries and other nonwage benefits, supplies, depreciation of tangible assets etc.), denoted $V(\{C_{ECB}, I\})$, where C_{ECB} stands for the cost of running the ECB in a period. The comprehensive net worth of the ECB is denoted $\hat{W}_{ECB}$. The ECB is insolvent if its comprehensive net worth is negative. The comprehensive net worth of a central bank is the maximum amount of resources the beneficial owner(s) can extract from the central bank in present discounted value terms without causing it to become insolvent. If this amount is negative, we call the central bank insolvent. Its beneficial owner(s) (or indeed any other interested party) could, of course, come to the rescue with a capital injection to return the comprehensive net worth of the central bank to a nonnegative value.

Unless there are material foreign-currency-denominated liabilities, insolvency is always a choice for the Governing Council of the

---

[17] We ignore the second component of the seigniorage profit stream, the PDV of the terminal monetary base, $V(\{\lim_{T\to\infty} M_{ECB,T}, I\})$, effectively assuming this to be zero. It would have to be considered if the economy were in a long-lasting liquidity trap.

ECB rather than a necessity. There could, however, be circumstances where the amount of additional base money that would have to be issued to meet the financial commitments of the ECB might be incompatible with its price stability mandate.

The comprehensive balance sheet of the ECB is given in Table 6.5.

The seigniorage number is based on an estimate in Buiter (2013) of Eurozone-wide seigniorage from the issuance of banknotes only. The calculations assume a constant long-run growth rate of real GDP of 1 percent, a constant long-run inflation rate of 2 percent and a constant long-run nominal interest rate of 4 percent. Translated to the present (with the total stock of banknotes in circulation on December 31, 2017, estimated at €1,170.7 bn) this would produce an estimate of the PDV of current and future seigniorage for the consolidated Eurosystem of around €4,062.3 bn. Assigning the ECB's share of this on the basis of its share of the stock of banknotes in circulation on December 31, 2017, gives us an estimate for the PDV of ECB seigniorage of €325.1 bn.

According to the ECB's Annual Report 2017 (Table 6.6), its operating expenses in 2017 were €1.086 bn.[18] We recognize that part of these costs reflect the regulatory and supervisory role of the ECB which is in principle operationally and institutionally separable from its monetary policy role. In 2013, the last year before the ECB assumed a regulatory and supervisory role, operating expenses were €527bn. We will use the 2017 number for our calculations, but the reader is free to substitute his/her own guestimates. We assume that operating expenses stay constant in real terms in the future and that the inflation rate of the operating expenses is 2 percent per annum. The nominal discount rate is again assumed to be 4 percent per annum.[19] Given these assumptions, the PDV of ECB operating costs in that case is

---

[18]   See ECB Annual Report 2017, www.ecb.europa.eu/pub/pdf/annrep/ecb.ar2017.en.pdf, Chart 11, p. A13.

[19]   Using market-consistent discount rates would result in infinite numbers both for the PDV of future seigniorage and the PDV of future operating costs.

Table 6.5 *Comprehensive balance sheet of the ECB, December 31, 2017; €bn*

Assets			Liabilities		
A_{ECB}^*	ECB Claims on foreigners	62.0	L_{ECB}^*	Foreign liabilities	19.5
$\sum_{i=1}^{K} D_{ECB}^{g_i}$	ECB Claims on EA governments	258.5	M_{ECB}	Monetary base	93.7
$\sum_{i=1}^{K} D_{ECB}^{p_i}$	ECB Claims on EA private sector		$\sum_{i=1}^{K} N_{ECB}^i$	Nonmonetary liabilities to EA	3.8
$\sum_{i=1}^{K} L_{ECB}^i$	ECB Target2 claims on NCBs	1,140.9	$\sum_{i=1}^{K} A_{ECB}^i$	Mostly Target2 liabilities to NCBs	1,304.8
$V\big(\{(i - i^M)M_{ECB}, I\}\big)$	Present value of ECB seigniorage	325.1	$V(\{C_{ECB}, I\})$	Present value of ECB running costs	54.8
			$\hat{W}_{ECB}$	ECB Comprehensive net worth	310.0
Total Assets		1,786.5	**Total liabilities**		1,786.5

Source: ECB and own calculations

Table 6.6 *NCB operating costs*

Eurosystem country	NCB operating (Millions EUR)
France	2,169
Italy	1,965
Germany	1,498
ECB	1,086
Spain	489
Belgium	440
Greece	391
Netherlands	379
Austria	379
Ireland	276
Portugal	208
Finland	82
Slovakia	81
Luxembourg*	81
Cyprus*	43
Slovenia	38
Latvia	38
Lithuania	34
Estonia	20
Malta	19
Total	**9,718**

Source: ECB and NCB financial statements
* Cyprus and Malta data for 2016, all others for 2017.

€54.8 bn. The estimated comprehensive net worth of the ECB is thus estimated to be €310 bn – almost the same as the PDV of its seigniorage.

6.4.b Conventional and Comprehensive Balance Sheets of an NCB

To determine how vulnerable an individual NCB is to insolvency risk, we first consider the conventional balance sheet of the NCB. In the

Eurosystem, it is key to distinguish between two kinds of activities undertaken by an NCB and the associated assets and liabilities. The first are "shared-risk" activities. In theory, this should include all assets and liabilities put on the balance sheet as part of the implementation of the common monetary, credit and exchange-rate policies. Any profits or losses incurred in the pursuit of "shared-risk" activities are shared in proportion to the capital key. In practice, as noted earlier, a significant share – 80 percent – of the PSPP asset purchases and all ELA asset acquisitions have been designated "own-risk." Any profits or losses incurred on these assets (and on the ANFA and tier-2 collateral mark-2 assets) are for the sole account of the NCB taking the asset on its balance sheet.

We consider an individual NCB, labeled i. $A_i^{*,o}$ is the value of the stock of gold and foreign exchange reserves and other foreign assets of NCB i held on an own-risk basis; $A_i^{*,s}$ is the value of the stock of gold and foreign exchange reserves and other foreign assets of NCB i held on a shared-risk basis; $L_i^{*,o}$ is the value of the stock foreign liabilities of NCB i held on an own-risk basis; $L_i^{*,s}$ is the value of the stock foreign liabilities of NCB i held on a shared-risk basis; $D_i^{g_j,o}$ is the stock of Eurozone government j debt held on an own-risk basis by NBC i; $D_i^{g_j,s}$ is the stock of debt of Eurozone government j debt held on a shared-risk basis by NBC i; $D_i^{p_j,o}$ is the stock of claims on the private sector of Eurozone member state j held on an own-risk basis by NBC i; $D_i^{p_j,s}$ is the stock of claims on the private sector of Eurozone member state j held on a shared-risk basis by NCB i; $A_{ECB}^{i,0}$ is the stock of claims on the ECB (mostly Target2) held on an own-risk basis by NBC i; $A_{ECB}^{i,s}$ is the stock of claims on the ECB (mostly Target2) held on a shared-risk bases by NCB i.[20] $L_{ECB}^{i,0}$ is the stock of liabilities to the ECB (mostly Target2) held by NBC i on an own-risk basis; $L_{ECB}^{i,s}$ is the stock of liabilities to the ECB (mostly Target2) held by NBC i on a shared-risk basis;[21] M_i is the stock of central bank money or the monetary base issued by NBC i; M_i^o is the own-risk component and M_i^s the

[20] $A_{ECB}^i = A_{ECB}^{i,o} + A_{ECB}^{i,s}$ [21] $L_{ECB}^i = L_{ECB}^{i,o} + L_{ECB}^{i,s}$

shared-risk component;[22] $N_i^{j,o}$ is the stock of nonmonetary liabilities to residents of Eurozone member state j held on an own-risk basis by NCB i; $N_i^{j,s}$ is the stock of nonmonetary liabilities to residents of Eurozone member state j held on a shared-risk basis by NCB i; W_i is the conventional net worth, equity or capital of NCB i; σ_i is the capital key share of NCB i, $\sum_{j=1}^{K} \sigma_j = 1$; and $\hat{W}_i$ is the comprehensive net worth of NCB i.

The conventional balance sheet of NCB i given in Table 6.7 for the Banca d'Italia is pretty self-explanatory. National central bank i has external liabilities and domestic monetary and nonmonetary liabilities. The nonmonetary liabilities are either to residents of Eurozone member state i or to residents of other Eurozone member states. There are both own-risk and shared-risk liabilities. On the asset side of the conventional balance sheet we have the stock of gold and foreign exchange reserves and other foreign assets (own-risk and shared-risk), Eurozone government bonds (own-risk and shared-risk) and claims on the Eurozone private sector (own-risk and-shared risk). There are also the (mostly) Target2 claims and liabilities of NCB i to the ECB. Note that conventional net worth, W_i can be negative without this implying insolvency of NCB i as long as that NCB can exercise its claim to its capital key share of the PDV of future shared profits of the Eurosystem.

The comprehensive balance sheet of the national central bank differs from the conventional one in three ways. First, it adds the intangible seigniorage asset: the NCB's share of the present discounted value of future profits earned by the Eurosystem through its ability to issue central bank money whose interest rate is normally below the interest rate on central bank assets. Second, it adds the intangible liability of the PDV of the own-risk cost of running NCB i, $V(\{C_i^o, I\})$, and the capital key share of the shared-risk cost of running the entire Eurosystem, $\sigma_i V\left(\left\{C_{ECB} + \sum_{j=1}^{K} C_j^s, I\right\}\right)$. We assume the

---

[22] $M_i = M_i^o + M_i^s$

Table 6.7 *Conventional balance sheet of NCB i, Banca d'Italia, December 31, 2017; €bn*

Assets			Liabilities		
Own-risk claims on foreigners	$A_i^{*,o}$	127.7	Own-risk liabilities to foreigners	$L_i^{*,o}$	11.1
Shared-risk claims on foreigners	$A_i^{*,s}$		Shared-risk liabilities to foreigners	$L_i^{*,s}$	
Own-risk claims on EA governments	$D_i^{g_i,o} + \sum_{\substack{j=1 \\ j\neq i}}^{K} D_i^{g_j,o}$		Own-risk monetary base	M_i^o	331.0
Shared-risk claims on EA governments	$D_i^{g_i,s} + \sum_{\substack{j=1 \\ j\neq i}}^{K} D_i^{g_j,s}$	757.3	Shared-risk monetary base	M_i^s	
Own-risk claims on EA private sector	$D_i^{p_i,o} + \sum_{\substack{j=1 \\ j\neq i}}^{K} D_i^{p_j,o}$		Own-risk nonmonetary liabilities to EA	$N_i^{i,o} + \sum_{\substack{j=1 \\ j\neq i}}^{K} N_i^{j,o}$	53.9
Shared-risk claims on EA private sector	$D_i^{p_i,s} + \sum_{\substack{j=1 \\ j\neq i}}^{K} D_i^{p_j,s}$		Shared-risk nonmonetary liabilities to EA	$N_i^{i,s} + \sum_{\substack{j=1 \\ j\neq i}}^{K} N_i^{j,s}$	
Own-risk mostly Target assets	$A_{ECB}^{i,o}$	47.2	Own-risk mostly Target2 liabilities	$L_{ECB}^{i,o}$	437.6
Shared-risk mostly Target assets	$A_{ECB}^{i,s}$		Shared-risk mostly Target Liabilities	$L_{ECB}^{i,s}$	
			Conventional net worth [23]	W_i	98.5
Total Assets		932.2	**Total Liabilities**		932.2

Assets and liabilities don't necessarily add up because of rounding errors.

[23]   This is the sum of provisions, revaluation accounts and capital and reserves.

ECB's running costs are entirely shared-risk. Third, it adds the (contingent) assets and liabilities associated with shared-risk activities that are omitted from the conventional balance sheet. This includes the NCB's capital key share of the own-risk assets and liabilities included in the conventional balance sheet. The comprehensive balance sheet for an NCB is shown in Table 6.8.

We cannot fill in the actual figures for the Banca d'Italia because we don't know the breakdown of assets and liabilities between own-risk and shared-risk. We will therefore only look at some special cases: first, when there is only shared risk and, second, when there is no shared risk or shared risk only through the ECB.

6.4.c Conventional and Comprehensive Balance Sheets of the Consolidated Eurosystem

The conventional balance sheet of the consolidated Eurosystem is given in Table 6.9 and the comprehensive balance sheet of the consolidated Eurosystem in Table 6.10; W denotes the conventional net worth of the consolidated Eurosystem and $\hat{W}$ its comprehensive net worth.

Note that the Target2 assets and liabilities cancel out in the consolidated balance sheets of the Eurosystem that covers all debtors and creditors – Target2 is a closed system.

In Tables 6.9 and 6.10 we could have added together own-risk and shared-risk assets and liabilities.

The total annual operating cost of the Eurosystem were €9,7 bn in 2017. Our assumption of constant real operating costs, 2 percent inflation and a 4 percent nominal discount rate then results in a PDV of current and future operating costs of €495.6 bn.

6.4.d What Is the Loss Exposure of an NCB?

The comprehensive NCB balance sheet in Table 6.8 presents a potentially very different picture of the financial strength or vulnerability of an NCB from that presented by the conventional balance sheet in Table 6.7. The own-risk assets and liabilities are, of course unaffected.

Table 6.8 Comprehensive balance sheet of NCB i

Assets		Liabilities	
Own-risk claims on foreigners	$A_i^{*,o}$	Own-risk liabilities to foreigners	$L_i^{*,o}$
Shared-risk claims on foreigners	$\sigma_i\left(A_{ECB}^* + \sum_{j=1}^K A_j^{*,s}\right)$	Shared-risk liabilities to foreigners	$\sigma_i\left(L_{ECB}^* + \sum_{j=1}^K L_j^{*,s}\right)$
Own-risk claims on EA governments	$D_i^{g_i,o} + \sum_{\substack{j=1 \\ j\neq i}}^K D_i^{g_j,o}$	Own-risk monetary base	M_i^o
Shared-risk claims on EA governments	$\sigma_i\sum_{\ell=1}^K\left(\dfrac{D_{ECB}^{g_\ell} + D_i^{g_\ell,s}}{K} + \sum_{\substack{j=1 \\ j\neq i}}^K D_\ell^{g_j,s}\right)$	Shared-risk monetary base	$\sigma_i\left(M_{ECB} + \sum_{i=1}^K M_i^s\right)$
Own-risk claims on EA private sector	$D_i^{p_i,o} + \sum_{\substack{j=1 \\ j\neq i}}^K D_i^{p_j,o}$	Own-risk nonmonetary liabilities to EA	$N_i^{i,o} + \sum_{\substack{j=1 \\ j\neq i}}^K N_i^{j,o}$
Shared-risk claims on EA private sector	$\sigma_i\sum_{\ell=1}^K\left(\dfrac{D_{ECB}^{p_\ell} + D_i^{p_\ell,s}}{K} + \sum_{\substack{j=1 \\ j\neq i}}^K D_\ell^{p_j,s}\right)$	Shared-risk nonmonetary liabilities to EA	$\sigma_i\sum_{\ell=1}^K\left(\dfrac{N_{ECB}^\ell + N_i^{\ell,s}}{K} + \sum_{\substack{j=1 \\ j\neq i}}^K N_\ell^{j,s}\right)$

$A_{ECB}^{i,o}$	Own-risk mostly Target2 claims	$L_{ECB}^{i,o}$	Own-risk mostly Target2 liabilities
$\sigma_i \sum_{i=1}^{K} A_{ECB}^{i,s}$	Shared-risk mostly Target2 claims	$\sigma_i \sum_{i=1}^{K} L_{ECB}^{i,s}$	Shared-risk mostly Target2 liabilities
$V\left(\left\{\{(i - i^M)M_i^o, I\right\}\right)$	Present value of own-risk seigniorage	$V(\{C_i^o, I\})$	Present value of own-risk running costs
$\sigma_i V\left(\left\{\left\{(i - i^M)\left(M_{ECB} + \sum_{j=1}^{K} M_j^s\right)\right\}, I\right\}\right)$	Present value of shared-risk seigniorage	$\sigma_i V\left(\left\{\left(C_{ECB} + \sum_{j=1}^{K} C_j^s\right), I\right\}\right)$	Present value of shared-risk running costs
	Shared-risk seigniorage	$\hat{W}_i$	Comprehensive net worth
Total Assets		Total Liabilities	

Table 6.9 *Conventional balance sheet of the consolidated Eurosystem, December 31, 2017; € bn*

Assets			Liabilities	
$\sum_{i=1}^{K} A_i^{*,o}$		Own-risk claims on foreigners	Own-risk liabilities to foreigners $\sum_{i=1}^{K} L_i^{*,o}$	421.9
$A_{ECB}^* + \sum_{i=1}^{K} A_i^{*,s}$	681.9	Shared-risk claims on foreigners	Shared-risk liabilities to foreigners $L_{ECB}^* + \sum_{i=1}^{K} L_i^{*,s}$	
$\sum_{i=1}^{K}\left(D_i^{g_i,o} + \sum_{\substack{j=1\\j\neq i}}^{K} D_i^{g_j,o}\right)$		Own-risk claims on EA governments	Own-risk monetary base $\sum_{i=1}^{K} M_i^o$	3,050.3
$\sum_{i=1}^{K}\left(D_{ECB}^{g_i} + D_i^{g_i,s} + \sum_{\substack{j=1\\j\neq i}}^{K} D_i^{g_j,s}\right)$	3,779.7	Shared-risk claims on EA governments	Shared-risk monetary base $M_{ECB} + \sum_{i=1}^{K} M_i^s$	
$\sum_{i=1}^{K}\left(D_i^{p_i,o} + \sum_{\substack{j=1\\j\neq i}}^{K} D_i^{p_j,o}\right)$		Own-risk claims on EA private sector	Own-risk nonmonetary liabilities to EA $\sum_{i=1}^{K}\left(N_i^{i,o} + \sum_{\substack{j=1\\j\neq i}}^{K} N_i^{j,o}\right)$	537.2
$\sum_{i=1}^{K}\left(D_{ECB}^{p_i} + D_i^{p_i,s} + \sum_{\substack{j=1\\j\neq i}}^{K} D_i^{p_j,s}\right)$		Shared-risk claims on EA private sector	Shared-risk nonmonetary liabilities to EA $\sum_{i=1}^{K}\left(N_{ECB}^i + N_i^{i,s} + \sum_{\substack{j=1\\j\neq i}}^{K} N_i^{j,s}\right)$	
			Conventional net worth $W = W_{ECB} + \sum_{i=1}^{K} W_i$	460.2
Total Assets	4,471.6		**Total Liabilities**	4,471.6

Source: ECB and own calculations

Table 6.10 *Comprehensive balance sheet of the consolidated Eurosystem, December 31, 2017; € bn*

Assets		Liabilities	
Own-risk claims on foreigners	$\displaystyle\sum_{i=1}^{K} A_i^{*,o}$ 681.9	Own-risk liabilities to foreigners	$\displaystyle\sum_{i=1}^{K} L_i^{*,o}$ 421.9
Shared-risk claims on foreigners	$\displaystyle A_{ECB}^{*} + \sum_{i=1}^{K} A_i^{*,s}$	Shared-risk liabilities to foreigners	$\displaystyle L_{ECB}^{*} + \sum_{i=1}^{K} L_i^{*,s}$
Own-risk claims on EA governments	$\displaystyle\sum_{i=1}^{K}\left(D_i^{g_i,o} + \sum_{\substack{j=1\\ j\neq i}}^{K} D_i^{g_j,o} \right)$	Own-risk monetary base	$\displaystyle\sum_{i=1}^{K} M_i^{o}$
Shared-risk claims on EA governments	$\displaystyle\sum_{i=1}^{K}\left(D_{ECB}^{g_i} + D_i^{g_i,s} + \sum_{\substack{j=1\\ j\neq i}}^{K} D_i^{g_j,s} \right)$ 3,779.7	Shared-risk monetary base	$\displaystyle M_{ECB} + \sum_{i=1}^{K} M_i^{s}$ 3050.3
Own-risk claims on EA private sector	$\displaystyle\sum_{i=1}^{K}\left(D_i^{p_i,o} + \sum_{\substack{j=1\\ j\neq i}}^{K} D_i^{p_j,o} \right)$	Own-risk nonmonetary claims on EA	$\displaystyle\sum_{i=1}^{K}\left(N_i^{i,o} + \sum_{\substack{j=1\\ j\neq i}}^{K} N_i^{j,o} \right)$
Shared-risk claims on EA private sector	$\displaystyle\sum_{i=1}^{K}\left(D_{ECB}^{p_i} + D_i^{p_i,s} + \sum_{\substack{j=1\\ j\neq i}}^{K} D_i^{p_j,s} \right)$	Shared-risk nonmonetary claims on EA	$\displaystyle\sum_{i=1}^{K}\left(N_{ECB}^{i} + N_i^{i,s} + \sum_{\substack{j=1\\ j\neq i}}^{K} N_i^{j,s} \right)$ 537.2

Table 6.10 (cont.)

Assets			Liabilities		
$V\left(\left\{(i-i^M)\sum_{j=1}^{K}M_j^o,\, I\right\}\right)$	Present value of own-risk seigniorage	4,062.3	$V\left(\left\{\sum_{j=1}^{K}C_j^o,\, I\right\}\right)$	Present value of own-risk running costs	496.4
$V\left(\left\{(i-i^M)\left(M_{ECB}+\sum_{j=1}^{K}M_j^s\right),\, I\right\}\right)$	Present value of shared-risk seigniorage		$V\left(\left\{C_{ECB}+\sum_{j=1}^{K}C_j^s,\, I\right\}\right)$	Present value of shared-risk running costs	
			$\hat{W}=\hat{W}_{ECB}+\sum_{i=1}^{K}\hat{W}_i$	Comprehensive net worth	4,017.1
Total Assets		8,522.9	**Total Liabilities**		8,522.9

Source: ECB and own calculations

On the liability side, the effective monetary liability is the sum of the own-risk money stock and the capital key share of the total stock of central bank money issued on a shared-risk basis in the Eurosystem.[24] The same applies to the nonmonetary liabilities. On the asset side, the capital key share of the total stocks of domestic and foreign government bonds held by the entire Eurosystem on a shared-risk basis represents an effective exposure. So does the capital key share of the total stock of shared-risk claims on the private sector held by the Eurosystem. Each NCB is also exposed to its capital key share of the gold and foreign exchange reserves and other foreign assets held by the ECB. Finally, there is the intangible asset of the present discounted value of future seigniorage revenue and the intangible liability of the PDV of future running costs. NCB i is entitled to its capital key share of the shared-risk seigniorage revenue of the Eurosystem as a whole, and can expect to receive it gradually, during normal times, through its capital key share of the profits distributed by the Eurosystem. It is also liable for its capital key share of the PDV of the shared-risk running costs of the Eurosystem.

6.4.e The Case of Full Risk Sharing

Consider the case where there are no own-risk activities, assets and liabilities. In that case, the comprehensive balance sheet of the NCB in Table 6.8 simplifies to the one given in Table 6.11 for Banca d'Italia. From Table 6.1, Italy's capital key share is 0.1749.

Note again that the terms involving the Target2 assets and liabilities cancel out, as there is full risk sharing both with the ECB and with all other NCBs. This means that the comprehensive balance sheet of an NCB under full risk sharing is the same as the comprehensive balance sheet of the consolidated Eurosystem with each of the assets and liabilities multiplied by its ECB capital key share – it is the

---

[24] Note that since central bank money is irredeemable, it is a liability in name only. The holder of a €10 banknote has no claim on the Eurosystem other than for banknotes jointly worth €10. So central bank money is viewed as an asset by the holder but not as a liability in any meaningful sense by the Eurosystem.

Table 6.11 *Comprehensive balance sheet of NCB i under full risk sharing, Banca d'Italia, December 31, 2017; €bn*

Assets			Liabilities		
$\sigma_i\left(A^*_{ECB} + \sum_{j=1}^K A^{*,s}_j\right)$	Shared-risk claims on foreigners	119.3	$\sigma_i\left(L^*_{ECB} + \sum_{j=1}^K L^{*,s}_j\right)$	Shared-risk liabilities to foreigners	73.8
$\sigma_i\sum_{\ell=1}^K\left(D^{g_\ell}_{ECB} + D^{g_\ell,s}_\ell + \sum_{\substack{j=1\\j\neq\ell}}^K D^{g_j,s}_\ell\right)$	Shared-risk claims on EA governments	661.2	$\sigma_i\left(M_{ECB} + \sum_{j=1}^K M^s_j\right)$	Shared-risk base money	533.5
$\sigma_i\sum_{\ell=1}^K\left(D^{p_\ell}_{ECB} + D^{p_\ell,s}_\ell + \sum_{\substack{j=1\\j\neq\ell}}^K D^{p_j,s}_\ell\right)$	Shared-risk claims on EA private sector	710.5	$\sigma_i\sum_{\ell=1}^K\left(N^i_{ECB} + N^{i,s}_i + \sum_{\substack{j=1\\j\neq\ell}}^K N^{j,s}_i\right)$	Shared-risk nonmonetary liabilities to EA	93.9
$\sigma_i V\left(\left\{(i-i^M)\left(\frac{M_{ECB}}{\sum_{j=1}^K M^s_j}\right)\right\}, I\right)$	Present value of shared-risk seigniorage		$\sigma_i V\left(\left\{C_{ECB} + \sum_{j=1}^K C^s_j, I\right\}\right)$	Present value of shared-risk running costs	86.5
			$\hat{W}_i = \sigma_i\left(\hat{W}_{ECB} + \sum_{j=1}^K \hat{W}_j\right)$	Comprehensive net worth	703.3
Total Assets		1,491.0	**Total Liabilities**		1,491.0

Source: Banca d'Italia and own calculations

ECB capital key share of the comprehensive balance sheet of the consolidated Eurosystem. Therefore, an individual NCB can become insolvent if and only if the entire Eurosystem becomes insolvent: $\hat{W}_{ECB} + \sum_{j=1}^{K} \hat{W}_j < 0$. Given limited foreign currency liabilities and a willingness to "print" to prevent default, the Eurosystem and the individual NCB cannot become insolvent. Note that the PDV of future seigniorage is just under 48 percent of total assets for Italy. Even if a disaster befell the other assets, central bank insolvency would be extremely unlikely if a central bank could realize without delay the full value of its share of the PDV of future seigniorage. Although the logic of the comprehensive balance sheet/intertemporal budget constraint appears not to be part of the intellectual and professional toolkit of most central bankers, in the case of full risk sharing a bailout is likely because every NCB is in the same position: if one needs a bailout, they all do.

6.4.f   The Case of No Risk Sharing

Now consider the polar opposite case where there are only own-risk activities, assets and liabilities.

The comprehensive balance sheet of the individual NCB in Table 6.8 now simplifies to the one given in Table 6.12 for Italy. Note that all assets and liabilities are assumed to be own-risk in this case.

Operating expenses for the Banca d'Italia in 2017 were €1,965 million.[25] Making the same assumptions as for the ECB and the consolidated Eurosystem, the PDV of its operating expenses is therefore €100.2 bn.

Table 6.12 represents the case where the Eurosystem has ceased to be an operationally deentralized central bank and has become a currency board system with the ECB at the center and the NCBs hoping that they can retain access to the Target2 system when the

---

[25]   The cumulative monthly net purchases under the PSPP were €1.95 trillion on April 6, 2018. Source: ECB.

Table 6.12 *Comprehensive balance sheet of NCB i without any risk sharing, Banca d'Italia, December 31, 2017; €bn*

Assets			Liabilities	
$A_i^{*,o}$	127.7		Own-risk liabilities to foreigners	$L_i^{*,o}$	11.1
$D_i^{g,o} + \sum_{\substack{j=1 \\ j \neq i}}^{K} D_i^{g,o}$	757.3	Own-risk claims on EA governments	Own-risk liabilities to EA governments	M_i^o	331.0
$D_i^{p,o} + \sum_{\substack{j=1 \\ j \neq i}}^{K} D_i^{p,o}$		Own-risk claims on EA private sector	Own-risk liabilities to EA private sector	$N_i^{i,o} + \sum_{\substack{j=1 \\ j \neq i}}^{K} N_i^{j,o}$	53.9
$A_{ECB}^{i,o}$	47.2	Own-risk claim on Target2	Own-risk Target2 liabilities	$L_{ECB}^{i,o}$	437.6
$V\big(\{(i - i^M)M_i^o, I\}\big)$	653.7	Present value of own-risk seigniorage	Present value of own-risk running costs	$V(\{C_i^o, I\})$	100.2
			Comprehensive net worth	$\hat{W}_i$	652.1
Total Assets	1,585.9		**Total Liabilities**		1,585.9

Source: Banca d'Italia and own calculations

intra-Eurosystem cross-border net balance of payments flows turn against them and there are doubts about their solvency.

In Table 6.12 we calculated "own-risk seigniorage" as the NCB's share of the seigniorage of the consolidated Eurosystem (given in Table 6.10), given by the ratio of the stock of euro currency notes outstanding (at the end of 2017) issued by NCB i to the outstanding stock of currency notes issued by the Eurosystem as a whole. This is the same method we used to calculate the ECB's seigniorage asset, plus the assumption that all currency issued by an NCB is own-risk. For Italy, the seigniorage is a big number – just under seven times conventional net worth.

Note that in Table 6.12 we have considered the extreme case where NCB i does not even share in the profits or losses of the ECB. If we assume instead that the only risk-sharing is through NCB i's equity stake in the ECB, Table 6.12 would be replaced by Table 6.13.[26]

Even if the claims on the ECB, $A_{ECB}^{i,o}$, are considered safe, the NCB is exposed to its national government, $D_i^{g_i,o}$, and private sector, $D_i^{p_i,o}$, and to claims on entities outside the Eurozone, $A_i^{*,o}$. It is even possible that, through legacy assets or ANFA, for instance, there is direct exposure to other Eurozone sovereigns, $\sum_{\substack{j=1 \\ j \neq i}}^{K} D_i^{g_j,o}$, and private debtors, $\sum_{\substack{j=1 \\ j \neq i}}^{K} D_i^{p_j,o}$. Because the individual NCB, as long as it remains part of the Eurosystem, cannot control its own seigniorage revenue, $PDV\{(i - i^M)M_i^o\}$ – since NCB monetary issuance is decided centrally by the Governing Council – it is certainly possible that an NCB goes bust even though all its liabilities are euro-denominated and the Eurosystem as a whole is solvent. In the shared-risk case, it is impossible for a single NCB (or a limited number of NCBs) to become insolvent while other NCBs and the consolidated Eurosystem remain solvent. Such an asymmetry between the financial health of different NCBs creates the risk that a bailout of an individual insolvent NCB by

---

[26] Note that $A_{ECB}^i = A_{ECB}^{i,o} + A_{ECB}^{i,s}$ and $L_{ECB}^i = L_{ECB}^{i,o} + L_{ECB}^{i,s}$

Table 6.13 *Comprehensive balance sheet of NCB i under risk sharing with ECB only, Banca d'Italia*

Assets			Liabilities		
$A_i^{*,o} + \sigma_i A_{ECB}^*$	Claims on foreigners	138.5	Liabilities to foreigners	$L_i^{*,o} + \sigma_i L_{ECB}^*$	14.5
$D_i^{g_i,o} + \sum\limits_{\substack{j=1 \\ j \neq i}}^{K} D_i^{g_j,o} + \sigma_i \sum\limits_{j=1}^{K} D_{ECB}^{g_j}$	Claims on EA governments	802.5	Monetary base	$M_i^o + \sigma_i M_{ECB}$	347.4
$D_i^{p_i,o} + \sum\limits_{\substack{j=1 \\ j \neq i}}^{K} D_i^{p_j,o} + \sigma_i \sum\limits_{j=1}^{K} D_{ECB}^{p_j}$	Claims on EA private sector		Nonmonetary liabilities to EA	$N_i^{i,o} + \sum\limits_{\substack{j=1 \\ j \neq i}}^{K} N_i^{j,o} + \sigma_i \sum\limits_{l=1}^{K} N_{ECB}^l$	54.6
$A_{ECB}^{i,o} + \sigma_i \sum\limits_{j=1}^{K} L_{ECB}^{L_i}$	Mostly Claims on Target2	246.7	Mostly Target2 liabilities	$L_{ECB}^{i,o} + \sigma_i \sum\limits_{j=1}^{K} A_{ECB}^i$	665.8
$V\left(\left\{\left((i - i^M)\binom{M_i^o}{+\sigma_i M_{ECB}}\right), I^i\right\}\right)$	Present value of seigniorage	710.6	Present value of running costs	$V(\{C_i^o + \sigma_i C_{ECB}, I^i\})$	109.8
			Comprehensive net worth	$\hat{W}_i + \sigma_i \hat{W}_{ECB}$	706.2
	Total Assets	1,898.3	**Total Liabilities**		1,898.3

Source: Banca d'Italia and own calculations

the rest of the Eurosystem will not occur. It is even possible that, because of central bankers' unwillingness or inability to think in terms of the comprehensive balance sheet rather than the conventional balance sheet, a financially challenged NCB might not be allowed to "run down" its comprehensive net worth, most of which is accounted for by the seigniorage assets. Indeed, "own-risk" base money issuance by NBC i in this de facto currency board system is a misnomer if "own-risk" is assumed to include discretion and control by the NCB, as $M_{ECB} + \sum_{j=1}^{K}(M_j^o + M_j^s)$ and each of its components are determined centrally.

Clearly, the extreme case of no risk sharing at all (Table 6.12) makes sense only as a description of a situation where the NCB has de facto left the Eurosystem and its nation no longer participates in the Economic and Monetary Union. In that case, the former Eurosystem member is likely to introduce its own currency and thus to restore control over its seigniorage. This is scant comfort if the former Eurozone member state cannot redenominate the bulk of its NCB's liabilities into the new national currency, say because they have not been issued under domestic law. Even if redenomination were possible for most of the sovereign liabilities, the new national currency could lose value in terms of the euro faster than the NCB can boost its seigniorage revenues. Such a high-inflation or hyperinflation episode would be likely if the NCB can cannot redenominate its debt or restructure it some other way. It remains possible even if material debt restructuring is engaged in.

6.4.g Target2 Balances as a Measure of Exposure of an NCB to the Rest of the Eurosystem

Consider the case of no risk sharing shown in Table 6.12. If there are no direct exposures of the NCB to other Eurozone governments $(D_i^{g_j,o} = 0, j = 1, ..., K;\ j{\neq}i)$, nor to the private sectors of other Eurozone member states $(D_i^{p_j,o} = 0, j = 1, ..., K;\ j{\neq}i)$, then the gross exposure of NCB i to the rest of the Eurozone is its gross Target2 assets, $A_{ECB}^{i,o}$. If, in addition, NCB i has no nonmonetary liabilities to the rest of the Eurozone $(N_i^{j,o} = 0, j = 1, ..., K; \ j{\neq}i)$, then the net exposure of NCB i to the rest of the Eurozone is its net Target2 balance, that is, its Target2 assets minus its Target2 liabilities, $A_{ECB}^{i,o} - L_{ECB}^{i,o}$. Note that the Target2 exposure is exposure to the ECB only.[27] The balance sheet becomes like Table 6.14:

Table 6.14 *Comprehensive balance sheet of NCB* i, *without any risk sharing and with exposure to the rest of the Eurosystem only through Target2*

Assets		Liabilities	
$A_i^{*,o}$	Own-risk claims on foreigners	$L_i^{*,o}$	Own-risk liabilities to foreigners
$D_i^{g_i,o}$	Own-risk claims on own government	M_i^o	Own-risk monetary base
$D_i^{p_i,o}$	Own-risk claims on own private sector	$N_i^{i,o}$	Own-risk liabilities to own country residents
$A_{ECB}^{i,o}$	Own-risk claim on Target2	$L_{ECB}^{i,o}$	Own-risk Target2 liabilities
$V\left(\{(i - i^M)M_i^o, I\}\right)$	Present value of own-risk seigniorage	$V(\{C_i^o, I\})$	Present value of own-risk running costs
		$\hat{W}_i$	Comprehensive net worth
Total Assets		Total Liabilities	

[27] Strictly speaking, there are bilateral intra-NCB balances during a trading day: "Intra-ESCB balances result primarily from cross-border payments in the EU that are settled in central bank money in euro. These transactions are for the most part initiated by private entities (i.e. credit institutions, corporations and individuals). They are settled in TARGET2 – the Trans-European Automated Real-time Gross settlement Express Transfer system – and give rise to bilateral balances in the TARGET2 accounts of EU central banks. These bilateral balances are netted and then assigned to the ECB on a daily basis, leaving each national central bank (NCB) with a single net bilateral position vis-à-vis the ECB only. Payments conducted by the ECB and settled in

Table 6.14 represents our interpretation of the view of the Bundesbank's exposure to the rest of the Eurosystem favored by Hans Werner Sinn (2011). Exposure is measured as gross claims of the Bundesbank on Target2 if, in the case of a Eurozone breakup, the Bundesbank honors its Target2 commitments; it is measured as net claims on Target2 if the Bundesbank reneges on its gross Target2 liabilities. Either there is no risk sharing at all in the Eurosystem *and* the equity in the ECB is worthless or NBC i has left the Eurosystem (or the rest of the Eurosystem has collapsed), and existing risk-sharing agreements (including the Buba's equity share in the ECB) are considered null and void. All Target2 assets and liabilities are own-risk in this perspective. The treatment of the own-risk (euro) monetary base for this case is not straightforward. If the Eurosystem has collapsed completely, its currency would, presumably be worthless unless national governments from the former Eurozone guarantee some positive exchange rate of the euros issued in the past by their national central banks vis-à-vis their new currencies.

Following a similar logic, Carmen Reinhart (2018) treats the (gross) Target2 liabilities as the right metric of the Banca d'Italia's debt to the rest of the Eurosystem. Even if the very strong assumptions required for this to be correct are satisfied, one cannot simply add the Banca d'Italia's Target2 gross liabilities (26 percent of GDP in March 2018) to the Italian general government debt to obtain a true picture of the Italian public debt. It is correct that, since the national sovereign is the beneficial owner of its central bank, the accounts of the national central bank should be consolidated with those of the general government. However, the Banca d'Italia also holds a considerable amount of Italian government debt, which should be netted out against the gross Italian government debt outstanding. Although the item "General Government Debt" in the March 31 balance sheet of the Banca

TARGET2 also affect the single net bilateral positions. These positions in the books of the ECB represent the net claim or liability of each NCB against the rest of the European System of Central Banks (ESCB)." Source: ECB, Annual Accounts of the ECB 2017, p. A30.

d'Italia was only €13.9 bn, "Securities of Euro-Area Residents" was €441.6 bn, of which €368.2 bn was "Securities held for monetary policy purposes." It is likely that a large share of this consists of Italian sovereign debt, either held directly or as collateral for lending to Italian banks.

6.4.h The General Case of Partial Risk Sharing

Table 6.8 represent the current operationally relevant case of partial risk sharing – a convex combination of the cases of no risk sharing and full risk sharing, for which we cannot provide the weights because the details of what assets, liabilities and activities are own-risk are not provided in the information made available by the ECB and the NCBs. Apart from the fact that, in our view, the "own-risk" feature infringes the spirit and, in the case of ELA and the own-risk component of the PSPP, likely also the letter of the TFEU, it turns, as noted earlier, the Eurosystem from an operationally decentralized monetary union into a system of currency boards (see also Buiter (2014b, 2015)). If the losses incurred by an NCB are large enough (say because of a default by the own sovereign of the NCB), that NCB can become insolvent because it cannot create euro central bank money at will.

The risk of NCB insolvency are clearly less when we recognize the seigniorage asset, as we do in the comprehensive balance sheet. Note that this intangible asset can only serve as a buffer against insolvency if the NCB can "borrow" against it – not by formally collateralizing future base money issuance but through the confidence it instills in the markets (and the other members of the Eurosystem), who believe that, despite suffering a large loss, the afflicted NCB will be able to meet its current and future obligations because of the (collectively approved) current and future base money issuance by that NCB and the rest of the Eurosystem and the associated profits of which the afflicted NCB will get its proper share.

The Banca d'Italia shows €932.2 bn worth of assets on its conventional balance sheet in Table 6.7, with conventional net worth (again generously interpreted to include revaluation accounts as well as capital and reserves) of €98.5 bn. Again, conventional net worth could easily be wiped out by rather modest capital losses. The comprehensive balance sheet without any risk sharing given in Table 6.12 adds own-risk seigniorage worth €653.7 bn to total assets and comprehensive net worth, which then looks highly secure at €652.1 bn. That picture remains qualitatively intact when we consider the comprehensive balance sheet of the Banca d'Italia under risk sharing with the ECB only, in Table 6.13. It has nonseigniorage assets of €1,187.7 bn (much of its exposure to the Italian sovereign and the Italian banking sector) and comprehensive net worth of €706.2 bn. Again, the Banca d'Italia looks secure against insolvency risk if and only if it is able to "realize" a sizeable share of its seigniorage asset, should it suffer a catastrophic loss.

6.5   HOW TO REDUCE THE RISK EXPOSURE OF THE NCBS

Risk exposures of an NCB that are out of line with the risk exposures of the consolidated Eurosystem are an existential threat to the monetary union. Should a highly exposed NCB suffer losses large enough to turn its comprehensive net worth negative, this NCB would become an ineligible counterparty in Target2. With no "foreign exchange flows" between the NCB and the rest of the Eurosystem, the NCB in question is de facto no longer part of the Eurosystem.

From the preceding discussion, it is apparent that there are only three strategies to reduce the risk exposure of an individual NCB. The first is to permit an NCB, following a capital loss, to borrow, in principle, up to the amount that would reduce its comprehensive net worth to zero. If the markets will not supply that amount of financing, the other members of the Eurosystem should. This was discussed in Section 6.3. This does not repair the fundamental flaw in the design of the Eurosystem – the existence of own-risk activities, assets and liabilities in a central banking system with twenty independent profit-and-loss centers – but it reduces the likelihood of this flaw turning out to be fatal. The second is to reduce the weight of risky assets in its balance sheet – risk reduction. The third is to increase the scale and scope of risk-sharing activities – risk sharing. Both could, severally or jointly, repair the existential defects of the Eurosystem.

6.5.a Increasing the Weight of Risk-Sharing Activities, Assets and Liabilities

Phasing out all "own-risk" activities should be the ultimate aim. The ideal outcome would be for the Eurozone NCBs to cease to be separate legal personalities with individual profit-and-loss accounts and balance sheets and to become instead mere branches of the ECB. But that will be a while in coming. Reducing the scope and size of the own-risk activities should and could start immediately. An immediate start can be made limiting the scale and scope of the four major own-risk activities.

Legacy ANFA assets and liabilities. Continue (and preferably speed up) the shrinking of legacy ANFA activities, assets and liabilities. Do not allow new ANFA activities. Zero ANFA exposure should be the long-run target.

ELA. Continue (and preferably speed up) the cleaning up of the balance sheets of systemically important banks and other financial institutions that need lender-of-last-resort support. When a country's banks have reduced their on- and off-balance sheet risks sufficiently and when they are regulated and supervised fully and effectively by the SSM rather than by national regulators and supervisors, that country's NCB's ELA facility can be turned into a shared-risk facility.

Idiosyncratic collateralized lending. This should and can be phased out promptly. Once the loans secured against this low-grade collateral mature, they should only be renewed against standard collateral acceptable by all NCBs. To replace this reincarnation of legacy tier-2 collateral with lending against collateral that is accepted by all NCBs, there should be a single list of generally acceptable collateral instruments – a "general framework" with no exceptions and no "temporary framework."

Own-risk PSPP purchases. This violation of the spirit and the letter of the TFEU should cease immediately. The flows of new purchases, including reinvestment of maturing debt, should be shared-risk. The existing stock of own-risk assets should be disposed of as soon as possible. If it is deemed desirable not to shrink the balance sheet as a result of the sale of the own-risk PSPP securities, the Eurosystem should replace them with safer assets (see Section 6.5.b).

CACs. All new euro area government securities with a maturity above one year issued on or after January 1, 2013, are subject to the model euro area CAC.[28] This makes hold-out problems less likely during a sovereign debt restructuring. More could be done, however, especially as regards aggregation clauses, to ensure that the pain of any sovereign debt restructuring is shared by the largest number of creditors. Since 2013, the euro area has required new domestic sovereign debt issuance to include a "dual limb" test. A dual restructuring vote requires a qualified majority of all bondholders of the relevant debt as well as a qualified majority of the holders of each individual bond involved in the restructuring. The "single limb" restructuring vote, which the Eurozone is supposed to be headed for by 2022, replaces this with a qualified majority of all the holders of any bonds included in a restructuring. It also deserves consideration to buy back outstanding debt issued before January 2013 and replace it with new debt that is subject to the model euro area CAC, and to repeat this after the single limb test becomes the binding constraint on sovereign debt restructuring.

6.5.b Increasing the Net Supply of Safe(r) Assets

The aim is for the Eurosystem to take the least possible credit risk when it is not engaged in crisis management; that is, not engaged in lender-of-last-resort operations or market-maker-of-last-resort operations. Any new measures, policies, rules, regulations and institutions that improve the creditworthiness of the Eurozone sovereigns and of the national banking systems of the Eurozone can contribute to the

---

[28] See https://europa.eu/efc/sites/efc/files/docs/pages/cac_-_text_model_cac.pdf.

required risk reduction in the assets of the Eurosystem. We will list some of these here. It is also possible, however, to increase the supply of safe(r) sovereign assets through financial engineering, without increasing the average credit quality of the outstanding stock of sovereign debt.

Longer-duration debt instruments issued by the ECB

The ECB could issue bills or bonds that would be held by parties outside the Eurosystem, who would in turn release holdings of safe sovereign debt that the Eurosystem could put on its balance sheet. This could be done without increasing the size of the Eurosystem's balance sheet, say by reducing the amount of excess reserves outstanding. There is an entry "Debt certificates issued" on the balance sheet of the consolidated Eurosystem. It has had a zero outstanding balance for quite some time, but there is no reason why this has to remain so. Private entities that currently hold low-risk sovereign debt may be willing to invest in ECB debt instruments instead, freeing their current holdings of safe sovereign debt for other investors, including the Eurosystem.

6.5.c Financial Engineering Solutions

A simple way to create additional safe(r) assets is through financial engineering.

Sovereign-debt-backed CDOs

Public or private financial entities, including banks, could issue asset-backed securities (ABS) or collateralized debt obligations (CDOs) backed by a pool of sovereign debt instruments and tranched according to seniority. European safe bonds (ESBies, as proposed by Brunnermeier et al. (2011, 2017a, b)) or SBBS (sovereign bond backed securities as proposed by the European Commission (2018)) are examples of such a synthetic safe-instrument proposal. It clearly makes sense to encourage the securitization and tranching of euro area sovereign debt. Debt instruments issued by different sovereigns but similar in other respects (remaining maturity and duration, fixed rate v. floating rate, index-linked etc., issued under domestic law or issued under, say, London law) could be pooled and tranched according to seniority. ABSs or CDOs created by pooling different Eurozone national sovereigns (with weights given by, say, their ECB capital key shares) could make part of the higher risk sovereign debt more liquid. It could help the Eurosystem not to violate the issuer limit and it could facilitate the meeting of any upper limits on exposures to individual sovereigns by commercial banks that may be imposed in the future as part of a deepening banking union.[29] It is not a game changer, but its likely impact would be positive.

Creating ABS backed by the debt of multiple Eurozone sovereigns will only be effective in resolving the shortage of safe assets if the resulting derivative instruments are treated for regulatory purposes, including meeting capital requirements and liquidity requirements, in a manner consistent with the treatment of the individual national sovereigns underlying the ABS and the risk transformation achieved by pooling and tranching. Under current rules, ESBies/SBBS would be treated significantly less favorably than the Eurozone sovereign bonds constituting their underlying portfolio, (e.g. in terms of capital requirements, the eligibility for liquidity coverage and collateral, etc.).

Of course, the junior tranch(es) would be riskier than the pool of underlying assets, but presumably a market can be found for these European unsafe bonds (EUBies) as well if the yield offered is high enough.

Subordinating debt issuance beyond some benchmark
Another way of creating additional safe(r) assets would be by making debt outstanding beyond some verifiable threshold or benchmark junior to the debt below that threshold. This could be applied to existing stocks outstanding or to net new flows, or both. Date of

---

[29] In the proposal of the European Commission (2018), the pool of Eurozone sovereign securities backing the new sovereign bond would be ECB capital key-weighted and the senior tranche would be 70 percent of the overall SBBS issuance.

issuance could determine which bonds are on either side of the threshold. Subordinating new debt issuance to existing debt if certain debt or deficit thresholds/criteria or other fiscal sustainability criteria are violated would, like ESBies/SBBS, not change the overall riskiness of the public debt outstanding, but would split it into riskier debt (the junior issuance) and safer debt (the senior issuance). Over time, making new sovereign debt issuance above the threshold riskier and therefore likely more costly might encourage government behavior conducive to less additional net debt issuance.

Safer issuance by new financial institutions

Another example of a pure financial engineering solution is the E-bond proposal of Leandro and Zettelmeyer (2018). A senior financial intermediary created for the purpose would purchase a portfolio of sovereign debt instruments from EA member states (according to the ECB capital key or some similar metric). By making the intermediary the senior creditor, its bonds would be lower risk: effectively the sovereign debt not purchased by the intermediary but held by other investors would constitute the junior tranche.[30]

Instead of making the intermediary the senior creditor, its debt could be made safer by adding a capital cushion to its balance sheet. This is Leandro and Zettelmeyer's second proposal. The holders of the equity would effectively play the role of the holders of the junior tranche in the tranching proposals. The third proposal of Leandro and Zettelmeyer (2018) turns the intermediary into a leveraged sovereign wealth fund with the initial capital provided by the Eurozone member state governments, in proportion, say, to the ECB capital key. It would invest in a globally diversified portfolio. Its debt could be made as safe as required either by raising the ratio of capital to assets or by changing the risk-return profile of the assets it invests in.

---

[30]   An earlier proposal by Beck and Uhlig (2011) only had the pooling of sovereign assets without granting senior creditor status to the intermediary or adding a material capital cushion.

6.5.d Financial Engineering with Risk Sharing

This refers to ways to increase the supply of safe assets through mutualization of (part of the) existing debt outstanding and/or future sovereign debt issuance (see e.g. De Grauwe and Moesen (2009), Issing (2009) and Rutte (2018); for a recent survey, see Cimadomo et al. (2018)).

Blue and Red bonds

Depla and von Weizsäcker (2010) made a Blue Bond proposal (really a Blue Bond–Red Bond proposal) to address the problems of managing the inherited excessive public debt overhang and creating the right incentives to avoid a recurrence in the future. Under the proposal, EU countries (not just Eurozone member states) should pool up to 60 percent of annual GDP worth of their national debt under joint and several liability as senior sovereign debt, thereby reducing the borrowing cost for that part of the debt. These would be the Blue Bonds. Any sovereign debt beyond a country's Blue Bond allocation should be issued as national and junior debt with sound procedures for an orderly default, thus increasing the marginal cost of public borrowing and helping to enhance fiscal discipline. These would be the Red Bonds. An independent Stability Council would propose annual Blue Bond allocations to member states (up to 60 percent of annual GDP). This would be voted on by member states' parliaments, supposedly to safeguard fiscal responsibility.

This proposal would lower the average cost of borrowing for high credit risk sovereigns. For low credit risk sovereigns, it is likely to raise the average cost of borrowing. It would increase the marginal cost of borrowing beyond the Blue Bond allocation for all sovereigns.

The proposal is likely to be of little interest to the non-Eurozone EU members. We will therefore consider only multicolored bond proposals for the Eurozone member states. Given the differences in economic size between the nineteen Eurozone member states, joint and several liability for all the senior sovereign debt could be viewed as

a bit silly from the perspective of the smaller joint and several guar-
antors, who could be forced into default should the larger member
states default. It might make more sense to have participating countries commit to responsibility/liability for their ECB capital key share
of the outstanding stock of Blue Bonds.

Upside down Blue and Red bonds

The German Council of Economic Experts (2012) proposed mutualizing the sovereign debt of eligible Eurozone governments *above* 60
percent of annual GPD. The program would create a European
Collective Redemption Fund. A European Redemption Pact (ERP)
includes a binding commitment of all participating countries to
bring public debt ratios below the reference value of 60 percent within
the next twenty to twenty-five years. To ensure that this objective can
be reached with realistic primary balances, participating countries can
transfer their excessive debt exceeding the 60 percent threshold at a
certain date, into a redemption fund for which participating member
countries are jointly and severally liable. In the original proposal, the
size of the Redemption Fund was set at €2.3 bn. This number would
likely be different if the proposal were to be implemented today. Only
countries that are not part of a bailout program are eligible to partici-
pate. This proposal looks like a no-hoper for two reasons. First, it relies
on a "binding commitment" that is unlikely to be self-enforcing and
cannot be enforced externally under any plausible future path of EU
supranational power evolution. Second, by mutualizing debt *above* 60
percent of annual GDP, it reduces the marginal cost of new net debt
issuance, creating a perverse incentive to borrow more rather than
less.

6.5.e Other Proposals for Mutualizing (Part of) the Sovereign Debt

The European Commission (2011), in its publications on "Stability
Bonds" considered three different ways to issue joint debt in the
Eurozone.

First, the full substitution by Stability Bond issuance of national issuance, with joint and several guarantees. This could apply to the outstanding stocks and/or future (gross or net) issuance. Without firm central control over national budgets – effectively full fiscal union – such a proposal is a political nonstarter. The transfer of national sovereignty to the supranational level required to achieve the necessary degree of central control over national public debt and deficits also likely makes it a political nonstarter for the time being, both North and South of the Rhine.

Second, the partial substitution by Stability Bond issuance of national issuance, with joint and several guarantees. This amounts to combinations of the Blue Bond–Red Bond and German Council of Economic expert proposals: some share of the existing debt and of new issuance would be converted to jointly and severally guaranteed Eurobonds with national governments remaining individually responsible for the rest.

Third, the partial substitution by Stability Bond issuance of national issuance, with several but not joint guarantees. This amounts to a (restricted version of) the pooling and tranching of (part of) the existing or future Eurozone sovereign debt already discussed.

Common bond issuance for specific programs or projects
There is a range of proposals for limited mutualized EU or Eurozone debt issuance to fund specific, limited projects or programs – with the debt in question either jointly and severally guaranteed or guaranteed according to some other risk sharing rule. Such de facto EU or Eurozone debt exists already, because the European Commission has borrowed €16 bn to fund programs for Hungary, Latvia and Romania under its balance of payments stabilization program.[31] The ESM at the end of 2016 had €85.7 bn worth of debt liabilities outstanding – de facto Eurozone debt guaranteed by capital subscriptions according to the ECB capital key. The next long-term EU budget 2021–2027

---

[31] The EU offers balance of payments assistance to EU countries outside the euro area that are facing problems with their balance of payments.

contains a proposal for a Reform Support Programme, with an overall budget of €25 bn that could be funded by EU debt issuance, in part or fully.[32]

6.5.f Strengthen the Creditworthiness of National Sovereigns

Encourage the pursuit of national sovereign risk-reducing policies
There are many ways to change the incentives and constraints faced by national budgetary policy makers when they make decisions on how much debt to issue. We already discussed the impact of the Blue Bond–Red Bond proposal and of the subordination of new debt to old debt as ways to raise the marginal cost of borrowing without affecting the average cost.

Part of the reason why there has been and continues to be excessive sovereign debt issuance by some sovereigns is the belief that the cost of sovereign default to parties other than the defaulting sovereign (the creditors and all those affected by a sovereign default but unable to express their views effectively through the ballot box or other political mechanisms) is simply too high, and that the creditors and other adversely affected third parties will choose to bail out the insolvent sovereign rather than bear the costs of the default. This may well be correct for large sovereign debtors, like Italy. It may also be correct for smaller sovereign debtors if there is a belief that contagion effects or other spillovers from even a small sovereign default could create a sudden funding stop for a systemically important sovereign.

One way to increase the expected cost of sovereign default to the sovereign is to make it more likely that an insolvent government will have to restructure its debt rather than being bailed out. This requires that there be an orderly sovereign debt restructuring mechanism for Eurozone sovereigns that makes restructuring possible without the defaulting sovereign having to exit the Eurozone and without creating

---

[32]   See European Commission – Press release: EU Budget: A Reform Support Programme and an Investment Stabilisation Function to strengthen Europe's Economic and Monetary Union, Brussels, 31 May 2018, http://europa.eu/rapid/press-release_IP-18-3972_en.htm.

chaos when it remains in the Eurozone. A sovereign debt restructuring facility (SDRF) would combine the ESM with a sovereign debt restructuring authority (SDRA). The SDRA (often referred to as the European Monetary Fund or EMF) would combine real-time debt sustainability analysis with the authority to make access to its funding facilities dependent on sovereign debt restructuring in a manner and of a magnitude it deems necessary. The power to call standstills for debt servicing and to overcome holdout problems should also be part of the SDRA's toolkit. "Single limb" CACs for all the sovereign debt involved in a restructuring would be helpful. The EMF would need enhanced access to whatever resources it may need to act credibly as a sovereign lender of last resort or sovereign debt market maker of last resort, including direct access to ECB funding with a capital key guarantee from the Eurozone sovereigns.

Other proposals for encouraging more responsible fiscal behavior by national sovereigns, such as increased supranational control over national fiscal decisions or more severe punishments for violating the budgetary norms, suffer from political feasibility problems and therefore from credibility problems. The political mood in the EU, including the Eurozone member states, does not favor a further transfer of national competencies to the supranational level. Imposing financial penalties on governments that are already likely to be in financial dire straits is like plucking feathers from a bald frog – unlikely to be effective and successful.

Creating fiscal risk-sharing facilities, including counter-cyclical facilities.

The previous paragraph also implies that proposals like those of French President Emmanuel Macron (2017) to create a supranational finance ministry with material tax, transfer and borrowing powers, and/or significant Eurozone-level counter-cyclical facilities, such as transfers to national governments that are increasing in the national rate of unemployment or the amount of national unemployment benefits paid, are unlikely to be politically feasible for the time being

(see also Marès (2017, 2018)).[33] The new multi-year EU budget proposal presented on May 2, 2018, by the European Commission included a
(small) €30 bn EU stabilization fund, called the European Investment
Stabilisation Function, that would help member state governments to
maintain investment during a cyclical downturn or other economic
rough patch.[34] If this proposal survives, it will be a small symbolic
victory for the principle of counter-cyclical risk sharing.

6.6   HOW TO COPE WITH AN NCB INSOLVENCY THAT CANNOT BE REPAIRED BY ITS SOVEREIGN?

We saw that it is possible for an NCB that is part of the Eurosystem to
become insolvent – unable to meet its financial commitments – presumably because its comprehensive net worth is perceived to be
negative or, more likely, because a majority of the Governing
Council is opposed to allowing an NCB to draw down significantly
the PDV of its future seigniorage entitlement. Italy represents the
most systemic sovereign default risk in the Eurozone and most of
the Italian sovereign debt held by the Eurosystem is held by the
Banca d'Italia for its own risk.

There are three possible scenarios when an NCB is no longer
able to meet its financial commitments and its sovereign is unable or
unwilling to come to the rescue. For concreteness, we assume the
sovereign has lost access to the financial markets and either has
defaulted on its debt or is about to default in the absence of external
financial support.

The first scenario is ex-post mutualization of the losses – a
bailout of the insolvent NCB by the rest of the Eurosystem. This
amounts to admitting that the "own-risk" attribute of 80 percent of
the PSPP should not have been taken seriously: the backdoor mutualization through the PSPP becomes front-door mutualization. That

---

[33]   See Marès (2017, 2018) for a presentation of the case that such significant steps towards
fiscal union are likely to be essential for the survival of the monetary union.

[34]   See European Commission, Press Release: EU budget: Commission proposes a modern
budget for a Union that protects, empowers and defends, Brussels, May 2, 2018, http://
europa.eu/rapid/press-release_IP-18-3570_en.htm.

would certainly solve the problem in the short run for the insolvent NCB and its sovereign, but would create the risk of EA breakup through a voluntary exit of the fiscally strong creditor nations.

It has been argued that the balance sheet destruction and the loss of competitiveness that would be suffered by the fiscally strong creditor nations should there be a Eurexit by a large member state (Italy, say) would dwarf the cost of a bailout. That line of reasoning ignores two arguments that would likely carry weight with Germany and the members of the "New Hanseatic League."[35]

The first argument is that the national fiscal irresponsibility that ultimately caused the insolvency of the NCB is a feature of a repeated game. A bailout today would encourage further fiscal irresponsibility and result in a potentially open-ended sequence of bailouts. Could the net contributors to a bailout make a credible commitment to fund a bailout this time but never again?

The second argument is that the risk of a sharp loss of competitiveness for the remaining members of the Eurozone following the exit of a fiscally weak member state can be controlled by aggressive foreign exchange market intervention aimed at preventing undue appreciation of the trade-weighted exchange rate of the euro, even if the bilateral exchange rate vis-à-vis the euro of the new currency of the exiting nation depreciates sharply.

In the second scenario, the insolvent NCB ceases to be an eligible counterparty in Target2 and thereby effectively ceases to be part of the Eurosystem. Its member state introduces a new national currency and redenominates euro-denominated assets and liabilities issued under national law into the new national currency. It leaves the Eurozone as quickly as possible, as it will be subject to a sovereign funding sudden stop and a bank run until it does. A temporary ban on cross-border financial flows and on bank withdrawals is likely to be part of this scenario.

---

[35] The expression "New Hanseatic League" is sometimes used to refer to the Netherlands, Estonia, Latvia, Lithuania, Sweden, Denmark, Finland and Ireland. Germany and Austria can be viewed as honorary members.

In the third scenario, the sovereign of the insolvent NCB signs up to an ESM program with serious conditionality in exchange for financial support through the outright monetary transactions (OMT) program of the ECB and/or from the ESM itself. Sovereign debt restructuring could be part of this scenario, so having a functioning EMF/SDRA would be helpful. This outcome would likely include capital controls, foreign exchange controls and strict limits on the amount of funds that can be withdrawn from banks in the afflicted nation, as it did in the cases of Greece (in place since 2015) and Cyprus (in place 2013–15). This should be seen as a temporary scenario. It either ends with a transition to the first or second scenario, or it leads to a gradual repair of the fiscal sustainability of the sovereign and with it the balance sheet of its NCB, followed by a lifting of the capital controls and the resumption of normal Eurozone membership.

6.7   CONCLUSION

The design of the Eurosystem was fatally flawed by allowing the nineteen NCBs to remain independent profit-and-loss centers and to continue – and indeed expand – own-risk financial activities that could threaten their solvency. The continued Eurozone membership of a member state whose NCB is insolvent would be at risk. The Eurosystem is not, in its current state, an operationally decentralized central bank but a system of currency boards.

This risk is not imaginary, as evidenced by leaked proposals (admittedly drafted in the heat of an election campaign) for the Eurosystem to forgive €250 bn worth of Italian sovereign debt.[36] If a financially challenged NCB could mobilize a material share of the present discounted value of its future seigniorage income (consistent with the achievement of the inflation target for the Eurozone), NCB insolvency would less likely. We fear that this is unlikely to be the case.

[36]   See: www.reuters.com/article/us-italy-politics-draft/5-star-league-want-ecb-to-for give-250-billion-euros-of-italy-debt-draft-idUSKCN1IG3EM.

The Chapter outlines institutional reforms and policies that could lower the risk of NCB insolvency, including (1) reduce and ultimately eliminate own-risk NCB activities; (2) financial engineering; (3) risk reduction and risk sharing through political and institutional reforms; and (4) recognition of the right of each NCB, in an emergency, to borrow, if necessary from the other Eurosystem participants, de facto against the security of its future inflation-target-compatible seigniorage entitlement.

The weaknesses in the design of the Eurosystem pose an existential risk. Unless they are addressed promptly and effectively, a breakup of the Eurozone, most likely triggered by an Italian sovereign default, is a material risk.

Concluding Remarks

Thirty-six years ago, I argued (in Buiter (1983)) that the comprehensive consolidated public sector balance sheet (now often referred to as the intertemporal budget constraint of the State) is the appropriate tool for analyzing the fiscal, financial and monetary options available to the sovereign. Regardless of the formal degree of operational and/or target independence of a central bank, it is beneficially owned by the fiscal authority/Treasury. Regardless of the formal ownership structures, which can be highly esoteric (some examples were given in Chapter 3), the Treasury receives the bulk of the profits of the central bank.

As regards the magnitude of the profits transferred from the central bank to the Treasury, two important lessons are contained in Chapter 1. First, when the economy is at the effective lower bound (in a liquidity trap), the amount of seigniorage that can be extracted is vast – in Japan up to 10 percent of annual GDP in a given year. This is the territory of Modern Monetary Theory. The reason is that at the ELB the demand for base money becomes effectively unbounded. However, once the economy is away from the ELB and base money demand is constrained by a standard base money demand function, the amount of seigniorage that can be extracted at any constant rate of inflation is small – less than half a percent of GDP on an annual basis in the USA. If we require that this seigniorage has to be extracted at the target rate of inflation, the numbers get even smaller. Even with seigniorage constrained to be extracted at the target rate of inflation, the present discounted value of current and future seigniorage can be a large number indeed. This matters, because it means the central bank has a noninflationary loss absorption capacity that is significantly larger than the conventional financial net worth recorded on the conventional central bank balance sheet. If the inflation constraint is absent (admittedly unlikely), the loss-absorption capacity of a central bank that does not have material foreign-currency-denominated liabilities is effectively infinite. With the Treasury as the beneficial owner of the central bank, sovereign default, when there is no material amount of sovereign foreign-currency-denominated debt outstanding, is always a choice rather than a necessity. Governments have, however, chosen to default on domestic currency debt if the alternatives were deemed sufficiently dire (Reinhart and Rogoff (2009, chapter 7)).

A key insight from Chapter 2 is that unless life at the ELB becomes the norm for the advanced economies, material fiscal tightening is required in most large advanced economies to ensure noninflationary fiscal sustainability. This conclusion assumes that the maximum amount of noninflationary annual seigniorage that can be extracted away from the ELB is 0.5 percent of GDP. If being stuck at the ELB is the new normal, few if any large advanced economies have to engage in material fiscal tightening.

Monetary issuance by the central bank relaxes the IBC of the State for two reasons. First, if the interest rate on central bank money is below the interest rate the central bank earns on its assets, monetary issuance is a profitable business. Second, central bank money is irredeemable. It is therefore an undoubted asset to the holder but not in any meaningful sense a liability to the issuer. This means that even at the ELB, when the interest rate on the central bank's assets (at the margin) does not exceed the own interest rate on the monetary base, monetary issuance by the central bank can relax the IBC of the State. All that is required is that, following an increase in the monetary base, the growth rate of the monetary base equals or exceeds the interest rate at the ELB.

This means that helicopter money drops (monetized public spending increases or tax cuts), analyzed in Chapter 3, can always be scaled up to the point that they boost nominal aggregate demand, both away from and at the ELB. Whether the increase in nominal aggregate demand shows up as an increase in real GDP or higher inflation depends on the amount of slack in the economy.

The importance of the IBC of the State both as a key analytical construct and as the organizing framework for practical analyses of the fiscal options open to the State, now and in the future, makes it all the more important that it be applied properly. This is why it is essential to refute the fiscal theory of the price level, as is done in Chapter 4. The FTPL confuses the IBC of the State, holding with equality and with sovereign debt priced at its contractual value (free of default risk), with an equilibrium bond pricing equation. It fails to recognize that this IBC of the State is implied, in equilibrium, by the IBC of the private sector (holding with equality and with sovereign debt priced at its contractual value) and the economy-wide real resource constraint. Using the same equilibrium condition twice is not acceptable economics. Treating the imposition of the IBC of the State (holding with equality and with sovereign debt priced at its contractual value) as an equilibrium selection mechanism in a world with a continuum of equilibria also has unacceptable economic implications.

The refutation of the FTPL is not just an academic exercise. A policy implication of the FTPL is that sovereign solvency is never a problem. This is not because a government with only domestic-currency-denominated public debt can always print itself out of trouble – the FTPL is supposed to apply even in a world where money exists only as a numeraire and standard of deferred value – and does not exist as a store of value, means of payment or medium of exchange. According to the FTPL, given the stock of nominal government bonds outstanding, the general price level will always assume the value required to make the real value of the bonds equal to the present value of current and future real augmented primary surpluses of the State. Should any real-world government be convinced by this argument, painful fiscal corrections, sovereign default or hyperinflation could be the result when it becomes clear that the FTPL will not come to the rescue of governments implementing arbitrary (non-Ricardian) fiscal-financial-monetary programs.

The logic of the IBC of the State applies at the ELB too. There is, however, a strong case for eliminating the policy asymmetry that prevents the monetary authorities from cutting the policy rate below the level defined by the ELB: zero (the rate of interest on currency) minus the carry cost of currency. We considered, in Chapter 5, three ways of lowering or eliminating the ELB. The first was eliminating currency, possibly replacing it with a central-bank-provided digital currency. A milder version of this approach raises the carry cost of currency by a finite amount by eliminating only the larger denomination currency notes. The second approach was to tax currency through one of a variety of deterministic or stochastic mechanisms. We believe that for this second proposal to work would require rather intrusive and coercive enforcement mechanisms. The third approach would be to keep currency but introduce a variable exchange rate between currency and deposits with the central bank. Arbitrage opportunities could be avoided if the interest rate on central bank deposits were set at, say, –5 percent, by appreciating deposits vis-à-vis currency at a rate of 5 percent. There is, unfortunately, one potential serious snag with this "solution": it requires that deposits rather than currency become the numeraire in the economy. If currency were to become the numeraire instead, the ELB would be restored at its original, currency-determined level.

The relationship between the Treasury and the central bank considered in the first five Chapters of this book is that of a traditional single central bank that is beneficially owned by a single Treasury. In addition we focused on the case where the central bank (and the sovereign) have no material foreign-currency-denominated liabilities. The Eurosystem differs from this benchmark case in a number of key

ways. First, there are nineteen national central banks, each one beneficially owned by its national Treasury, plus the ECB, which is owned
by the nineteen NCBs according to the capital key. Each NCB is
engaged in a significant amount of "own-risk" activities. Second,
monetary issuance (seigniorage) by the Eurosystem as a whole, by
each of the individual NCB and by the ECB, is a collective decision
taken by the twenty-five-member Governing Council of the ECB. This
means that, from the perspective of each individual NCB and its
sovereign, de facto all euro-denominated debt is foreign-currency-
denominated debt. Even if each individual NCB could borrow against
its capital key share of the current and future seigniorage of the
Eurosystem as a whole, an individual NCB can become insolvent
even though the consolidated system as a whole is solvent.

Insolvency of an individual NCB will most likely be the result of
a default by its sovereign, when the NCB in question is highly exposed
to its sovereign. Such is the case in Italy today. How can the
Eurosystem be reformed to turn it into a "normal" operationally
decentralized central bank? Ending all own-risk activities is the
most direct way to address this issue. Unfortunately, this can at best
happen gradually. Reducing the risk that NCBs hold on their balance
sheet by increasing the supply of safer assets is an obvious comple-
mentary strategy. Different approaches are under discussion, from
ECB debt issuance to pure financial engineering and (partial) mutualization of the outstanding stock of national sovereign debt or of new
sovereign debt issuance. Encouraging the pursuit of national sovereign
risk-reducing policies, for instance, by creating a mechanism for the
orderly restructuring of sovereign debt, could also make a material
contribution. It will be a great day for the Eurosystem when it can be
analyzed using the simple framework of Chapter 2 rather than the
complex one of Chapter 6.

References

Abai, K., and K. Murashima. (2017). *On the Fiscal Theory of the Price Level.* Citi Research, Economics, Japan Economics Flash, 9 February.

Bassetto, Marco. (2002). "A Game-Theoretic View of the Fiscal Theory of the Price Level." *Econometrica,* LXX, 2167–2196.

Beck, T., W. Wagner, and H. Uhlig. (2011). "Insulating the Financial Sector from the European Debt Crisis: Eurobonds without Public Guarantees." VoxEU. http://voxeu.org/article/eurobonds-without-public-guarantees-insulating-financial-sector-european-debt-crisis.

Bell, Stephanie. (2000). "Do Taxes and Bonds Finance Government Spending?" *Journal of Economic Issues,* 34(3), September.

Bergin, Paul R. (2000). "Fiscal Solvency and Price Level Determination in a Monetary Union." *Journal of Monetary Economics,* XLV, 33–53.

Bindseil, Ulrich, Marco Corsi, Benjamin Sahel and Ad Visser. (2017). "The Eurosystem Collateral Framework Explained." European Central Bank Occasional Paper Series, No. 189, May. www.ecb.europa.eu/pub/pdf/scpops/ecb.op189.en.pdf.

Borio, Claudio, Piti Disyatat and Anna Zabai. (2016). "Helicopter Money: The Illusion of a Free Lunch." Vox CEPR Policy Portal, 24 May. https://voxeu.org/article/helicopter-money-illusion-free-lunch.

Brunnermeier, M. K., L. Garicano, P. Lane, et al. (2011). *European Safe Bonds (ESBies).* The Euronomics Group.

Brunnermeier, Markus, Marco Pagano, Ricardo Reis, Stijn van Nieuwerburgh and Dimitri Vayanos. (2017a). "ESBies: Safety in the Tranches." *Economic Policy,* 32(90, 1 April 2017): 175–219. https://doi.org/10.1093/epolic/eix004.

Brunnermeier, Markus, Marco Pagano, Ricardo Reis, Stijn van Nieuwerburgh and Dimitri Vayanos. (2017b). "A Safe Asset for Europe." *Financial Times,* Alphaville Guest Post, April 28. https://ftalphaville.ft.com/2017/04/28/2188024/guest-post-a-safe-asset-for-europe/.

Buiter, Willem H. (1983). "Measurement of the Public Sector Deficit and Its Implications for Policy Evaluation and Design." *IMF Staff Papers,* 30, June, 306–349.

Buiter, Willem H. (1998). "The Young Person's Guide to Neutrality, Price Level Indeterminacy, Interest Rate Pegs, and Fiscal Theories of the Price Level." National Bureau of Economic Research Working Paper No. 6396, 1998 and CEPR Discussion Paper No. 1799, Mar. 1998.

Buiter, Willem H. (1999) "The Fallacy of the Fiscal Theory of the Price Level." Centre for Economic Policy Research Discussion Paper No. 2205, 1999.

Buiter, Willem H. (2001). "The Fallacy of the Fiscal Theory of the Price Level, Again." Bank of England Working Paper Series No. 141, July 2001.

Buiter, Willem H. (2002). "The Fiscal Theory of the Price Level: A Critique." *Economic Journal*, CXII, 459–480.

Buiter, W. H. (2003). "Helicopter Money: Irredeemable Fiat Money and the Liquidity Trap." NBER Working Paper No. 10163. https://willembuiter.com/Heliw10163.pdf.

Buiter, Willem H. (2004). "Overcoming the Zero Bound: Gesell vs. Eisler, Discussion of Mitsuhiro Fukao's 'The Effects of 'Gesell' (Currency) Taxes in Promoting Japan's Economic Recovery'." *International Economics and Economic Policy*, 2(2–3, November 2005): 189–200.

Buiter, Willem H. (2005). "New Developments in Monetary Economics: Two Ghosts, Two Eccentricities, a Fallacy, a Mirage and a Mythos." *The Economic Journal*, 115(502): C1–C31. https://doi.org/10.1111/j.0013-0133.2005.00978.x.

Buiter, Willem H. (2007a). "Seigniorage." *Economics, the Open-Access, Open-Assessment E-Journal*, 10.

Buiter, Willem H. (2007b). "Is Numérairology the Future of Monetary Economics? Unbundling numéraire and Medium of Exchange through a Virtual Currency with a Shadow Exchange Rate." *Open Economies Review*. Springer Netherlands; ISSN 0923-7992 (Print); 1573-708X (Online). Electronic publication date: Thursday, May 03, 2007. See Springer website.

Buiter, Willem H. (2009). "Negative Nominal Interest Rates: Three Ways to Overcome the Zero Lower Bound." *North American Journal of Economics and Finance* 20(3,December): 213–238. https://willembuiter.com/threewaysfinal.pdf.

Buiter, Willem H. (2010). "Games of 'Chicken' Between Monetary and Fiscal Authority: Who Will Control the Deep Pockets of the Central Bank?" *Citi Global Economics View*, 21 July 2010.

Buiter, Willem H. (2013) "The Role of Central Banks in Financial Stability: How Has It Changed?" In Douglas D. Evanoff, Cornelia Holthausen, George G. Kaufman and Manfred Kremer (eds.), *The Role of Central Banks in Financial Stability*, World Scientific Studies in International Economics: Volume 30, pp. 11–56. London: World Scientific Publishing Co.

Buiter, Willem H. (2014a). "The Simple Analytics of Helicopter Money: Why It Works – Always." *Economics: The Open-Access, Open-Assessment E-Journal*, 8(2014–28): 1–45 (Version 3). http://dx.doi.org/10.5018/economics-ejournal .ja.2014–28.

Buiter, Willem H. (2014b). "Central Banks: Powerful, Political and Unaccountable?." British Academy Keynes Lecture, given on 18 September 2014, published in the *Journal of the British Academy*, 2014. www.thebritishacademy.ac.uk/sites/ default/files/10%20Buiter%20Keynes%201803.pdf.

Buiter, Willem H. (2015). "The Euro Area: Monetary Union or System of Currency Boards?" *Citi, Citi Research, Economics, Global Economics View*, 19 March.

Buiter, Willem H. (2017a). "Bad and Good 'Fiscal Theories of the Price Level'." *Citi, Citi Research, Multi-Asset, Global Economics View*, 17 March.

Buiter, Willem H. (2017b). "The Fallacy of the Fiscal Theory of the Price Level – Once More." Unpublished paper, 2 April 2017. Also available as Columbia University, SIPA, CDEP and CGEG Working Paper No. 37, March 2017; also available as CEPR Discussion Paper No. 11941, 27 March 2017.

Buiter, Willem H. (2017c). "The Good and the Bad Fiscal Theory of the Price Level." Sixteenth C. D. Deshmukh Memorial Lecture, Reserve Bank of India, Mumbai, 11 April 2017. https://rbi.org.in/Scripts/BS_PressReleaseDisplay.aspx? prid=40123.

Buiter, Willem H., and Nikolaos Panigirtzoglou. (2001). Liquidity Traps: How to Avoid Them and How to Escape Them. In Wim F. V. Vanthoor and Joke Mooij (eds.), *Reflections on Economics and Econometrics: Essays in Honour of Martin Fase* (pp. 13–58). Amsterdam: De Nederlandsche Bank NV.

Buiter, Willem H., and Panigirtzoglou, Nikolaos. (2003). "Overcoming the Zero Bound on Nominal Interest Rates with Negative Interest on Currency: Gesell's solution. *Economic Journal*, 113(October (490): 723–746.

Buiter, Willem H., and E. Rahbari. (2012a). "Why Does the ECB Not Put Its Mouth Where Its Money Is? The ECB as Lender of Last Resort for Euro Area Sovereigns and Banks." *Citi Global Economics View*, 27 February 2012.

Buiter, Willem H., and E. Rahbari. (2012b). "Looking into the Deep Pockets of the ECB." *Citi Global Economics View*, 27 February 2012.

Buiter, Willem H., and Anne C. Sibert. (2007). "Deflationary Bubbles." *Macroeconomic Dynamics* 11(4, Sept.): 431–454.

Buiter, Willem H., and Anne C. Sibert. (2018). "The Fallacy of the Fiscal Theory of the Price Level – One Last Time." *Economics, The Open-Access, Open-Assessment E-Journal*, 12(2018–48): 1–56.

Cagan, P. (1956). "The Monetary Dynamics of Hyperinflation." In M. Friedman (ed., *Studies in the Quantity Theory of Money* (pp. 25–117). Chicago, IL: The University of Chicago Press.

Christiano, Lawrence J., and Terry J. Fitzgerald. (2000). "Understanding the Fiscal Theory of the Price Level." *FRB Cleveland – Economic Review*, 36(2,Qtr-2): 2–37.

Cimadomo, Jacopo, Sebastian Hauptmeier, Alessandra Anna Palazzo and Alexander Popov. (2018). "Risk Sharing in the Euro Area." *ECB Economic Bulletin*, 3/2018. www.ecb.europa.eu/pub/pdf/other/ecb.ebart201803_03 .en.pdf?b2711dd29e17c49b39397ba881286275.

Cochrane, J. H. (1999). "A Frictionless View of U.S. Inflation." NBER Working Paper No. 6646. www.nber.org/papers/w6646.

Cochrane, J. H. (2001). "Long-Term Debt and Optimal Policy in the Fiscal Theory of the Price Level." *Econometrica*, 69(1): 69–116. https://doi.org/10.1111/1468–0262.00179.

Cochrane, J. H. (2005). "Money as Stock." *Journal of Monetary Economics*, 52(3): 501–528. https://doi.org/10.1016/j.jmoneco.2004.07.004.

Cochrane, J. H. (2016a). "Do Higher Interest Rates Raise or Lower Inflation." Working Paper. http://faculty.chicagobooth.edu/john.cochrane/research/paper s/fisher.pdf.

Cochrane, J. H. (2016b). "The Fiscal Theory of the Price Level and its Implications for Current Policy in the United States and Europe." https://faculty.chicagobooth.edu /john.cochrane/research/papers/cochrane_fiscal_theory_panel_bfi. Pdf.

Cochrane, J. H. (2016c). "Next Steps for the FTPL." *The Grumpy Economist*. http:// johnhcochrane.blogspot.com/2016/04/next-steps-for-ftpl.html.

Cushing, Matthew J. (1999). "The Indeterminacy of Prices under Interest Rate Pegging: The Non-Ricardian Case." *Journal of Monetary Economics*, XLIV, 131–148.

Daniel, Betty C. (2001). "The Fiscal Theory of the Price Level in an Open Economy." *Journal of Monetary Economics*, XLVIII (2001). 293–308.

Daniel, Betty C. (2007). "The Fiscal Theory of the Price Level and Initial Government Debt." *Review of Economic Dynamics*, 10(2, April): 193–206. http://citeseerx .ist.psu.edu/viewdoc/download?doi=10.1.1.589.7022&rep=rep1&type=pdf.

De Grauwe, P. (2011). "The Governance of a Fragile Eurozone." CEPS Working Documents, 04 May 2011.

De Grauwe, Paul, and Wim Moesen. (2009). "Gains for All: A Proposal for a Common Eurobond." *CEPS Commentary*, 3 April. www.ceps.eu/publica tions/gains-all-proposal-common-eurobond.

Depla, Jacques, and Jakob von Weiszäcker. (2010). "The Blue Bond Proposal." Bruegel Policy Brief, Issue 2010/03, May.

Detter, Dag, and Stefan Fölster. (2015). *The Public Wealth of Nations: How Management of Public Assets Can Boost or Bust Economic Growth*. London: Palgrave Macmillan.

Detter, Dag, and Stefan Fölster. (2017). *The Public Wealth of Cities: How to Unlock Hidden Assets to Boost Growth and Prosperity*, Washington, DC: Brookings Institution Press.

Dupor, Bill. (2000). "Exchange Rates and the Fiscal Theory of the Price Level." *Journal of Monetary Economics*, XLV, 613–630.

Eberl, Jakob, and Christopher Weber. (2014). "ECB Collateral Criteria: A Narrative Database 2001–2013." IFO Working Paper No. 174, February. www.cesifo-group.de/DocDL/IfoWorkingPaper-174.pdf.

Eisler, Robert. (1932). *Stable Money: The Remedy for the Economic World Crisis: A Programme of Financial Reconstruction for the International Conference 1933;* with a preface by Vincent C. Vickers. London: The Search Publishing Co.

European Commission. (2011). "Green Paper on the feasibility of introducing Stability Bonds." MEMO/11/820, Brussels, 23 November 2011, http://ec.europa.eu/economy_finance/articles/governance/2011–11-23-green-paper-stability-bonds_en.htm.

European Commission. (2018). "Frequently asked questions: Enabling framework for sovereign bond-backed securities." Press Release Database, Brussels, 24 May 2018. www.europa.eu/rapid/press-release_MEMO-18-3726_en.htm.

Financial Stability Board. (2018). "Global Shadow Banking Monitoring Report 2017, March."

Fisher, Irving. (1933). "Debt-Deflation Theory of Great Depressions." *Econometrica*, 1(4 October): 337–357.

Forstater, Mathew, and Warren Mosler. (2005). "The Natural Rate of Interest Is Zero." *Journal of Economic Issues*, 39(2):535–542, June, DOI:10.1080/00213624.2005.11506832.

Fullwiler, Scott, Rohan Grey and Nathan Tankus. (2019). "An MMT Response on What Causes Inflation." *Financial Times*, Alphaville.

German Council of Economic Experts. (2012). "The European Redemption Pact: An Illustrative Guide." Working Paper 02/2012*) February 2012. www.sachverstaendigenrat-wirtschaft.de/fileadmin/dateiablage/download/publikationen/working_paper_02_2012.pdf.

Gesell, Silvio. (1916). *Die Natuerliche Wirtschaftsordnung*. Rudolf Zitzman Verlag. Available in English as *The Natural Economic Order*. London: Peter Owen Ltd., 1958.

Goodfriend, Marvin. (2000). "Overcoming the Zero Bound on Interest Rate Policy." *Journal of Money, Credit, and Banking*, 32(4): S.1007–1035.

Gros, D., and T. Mayer. (2010). "Towards a European Monetary Fund." CEPS Policy Brief.

IMF (2018). "Managing Public Wealth." *Fiscal Monitor*, October, World Economic and Financial Surveys.

Issing, Otmar. (2009). "Why a Common Eurozone Bond Isn't Such a Good Idea." Center for Financial Studies, White Paper No. III, July.

Jacobson, M., E. M. Leeper and B. Preston (2016). "Fiscal Inflation in 1933." Lecture Slides. https://bfi.uchicago.edu/wp-content/uploads/BFI_Jacobson_Leeper_Preston.pdf.

Kocherlakota, N., and C. Phelan (1999). "Explaining the Fiscal Theory of the Price Level." *Federal Reserve Bank of Minneapolis Quarterly Review* 2342: 14–23. https://minneapolisfed.org/research/quarterly-review/explaining-the-fiscal-theory-of-the-pricelevel.

Kopf, C. (2011). "Restoring Financial Stability in the Eurozone." CEPS Policy Briefs

Lara Resende, André. (2017). "Juros e conservadorismo intellectual." *Valor Econômico*, 13 January. www.valor.com.br/cultura/4834784/juros-e-conserva dorismo-intelectual.

Leandro, Alvaro, and Jeromin Zettelmeyer. (2018). "Safety Without Tranches: Creating a 'Real' Safe Asset for the Euro Area." Centre for Economic Policy Research, Policy Insight No. 93, June.

Leeper, E. M. (1991). Equilibria under 'Active' and 'Passive' Monetary and Fiscal Policies. *Journal of Monetary Economics*, 27(1): 129–147. https://doi.org/10.1016/0304-3932(91)90007-B.

Leeper, E. (2015). "Real Theory of the Price Level." The Becker Friedman Institute. https://bfi.uchicago.edu/sites/default/files/file_uploads/Leeper_Background_3%20copy.pdf.

Loyo, Eduardo. (1999). "Tight Money Paradox on the Loose: A Fiscalist Hyperinflation," mimeo. Kennedy School of Government, Harvard University.

Lukkezen, Jasper, and Hugo Rojas-Romagosa. (2016). "A Stochastic Indicator of Sovereign Debt Sustainability." 15 July. www.ris.uu.nl/ws/files/22780838/Lukkezen_Rojas_Romagosa_15jul2016_longversion.pdf.

Macron, Emmanuel. (2017). "Initiative for Europe." Sorbonne speech of Emmanuel Macron – Full Text / English Version, 26 September, http://international.blogs.ouest-france.fr/archive/2017/09/29/macron-sorbonne-verbatim-europe-18583.html.

Mankiw, N. Gregory. (2009). It May Be Time for the Fed to Go Negative. *New York Times*, April 18, 2009. www.nytimes.com/2009/04/19/business/economy/19view.html? r=1.

Marès, Arnaud. (2017). "Of the Consequences of Driving (the Economy) without a Safety Belt." *Western Europe Economics View*, 12 December.

Marès, Arnaud. (2018) "Fiscal Union, or Else." *European Economics View*, 3 May.

McCallum, Bennett T. (2001). "Indeterminacy, Bubbles, and the Fiscal Theory of Price Level Determination." *Journal of Monetary Economics*, XLVII, 19–30.

Minford, Patrick. (2017). "Comments on Buiter and Sibert, Invited Reader Comment." *Economics, The Open-Access Open-Assessment E-Journal*, November. www .economics-ejournal.org/economics/discussionpapers/2017–84.

Mosler, Warren. (2010) "Seven Deadly Innocent Frauds of Economic Policy." Valance Co. Inc.

Niepelt, D. (2004). "The Fiscal Myth of the Price Level." *Quarterly Journal of Economics*, 119(1, February): 277–300.

Reinhart, Carmen. (2018). "Italy's Long, Hot Summer." *Project Syndicate*, 31 May. www.project-syndicate.org/bigpicture/toward-another-eurocrisis.

Reinhart, Carmen, and Kenneth Rogoff. (2009). *This Time is Different: Eight Centuries of Financial Folly*. Princeton University Press

Roche, Cullen. (2019). "MMT – The Good, the Bad and the Ugly," Pragmatic Capitalism, Practical Views on Money & Life, 01/31/2019. https://www .pragcap.com/mmt-good-bad-ugly/.

Rogoff, Kenneth. (2016). *The Curse of Cash*. Princeton, NJ: Princeton University Press

Rogoff, Kenneth. (2017). "Dealing with Monetary Paralysis at the Zero Bound." *Journal of Economic Perspectives*, 31(3): 47–66.

Rogoff, Kenneth. (2018). "Data for the Curse of Cash." https://scholar.harvard.edu /rogoff/curse_of_cash_data.

Rutte, Mark. (2018). "Underpromise and Overdeliver: Fulfilling the Promise of Europe." Speech by the Prime Minister of the Netherlands, Mark Rutte, at the Bertelsmann Stiftung, Berlin, 2 March. www.government.nl/documents/spee ches/2018/03/02/speech-by-the-prime-minister-of-the-netherlands-mark-rutte -at-the-bertelsmann-stiftung-berlin.

Sargent, Thomas J. (1987). *Dynamic Macroeconomic Theory*. Cambridge, MA: Harvard University Press.

Sargent, Thomas J., and Neil Wallace. (1981). "Some Unpleasant Monetarist Arithmetic." *Federal Reserve Bank of Minneapolis Quarterly Review*, V (3): 1–17.

Schmitt-Grohé, Stephanie, and Martin Uribe. (2000). "Price Level Determinacy and Monetary Policy under a Balanced-Budget Requirement." *Journal of Monetary Economics*, XLV, 211–246.

Sims, C. A. (1994). A Simple Model for Study of the Determination of the Price Level and the Interaction of Monetary and Fiscal Policy. *Economic Theory*, 4(3): 381–399. https://doi.org/10.1007/BF01215378.

Sims, C. A. (1999a). "Domestic Currency Denominated Government Debt as Equity in the Primary Surplus." Presentation at the August 1999 Latin American Meetings of the Econometric Society at Cancun, Mexico. http://sims .princeton.edu/yftp/Cancun/DebtEquity.pdf.

Sims, C. A. (1999b). The Precarious Fiscal Foundations of EMU. *De Economist*, 147 (4): 415–436. https://doi.org/10.1023/A:1003819626903.

Sims, C. A. (2001). Fiscal Consequences for Mexico of Adopting the Dollar. *Journal of Money, Credit and Banking*, 33(2): 597–616. https://ideas.repec.org/a/fip/fe dcpr/y2001p597-625.html.

Sims, Christopher. (2011). "Stepping on a Rake: The Role of Fiscal Policy in the Inflation of the 1970's." *European Economic Review*, 55(1): 48–56.

Sims, Christopher. (2013). "Paper Money." *American Economic Review*, 103(2): 563–584.

Sims, Christopher. (2016a). "Active Fiscal, Passive Money Equilibrium in a Purely Backward-Looking Model." Princeton University Discussion Paper. http://sims .princeton.edu/yftp/OldKeynesianFTPL/BackwardAFPM.pdf.

Sims, C. A. (2016b). "Making Government Paper a Bad Investment." Slides presented at the Next Steps for the Fiscal Theory of the Price Level conference at the Becker Friedman Institute for Research on Economics at the University of Chicago, April 1, 2016. https://bfi.uchicago.edu/sites/default/files/file_up loads/6_MplsFedExpctns.pdf.

Sims, C. A. (2016c). "Fiscal Policy, Monetary Policy and Central Bank Independence." Paper presented at the Kansas Citi Fed Jackson Hole Conference, August 26, 2016.

Sinn, Hans-Werner. (2011). "The ECB's stealth bailout." VoxEU.org, 1 June.

Tcherneva, Pavlina R. (2002). "Monopoly Money: The State as a Price Setter." *Oeconomicus*, V, Winter.

Turner, Adair. (2016). "Demystifying Monetary Finance." *Project Syndicate*, August 10. www.project-syndicate.org/commentary/defending-helicopter-money-stimulus-by-adair-turner-2016–08?barrier=accesspaylog.

Uhlig, Harald. (2016). "The FTPL: Some Skeptical Remarks." Slides presented at the Next Steps for the Fiscal Theory of the Price Level conference at the Becker Friedman Institute for Research on Economics at the University of Chicago,

1 April. https://bfi.uchicago.edu/sites/default/files/file_uploads/10_FTPL_Re marks_Uhlig.pdf.

Woodford, M. (1994). "Monetary Policy and Price Level Determinacy in a Cash-In-Advance Economy." *Economic Theory*, 4(3): 345–380. https://doi.org/10.1007/BF01215377.

Woodford, M. (1995). Price Level Determinacy without Control of a Monetary Aggregate. *Carnegie-Rochester Conference Series on Public Policy*, 43: 1–46. https://doi.org/10.1016/0167-2231(95)90033-0.

Woodford, M. (1996). "Control of the Public Debt: A Requirement for Price Stability?" NBER Working Paper No. 5684. www.nber.org/papers/w5684.

Woodford, M. (1998a). "Doing without Money: Controlling Inflation in a Post-Monetary World." *Review of Economic Dynamics*, 1(1): 173–219. https://doi.org/10.1006/redy.1997.0006.

Woodford, M. (1998b). "Comment on John Cochrane, 'A Frictionless View of U.S. Inflation'." *NBER Macroeconomics Annual*, 13: 390–418.

Woodford, M. (1998c). "Public Debt and the Price Level." National Bureau of Economic Research Summer Institute. Conference draft. www.columbia.edu/~mw2230/BOE.pdf.

Woodford, M. (1999). "Price-Level Determination under Interest-Rate Rules." Princeton University. Unpublished.

Woodford, M. (2001). "Fiscal Requirements for Price Stability." *Journal of Money, Credit and Banking*, 33(3): 669–728. www.researchgate.net/publication/2436225_Fiscal_Requirements_for_Price_Stability.

Wray, L. Randall. (2015). *Modern Money Theory: A Primer on Macroeconomics for Sovereign Monetary Systems*, second edition. London: Palgrave Macmillan.

Wray, L. Randall. (2018). "Public Service Employment: A Path to Full Employment." Research Projects Reports, April. www.levyinstitute.org/pubs/rpr_4_18.pdf.

Wray, L. Randall, and Mathew Forstater, (eds.). (2005). *Contemporary Post Keynesian Analysis*. Cheltenham, UK: Edward Elgar.

Index

Printed in the United States
By Bookmasters